GROW
YOUR OWN
FOOD

RICHARD GIANFRANCESCO

APPLE

A QUARTO BOOK

First published by Apple Press
in the UK in 2011
7 Greenland Street
London NW1 0ND
www.apple-press.com

ISBN: 978-1-84543-377-2

Conceived, designed and produced by
Quarto Publishing plc
The Old Brewery
6 Blundell Street
London N7 9BH

QUAR.HGF

Senior Editor: Ruth Patrick
Editor: Corinne Masciocchi
Designer: John Grain
Art Director: Caroline Guest
Illustrators: Kuo Kang Chen, Rob Shone,
 John Woodcock
Photographers: John Grain, Colin and Jenny
 Guest, Mark Winwood

Creative Director: Moira Clinch
Publisher: Paul Carslake

Colour separation in China by
 Modern Age Pte Ltd
Printed in China by 1010 Printing
 International Ltd

10 9 8 7 6 5 4 3 2 1

CONTENTS

Foreword 6
About this book 7
Introduction 8

PART ONE
WHERE TO GROW 12

Types of gardens 14
Choosing the best site 18
Designing your food garden 20
Growing undercover 24

PART TWO
GROWING DIRECTORY 26

VEGETABLE AND SALAD CROPS 28
ROOT CROPS 30
Potato 31
Sweet potato 35
Carrot 36
Parsnip 38
Beetroot 40
Turnip 41
Radish 42
Swede 44
Onion 45
Shallot 48
Garlic 49
Jerusalem artichoke 50
Celeriac 51

LEAFY CROPS 52
Cabbage 53
Brussels sprouts 56
Kale 57
Mizuna and Mibuna 58
Chinese cabbage and Pak choi 60
Spinach 62
Perpetual spinach and Swiss chard 63
Lettuce 64
Chicory and Endive 66
Rocket 67

SEED AND FRUIT CROPS 68
Climbing beans 69
Dwarf beans 71
Broad beans 72
Peas 74
Mangetout and Sugar-snap peas 76
Courgette 78
Squash and Pumpkin 80
Marrow 82
Cucumber 83
Sweetcorn 86
Aubergine 88
Pepper 90
Chilli 92
Tomato 94

STEM AND FLOWER CROPS 98
Broccoli and Calabrese 99
Cauliflower 101

Kohlrabi 102
Fennel 103
Leek 104
Salad onion 106
Celery 108
Asparagus 110
Globe artichoke and Cardoon 112
Sprouting seeds 114
Microgreens 115
Edible flowers 116

HERBS 118
Bay 119
Basil 120
Chervil 122
Chives 123
Coriander 124
Dill and Fennel 125
Lovage 126
Oregano 127
Mint 128
Parsley 130
Rosemary 132
Sage 133
Tarragon 134
Thyme 135

FRUIT CROPS 136
TREE FRUIT 138
Apple 139
Pear 144

Plum, Gage and Damson 146
Sweet cherry 148
Acid cherry 150
Peach, Nectarine and Apricot 152
Fig 154

SOFT FRUITS 156
Strawberry 157
Raspberry 160
Blackberry and hybrid berries 164
Blackcurrant 166
Red and White currants 168
Blueberry 170
Cranberry 172
Grapes 173
Gooseberry 176
Rhubarb 178

TENDER FRUIT 180
Kiwi 181
Passion fruit 182
Physalis 183
Melon 184
Citrus fruit 186

NUTS 188
Cobnut and Filbert 190
Almond 192
Walnut 193

PART THREE
HOW TO GROW 194

Tools and equipment 196
Growing from seed 200
Buying plants 204
Pruning and training fruit trees 206
Growing in containers 210
Watering in the garden 214
Organic gardening 216
All about soil 218
Making compost 222
Dealing with weeds 224
Pests and diseases 226

PART FOUR
PRESERVING YOUR CROP 228

Preserving equipment 230
Jams 232
Jellies 232
Pickles 236
Chutneys 238
Drying 240
Freezing 242

Sowing summary 244
Crop selection summary 246
Hardiness zones 248
Index 250
Acknowledgements 256

FOREWORD

When I was a child, the joy of gardening was all in the eating! Picking fresh peas, raspberries and plums from the garden and eating them was one of my favourite summer activities. As gardening has become a much bigger part of my life, the practice of growing and nurturing the plants has become much more important. Fortunately for me, I now have my own children who share my childhood passion, and as long as I grow what they like, I can spend as much time as I need tending my garden.

As a garden researcher for the past 10 years I've conducted many trials on how to use your time most effectively in the garden and how to get the best out of your plot. How to improve your soil, reduce watering, select appropriate crops and specific varieties and reduce pest and disease damage will all save time in the long run, whatever the size of your garden. Spending time on learning the basics as well as debunking some of the time-heavy myths that many gardening books still profess are worth learning now. But whatever you do, make sure gardening stays a pleasure and not a chore.

ABOUT THIS BOOK

This book is a practical step-by-step guide to planning, growing and maintaining a productive vegetable and fruit garden, with information on getting the most from whatever kind of plot you choose. Using the features described here will quickly provide you with all you need to know.

Part 1: Where to grow (pages 12–25)
Helping you to design your growing food garden and how to get the most from your plot.

DESIGN IDEAS

Packed with photographs of inspirational garden designs, helping you to visualise the layout.

STAR PLANT STAMP
Crops marked with a stamp are specially recommended.

STAR RATING
On a scale of one to five, each entry is graded for a range of criteria.

STEP-BY-STEP SEQUENCES
Detailing techniques such as sowing, growing and maintaining your crops.

Part 2: Growing directory (pages 26–193)
Information on how to grow, maintain, harvest and store vegetable and salad crops, fruit and nuts.

CALENDAR
What to do when for optimum results.

VARIETY SELECTOR
Lists of recommended varieties.

SUPPLEMENTARY INFORMATION
Features topics and techniques in more detail, helping you to raise and maintain your plants.

Part 3: How to grow (pages 194–227)
Core information on foundation gardening techniques.

INSPIRATIONAL PHOTOGRAPHY
Clear photography accompanies each topic, detailing techniques and providing inspiration.

STEP-BY-STEP TECHNIQUES
Clear photographs and descriptions of the key preserving techniques.

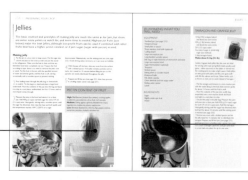
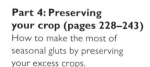

Part 4: Preserving your crop (pages 228–243)
How to make the most of seasonal gluts by preserving your excess crops.

RECIPES
Recipes included for each preserving technique.

INTRODUCTION

Is it because we're concerned about our diets, worried about the pesticides we're ingesting with supermarket food or just a desire to get closer to nature? Whatever the reason, more of us than ever are gardening, and gardening to grow food has become an achievable reality for everyone. Whether you have a window box or an allotment, it has become clear that growing food in your garden that you can take into your kitchen gives a real sense of achievement. Whether you're producing some herbs as a garnish, or growing all the ingredients you need for a dish, it can give the gardener and the cook an added dimension to both garden and food.

Fresh fruit and vegetables are good for you. Full of vitamins, antioxidants and other nutritional benefits, food from your garden couldn't be healthier.

Freshness affects taste too, and anyone who has eaten fresh strawberries, peas or asparagus from the garden will attest that the flavour is just so much better than those you buy in the supermarket.

Growing your own is good for the environment, too. No food miles, fewer pesticides and fertilisers, and less wastage. But if growing your own is so good, why isn't everyone doing it?

Growing your own food does take time. It also isn't necessarily the cost-saving hobby some would like you to believe either. However, the advice in this book will help you make the most of the time you have available, and where you do want to save money, the book points out some expensive supermarket delicacies or those that produce large quantities of staple foods. So the arguments for growing some of your own food definitely outweigh the costs.

Perennial spring treat
Asparagus is actually one of the easiest crops to grow. Once planted, this perennial vegetable will reward you with tender green spears every spring for years to come.

Potato harvest
Digging up your own home-grown potatoes is one of the most enjoyable events of the growing year.

How to grow For many, growing fruit and vegetables can last just a single year, being put off by failure and a lack of time to keep your plot in order.

This book will not only help you get started, but stay gardening for years to come. The How to Grow section (see pages 194–227) will provide reassurance to existing gardeners, and straightforward advice to new ones.

To begin with, get to know your plot. Understanding some of the basics, such as soil and climate, as well as knowing about some of the problems that you are likely to face, such as weeds and pests and diseases, are all worth reading and thinking about. It's also worth considering whether you'll be growing in the ground, the greenhouse or in containers, whether you'll be growing everything from seed and how and where you might do this, or whether you want to devote more space to fruit crops that require little maintenance, but more space.

Growing food doesn't need to be all about rows of vegetables and spending hours watering and weeding. Grow smart and select the right plants for your plot and you can really enjoy your gardening without it becoming a burden.

Seeds of potential
Just a few packets of seeds are all you need to start off your growing food year.

The importance of design
Good garden design, for example, incorporating raised beds, not only makes your garden look good, but makes growing food easier too.

Where to grow It's also worth thinking about what sort of gardener you are – are you into straight rows of neat crops, or do you prefer a more informal approach to your garden? Also, what sort of space do you have available? While those with large plots can afford to space their crops out well to get the maximum yield, others with smaller plots will want to cram their plants to cover every piece of soil with a plant. How to select the best site and design your plot are worthy of consideration before the spade is even lifted. The Where to Grow section (see pages 12–25) will help you answer all these questions.

What to grow Selecting plants that fit in with your lifestyle is of most importance. Not only choosing crops you enjoy eating and will use, but also plants that fit in with the time you have available. It's no point tending tomato plants all spring to find you're on holiday when they're ready to be harvested. Similarly, while growing rows of runner beans couldn't be easier, have you got a spare hour every week to pick them? And what will you do with several kilos of beans every week? Think about not just what you want to eat, but also how much time and effort the plants will need for growing, watering and picking.

Productive plants
If you're not careful, a single packet of seed will inundate you with a glut of vegetables. However, with most crops there are either ways to avoid a glut, or ways to store or preserve your produce for later use.

The Growing Directory (see pages 26–193) deals individually with every crop you may want to grow including fruit, salads, vegetables, nuts and even flowers. Each section begins with a star rating – a quick guide to how easy and productive each crop is. Importantly, we also consider how well the crop stores. While some will need to be eaten immediately, others can be stored for months, providing home-grown produce right through the winter. Temperature ranges are supplied for perennial vegetables and fruit, so you can check that your winter isn't too severe to support these crops.

Each entry looks at the best way to grow the crop, and whether it's suitable for containers. There's also a calendar for each entry, providing a guide to when you'll need to do annual tasks such as sow, plant out, prune and harvest each crop.

Once you've decided what to grow, you'll then be presented with recommended varieties of each. Each entry features a variety selector, which provides some straightforward advice from either independent horticultural trials or from my own experience on the best varieties to grow. These have been selected on the basis of their yield, quality and storage of produce, and taste, as well as their ability to fend off pests and diseases where appropriate. Finally, each entry comes with ideas for use in the kitchen as well as specific methods for storing the crop for longer-term use.

Attractive display
Vegetables and edible flowers can make attractive ornamental – and functional – beds if you plan the positioning of your crops.

PART 1: WHERE TO GROW

Before you rip open your first packet of seeds, or purchase a bundle of raspberry canes, you need to consider your growing space. How big is your garden? Is it shaded or in full sun? What sort of garden style do you prefer? Spend some time designing your garden around your requirements. In the long run, having a growing food garden-space that works for you, your family and your kitchen will pay dividends.

Types of gardens

Wherever you decide to start growing your food garden, it's worth giving some consideration to the style of garden you want and how you might use it. Of course, this is determined in some way by the plot you have available, but whether you have a small balcony or patio, or a larger plot, it's worth thinking about not just what you want to grow, but how you want to use your garden.

Raised beds
Raised beds were first used where the soil or climatic conditions made gardening tricky. Now, they're used as design features in their own right. Raised beds are also easier to weed and tend to, being that bit nearer.

There are lots of garden styles to choose from when deciding how to lay out an ornamental garden, and it's similar for the vegetable plot too. Traditional vegetable gardens consist of neat, parallel beds with narrow paths in between to access the produce and maximise the growing space. Raised beds are a newer technique that, oddly enough, can evoke a traditional look. In smaller plots, the growing food garden often means incorporating it into the rest of the garden. A more ornamental kitchen garden, or potager, where flowers and vegetables sit happily side by side, can be both attractive and productive. On an even smaller plot, growing in containers and small raised beds may be the only option. While the space in these gardens may be limited, with decent planning they can still be extremely productive.

Perfect for smaller gardens
Patio gardening can be productive too. Crops like peppers, aubergines and tomatoes all do well on a sunny patio, as long as they're well watered and fed.

Productive plots
An allotment plot like this could require 16–20 hours per week to keep in good order during the peak growing season.

The allotment plot

This is a term used to describe a large section of your garden given over entirely to growing food. Allotments in their true sense are pieces of land, often from the local or parish council, loaned to private individuals to grow fruit and vegetables. Just like your own garden, they'll need a big investment of time to get them right, so should be treated just like your own. The effort you put into the site when you first take it over will pay dividends in years to come, and creating a good basic structure to the plot is essential. There are some simple rules to follow here that should be considered before even a spade is sunk into the ground (see pages 18–25).

Large plots dedicated solely to fruit- and vegetable-growing do not always look fantastic. Winter especially will be fairly bleak, with bare stems and trunks, and little to look at and enjoy. There may be limited pickings too, except for winter brassicas such as Brussels sprouts, and root vegetables such as parsnips, and also perhaps lettuce and other greens, depending on your climate. If you want your garden to be attractive all year round, then this style isn't for you. If, however, your site is out of sight for most of the time, and you visit it only to garden and pick your produce, then this type of plot, where every square

centimetre is devoted to productive gardening, will be both the easiest to manage and give the highest returns.

Most large garden vegetable and fruit plots are usually designed to have everything that's required in one spot: a shed, compost bin and cold frames are all useful structures to have, as is a seat or bench to enjoy looking at the fruits of your labour. Plots are usually laid out as a series of narrow beds, sometimes raised off the ground, with paths in between. To make them easier to create, the beds are often not edged, but in the long run, it's better to edge them with planks of wood to help keep a distinction between your paths and beds. Paths are usually grass, chipped bark or straw, but for the more ornamental plot there is no reason why you can't use paving, brick or concrete paths. Whatever you use, in this type of garden it's about devoting as much soil as you can to growing produce.

Permanent fruit trees and berries, as well as perennial vegetables such as asparagus, will have their own areas of the plot. These will help provide the plot with some structure, especially in the winter months. The other beds should be devoted solely to annual vegetables and herbs, and a rotation system implemented (see pages 22–23).

The kitchen garden or potager

For many gardeners, growing food in their back garden is what gardening is all about. Being able to pop out into the garden and dig up some potatoes or pick a few mangetout for dinner makes this type of gardening very rewarding. However, many of us don't have huge plots of land where whole areas can be devoted solely to growing food – many of us want our garden to be not only productive but attractive too.

This is where the idea of the kitchen garden, or potager, comes in. Mixing flowers, vegetables, herbs and fruit is not a new idea, but it's a solution that can work extremely well for many modern gardeners. It is important to realise, however, that your plants may not grow to the size they would in a dedicated growing food plot, and crops will not be quite as bountiful. Managing a potager where plants are grown in a more haphazard fashion than in the straight rows or blocks of an allotment plot may also mean more work for you. But in the end, it's about working with what you've got, and if you want your garden to produce cut flowers for your house as well as food for your kitchen, and for it to be full of scent, buzzing insects and colour, then a kitchen garden is definitely for you.

Kitchen gardens vary in their formality and devotion to growing food. On the one hand, they can be truly ornamental gardens, with a selection of vegetables, herbs and fruit planted just occasionally around the flowers. On the other, they may be more dedicated to growing food, with the use of flowers limited to entrances and path edges. The best potagers, however, feature an equal mix of flowers and food – they are usually laid out in beds with a series of paths, just like an allotment garden, as whenever you're growing food you need to make sure you can always reach the middle of the bed from the path, without having to walk on the soil.

IDEAS: KITCHEN GARDEN

There are no clear rules to follow with a kitchen garden, and it's worth experimenting with flowers, vegetables and fruit to see what works for you. Here are some ideas for you to consider:

- You may choose a pear tree instead of an ornamental crab apple, and a blackberry or acid cherry to grow against a fence instead of a rose. These choices mean that while you may loose out on some colour, you'll be rewarded with a harvest.

- Think about the vegetable varieties that you grow. While some can be plain and productive, others can be ornamental. A beautiful cavolo nero kale plant looks incredible in any garden, as can the two-tone flowers of some varieties of climbing runner beans. Edging plants of frilly lettuce or herbs such as chives or parsley can be both ornamental and productive.

- Use height in the garden, not just for vegetables that climb such as beans and peas, but also for those that can be trained to climb such as pumpkins, squashes and marrows. Mix these with climbing annuals such as sweet peas that can be used as cut flowers.

- Add other flowers that can be used for cutting: marigold, chrysanthemum, sunflowers and cornflowers, for example, as well as flowers that you can eat (see pages 116–117).

Interplanting flowers and vegetables

Growing flowers alongside vegetables can provide extra benefits. Some flowers, such as nasturtiums, may be edible, while others, such as marigolds, may deter pests. Best of all, they brighten up your edible garden and turn a vegetable patch into a kitchen garden.

The patio garden

In smaller plots you may not have the luxury of being able to grow flowers and food side by side, but it doesn't mean that the productive patio garden has to look miserable for much of the year. Ornamental pots and bedding plants can still be used to great effect to make your patio or balcony a cheery and welcoming place to sit. The best productive patio gardens also include scented plants as well as a place nearby, situated in the sun, where you can sit and relax.

Some patio gardens will be big enough to squeeze in a single raised bed – a good idea to boost your productivity. This amount of space allows for growing larger vegetables such as brassicas and sweetcorn that don't typically do well in containers, but rows of cut-and-come-again lettuce, as well as fruit such as strawberries, and herbs, also look attractive.

Create a spectacle

Growing food doesn't have to mean an allotment-style with lots of bare soil. Edible plants can look good in the garden too as with this row of tomato plants growing in pewter-style containers. Kitchen and patio gardens should contain just as many flowers as they do crops.

IDEAS: PATIO GARDEN

Again, there are no hard and fast rules to growing food on the patio, but consider these options:

- If you're restricted to pots, the most productive patio gardens are those where just one type of vegetable per pot is grown. A number of pots all filled with different vegetables placed together means you wouldn't even notice this monoculture.

- Herbs always do well in pots, and evergreen ones such as bay and rosemary may help to provide a backbone.

- Some fruit in pots always do well – blueberries are a must, but even raspberries and currants can thrive in containers.

- Annual herbs such as coriander and parsley look attractive in containers and their diminutive size means they thrive.

- Position the best-looking containers at the front of the patio, and move the less attractive ones, such as potatoes, towards the back.

- Try growing vegetables and fruit in hanging baskets too – cucumbers, tomatoes and melons on a sunny patio, squashes and marrows where it's cooler.

Choosing the best site

Whatever your garden size, you will probably have some choice about where to site your productive garden. If you really have no choice, you'll need to select the plants that suit the situation you have. Otherwise, it's worth considering your options before you start to design it. Whatever you do, don't always opt for the piece of land at the end of the garden. Large trees, poor drainage or frost pockets may mean that these areas will not be particularly productive. There are six physical considerations to bear in mind.

Sun and shade

It's a good idea to work out how sunny or shady your proposed plot is likely to be. While it may not receive much sun in the winter, it's important that the sun reaches it during the summer months. Although some fruit and vegetables grow well in shade, they will all be outperformed by those grown in sun. It's a good idea to have an open site away from large buildings, walls and trees. This may not be always possible, but it is worth attempting to maximise the amount of sun your plot receives. Consider, for example, reducing the height of any existing trees

Consider additional features
Selecting a position for all the additionals such as a water butt, shed and greenhouse is important. The best place for a water butt is below a roof, but consider how far you need to carry the water, and if necessary invest in a water-butt pump.

or raising the canopy. Swapping fence panels for see-through trellises will not only allow you to grow climbing plants, but also allow more sunlight to enter into the garden.

Soil

Most sites will have the same soil right across the plot (see page 218). You'll need to consider what soil you have, and where necessary, how to improve its structure, texture and fertility. Where drainage is a problem, consider creating land drains to allow excess water to drain off your site.

Wind

It's worth avoiding areas of your garden that you know are exposed to strong wind. In coastal areas, this can be challenging, but there are some tricks you can use to increase the amount of shelter your plants receive.

The first is to consider the boundaries of your garden. Solid fences and walls may seem like a good idea, but this creates turbulence and the strength of the winds in the garden may actually increase. Much better are barriers that allow some of the air to come through, but the barrier both filters and slows the air movement. Hedges are ideal for this, but will take some years to grow. Alternatively, windbreak materials can be erected as a temporary measure while the hedges develop.

Water

All plants need water, and it's important that you have a ready supply. If you tend to use the tap to water your plants, consider how far away the tap is from your plot, and if necessary add an extension to this.

Most of the watering, though, will come from the sky, but walls and especially trees can really reduce how much water reaches both the soil and the roots of your plants. In the summer, trees and ornamental shrubs will be taking up gallons of water from the ground and can make the surface dry and unproductive. For this reason, avoid siting your garden next to large trees.

A traditionally designed plot
A well-designed food garden means providing your plants with the best conditions available to you – lots of sunshine, good soil and little competition from other plants growing nearby. This open, flat plot provides just that.

Temperature

Temperature affects all gardens, but there is not really very much we can do to change it, except when it comes to frost. In some gardens, particularly those that lie on a slope, there will be areas that will remain frostier for longer. These are called frost pockets and occur when cold air runs down a slope and settles in a dip. Where you think you have a frost pocket, it's worth making sure you avoid that area for your growing food plot. If you find that your plot sits right on a frost pocket, consider ways of dealing with the problem area. Simply creating a gap at the bottom of a fence to allow the cold air to continue on its way may be possible, for example.

Slopes

Slopes can be tricky to use for the productive gardener. Very slight slopes shouldn't cause much concern, and if you're creating raised beds it may be possible to flatten out the slopes within the beds. Where slopes are steeper, creating terracing is the best option. Use terracing perpendicular to the slope to create a series of level beds with steps down.

Crops in blocks
Crops are often planted in blocks or squares. This allows you to get the soil and conditions right for each crop, as well as maximising the use of space – as soon as one crop is harvested, another one should be planted in its place.

Designing your food garden

Once you've decided on the style of garden you are going to create and have set out the plot that is available to you, it's important to spend some time designing the plot. Once you've dug out the beds and planted some fruit, it's hard to go back and start again, so it's important to be organised. Your best bet is to sketch out some rough plans on paper. Only in this way can you really start to understand what you can fit in your plot and where it should all go.

CREATING THE PERFECT GROWING FOOD GARDEN PLAN

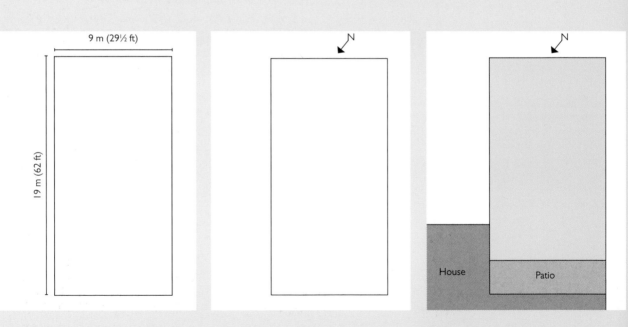

1 First take some measurements and work out the area you have available. Draw this to a known scale on a piece of paper.

2 Work out where north is in relation to your plot and draw this on the paper as an arrow.

3 Draw in any structures that surround your plot or are within it, such as houses or garages. Think about the amount of shade they can cast.

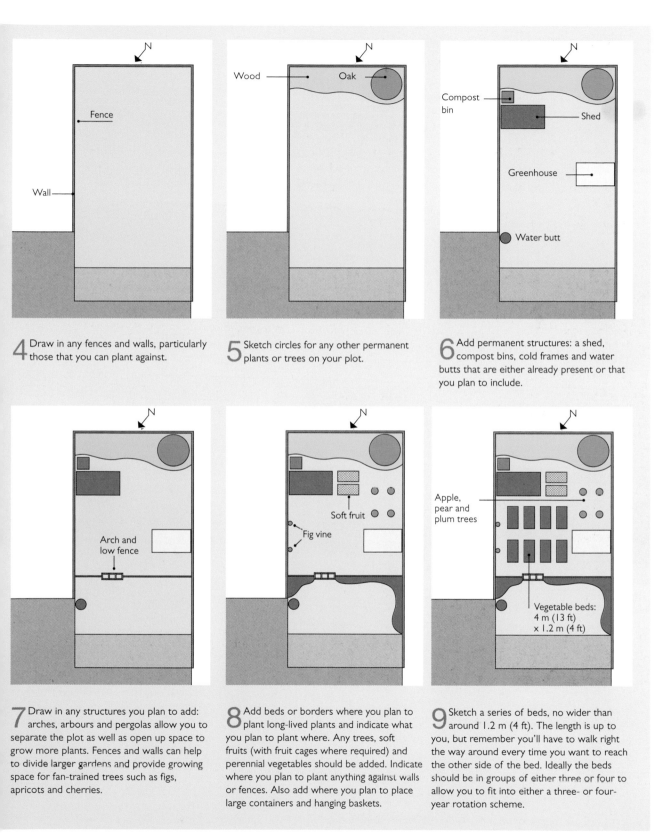

4 Draw in any fences and walls, particularly those that you can plant against.

5 Sketch circles for any other permanent plants or trees on your plot.

6 Add permanent structures: a shed, compost bins, cold frames and water butts that are either already present or that you plan to include.

7 Draw in any structures you plan to add: arches, arbours and pergolas allow you to separate the plot as well as open up space to grow more plants. Fences and walls can help to divide larger gardens and provide growing space for fan-trained trees such as figs, apricots and cherries.

8 Add beds or borders where you plan to plant long-lived plants and indicate what you plan to plant where. Any trees, soft fruits (with fruit cages where required) and perennial vegetables should be added. Indicate where you plan to plant anything against walls or fences. Also add where you plan to place large containers and hanging baskets.

9 Sketch a series of beds, no wider than around 1.2 m (4 ft). The length is up to you, but remember you'll have to walk right the way around every time you want to reach the other side of the bed. Ideally the beds should be in groups of either three or four to allow you to fit into either a three- or four-year rotation scheme.

Allotment plots

These plots are often situated away from the house, either in another part of the garden or in a different location.

A shed may be useful to store your tools, pots, fertilisers and pest controls. Sheds should be positioned in the most shady and dry part of the plot so that they don't take up valuable growing space. It's a good idea to site some other essentials nearby, such as a compost bin for all your waste plant material. While these work best when sited in the sun, most people tend to keep them out of the way in a shady corner, but this does mean that decomposition will take a little longer. If you are thinking of having a greenhouse, this needs to be considered from the outset too as you'll need a sunny site on level ground.

Next are the beds. First think about any fruit trees you want to grow. Ideally, these should be positioned so they cast as little shade as possible onto your site.

Potagers and kitchen gardens

It's not necessary to lay out potagers and kitchen gardens in a very formulaic way. It is a good idea to have a series of paths that are intersected by narrow beds. These can be laid out in a pattern of symmetry to provide some order to your kitchen

CROP FAMILIES

Crops are put into families and these families move around the plot together.

Family		Why group together?	What soil conditions do they prefer?
PEA AND BEAN Includes all peas, mangetout, broad beans, runner beans and dwarf beans.		These plants have root nodules that turn nitrogen in the air into nutrients the plants can use.	Because they make their own nitrogen, they require little fertiliser but need plenty of water, so prefer soil that has had plenty of organic matter, such as compost or manure, added.
POTATO Also includes tomatoes, aubergines and peppers.		Can suffer from blight, so best moved around together to stop re-infection. Other problems, such as scab and eelworm, can be avoided if moved around the garden together.	All like a decent amount of organic matter and nutrients.
ROOT CROP Includes carrots and parsnips, but also parsley.		Carrot fly can be avoided if the crops are netted together.	Don't like soil with fresh compost added. They don't require much in the way of additional fertiliser either.
BRASSICA Includes cabbages, cauliflowers, Brussels sprouts, Chinese vegetables such as Chinese cabbage and pak choi, radishes, kohlrabi, kale, as well as some salads such as mizuna and rocket.		These plants can suffer from clubroot and prefer an alkaline soil. They suffer from flying pests so should be covered with fine mesh. Protect winter crops from bird damage.	Compost or manure should have been added for the previous crop. They require high levels of nutrients.
ONION Includes all onions, shallots, garlic, leeks and chives.		Plants can suffer from allium leaf miner and white rot. Mesh can be used on the crop to control insect pests.	An average amount of fertiliser and soil that has had compost or manure added to it for the previous crop.
EVERYTHING ELSE		All other crops should be moved around the garden, but it's not vital; they can be fitted in with any of the above families where there is space.	

garden. However, don't necessarily restrict yourself to rectangular beds. A series of 1-m (3 ft 2-in) square beds can work just as well, as can triangular or curved beds. Most importantly the kitchen garden has to fit in with the style of your house. Replicate and complement the materials used in your house and garden in the structure of your kitchen garden so it seamlessly flows on. Think about creating arches to enter and exit the garden, as well as some areas where fencing or walls allow you to grow climbing plants.

Because many of the plants take up residence for just the summer months, think about how you can fill in these gaps during the winter. Use permanent obelisks in the centre of beds, which can be used by climbing plants in the summer, but provide a feature during the winter too. Consider the positioning of trees and soft fruit. These can provide structure to your garden in the winter, but you don't want them to shade out your summer vegetables.

Patios and balconies

These are the gardens that provide the most design limitations. You are restricted in space, and have little choice when it comes to sun or shade. To maximise your growing space, consider any structures that allow you to grow in a three-dimensional space. Pergolas, arches and even simple posts allow you to grow plants vertically, making the most of the space you have available.

When choosing containers, go for a range of styles and sizes, but remember that the larger the pots, the less watering they'll require (if you have a balcony, make sure that it will hold the extra weight of the containers). Lastly, think about adding a series of hanging baskets or other systems to grow plants against walls and fences. These again open up growing space to you that otherwise wouldn't be available.

Crop rotation

Within your plan it's likely you'll have some space to grow vegetables each year. If you've followed the advice given on the previous pages, you'll have beds in groups of three or four. This allows you to rotate your crops around the garden each year.

The most important reason for this is to stop the build-up of pests and diseases. If you grew all your plants from the onion family in a single bed every year, for example, it's likely that onion white rot will strike and affect crops in future years. Moving crops regularly means this build-up of disease is less likely. Crop rotation ensures that additions of nutrients are kept to a minimum while ensuring plants grow to their maximum potential. With crop rotation, you should need to add bulky organic matter, such as compost or manure only every three years – while some crops like freshly manured ground, and others, such as carrots, dislike it.

Where full crop rotation isn't possible, try to move at least the potatoes, onions and brassicas around the garden, even if it's just by a metre or so.

THREE-YEAR THREE-BED ROTATION

YEAR 1

Plot A Peas, beans and onions (add manure/compost)

Plot B Potatoes and root crops (add fertiliser)

Plot C Brassicas (add fertiliser)

YEAR 2

Plot A Brassicas (add fertiliser)

Plot B Peas, beans and onions (add manure/compost)

Plot C Potatoes and root crops (add fertiliser)

YEAR 3

Plot A Potatoes and root crops (add fertiliser)

Plot B Brassicas (add fertiliser)

Plot C Peas, beans and onions (add manure/compost)

FOUR-YEAR FOUR-BED ROTATION

YEAR 1

Plot A Peas and beans (add compost)
Plot B Brassicas (add plenty of fertiliser)
Plot C Onions and root crops (no compost, little fertiliser)
Plot D Potatoes (add compost and fertiliser)

YEAR 2

Plot A Potatoes (add compost and fertiliser)
Plot B Peas and beans (add compost)
Plot C Brassicas (add plenty of fertiliser)
Plot D Onions and root crops (no compost, little fertiliser)

YEAR 3

Plot A Onions and root crops (no compost, little fertiliser)
Plot B Potatoes (add compost and fertiliser)
Plot C Peas and beans (add compost)
Plot D Brassicas (add plenty of fertiliser)

YEAR 4

Plot A Brassicas (add plenty of fertiliser)
Plot B Onions and root crops (no compost, little fertiliser)
Plot C Potatoes (add compost and fertiliser)
Plot D Peas and beans (add compost)

Crop rotation examples
Above are two crop-rotation schemes to try, depending on the size of your garden. Using a rotation scheme will ensure that your soil stays nutrient-rich and low in pests and diseases.

Growing undercover

Growing undercover gives you a head start with many of your summer crops, allowing you to sow earlier than you would otherwise be able to.

GREENHOUSE TIPS

The most traditional-looking undercover space, a greenhouse is ideal for most vegetable and fruit growers. Greenhouses can be expensive, but it's worth investing in a decent one.

What materials? You'll be able to choose between an aluminium and wood greenhouse. While aluminium greenhouses are cheaper, they are much more difficult to dismantle and reassemble, so if you think you may move home in the next few years, wood is a better option.

What size? It's best to go for a greenhouse as big as you can afford and fit into your garden. 1.8 × 2.4 m (6 × 8 ft) is the most popular size and a good one to start with. Anything less than this and you'll soon run out of space.

What extras? Consider buying staging and shelving for at least one side. It's much easier to buy this with the greenhouse so it all fits into place. These give you space to raise plants from seed and grow vegetables in small containers. The other open side can be used for growing cordon vegetables such as tomatoes and cucumbers.

Windows and vents Most greenhouse come with windows in the roof and the side. Consider buying some automatic openers, which open as the temperature rises.

Electrical supply It's well worth installing an electrical supply, with a waterproof socket or two. Always use an RCD device when using electricity outdoors. An electric supply will allow you to use a thermostatically controlled electric greenhouse heater and a heated propagator to get your seedlings going.

Watering Consider fixing a water butt to the side of your greenhouse for a nearby supply, or run a fixed pipe and attach a tap next to your greenhouse, which will save both trailing a hosepipe across your garden and carrying cans of water.

You can also fit an irrigation system inside your greenhouse, and using a water timer means that watering by hand twice a day in midsummer to keep your plants going becomes a thing of the past (see pages 214–215).

While we can improve our soil, select good-quality varieties and monitor pest control, one thing we can't govern is the weather. Investing in a frost-free environment for your plants means you'll be able to garden and harvest all through the year. For example, you can start tender vegetables early, which means harvesting comes earlier too. They also allow you to grow tender fruit as well as salads through the winter. Although a greenhouse is the most popular choice, there are other options.

Conservatory

If your house has a conservatory, it's an ideal space for growing food. It's likely everything will have to be grown in a container, but it's more than possible to grow all sorts of fruit and salad crops – anything from a nectarine to large pots of herbs. It may be difficult to keep a conservatory cool in the summer, so if yours receives lots of direct sun, consider installing blinds.

Polytunnel

A polytunnel is basically a plastic tunnel greenhouse. As they're made of aluminium hoops and sheet plastic, they are much cheaper to buy than a greenhouse and because they don't need a solid base, they're much cheaper to install too. They do not

Greenhouse
Western red cedar timber makes for a long-lasting and attractive greenhouse. Its natural oils means that it's not necessary to stain, and the colouring will slowly lighten with age.

Polytunnel protection
Polytunnels are cheap and quick to erect. They are ideal where the climate isn't quite warm enough for the crops you want to grow, or when you want to raise plants slightly out of season.

WHAT TO GROW IN A GREENHOUSE

- It's a great place to raise seedlings, both tender crops such as sweetcorn and French beans, but also a good place to start hardy crops such as brassicas, onions and peas.
- If you want an early crop of potatoes, carrots or courgettes, consider growing them in a pot and starting in the greenhouse very early in the season.
- Herbs can be overwintered in the greenhouse and remain productive for much of the year.
- Aubergines, peppers and chillies can be grown in the greenhouse all summer. They can make the greenhouse both look good and be productive.
- Propagating plants such as strawberries can be left in a greenhouse where they will root quickly.

give the same insulation or light quality as a greenhouse but are perfectly good for growing all sorts of fruit and vegetables. Unheated, a polytunnel will allow you to extend your season by a month or two, but if you add a heater, you can use it just as a greenhouse. However, they're not things of beauty so are best used in a devoted vegetable garden.

Cold frame

For those with little space, a cold frame is a worthy investment. Even for those with a greenhouse, a cold frame provides a space to transfer your plants to harden them off.

Many plants will suffer if you move them straight from the protection of a greenhouse to outside, so a cold frame, where the lid can be opened in the day and closed at night, allows a plant to acclimatise to the harsher conditions outside.

Mini greenhouse

If a cold frame doesn't give quite enough space, a mini greenhouse can be perfect. These come in a range of materials and prices. The cheapest are plastic covers over a thin metal frame; the more expensive are fixed to the side of the house and made of wood or aluminium and glazed with glass. While expensive versions should be avoided unless you really cannot fit a full-sized greenhouse in your garden, a cheap version is perfect for raising seedlings in a small garden. Choose one with plenty of shelving, and a width to fit a standard seed tray. This way you can raise lots of plants in one go.

If the shelves can be removed, it can be used later in the summer for larger crops such as a couple of tomatoes or cucumbers.

Pest and disease problems

The one problem of growing in a hot environment is that the seedlings can be a magnet for lots of pests and diseases. And the fact that they never become really cold means these pests and diseases rarely die out naturally. At least once a year it's a good idea to take all your plants out of the greenhouse and give it a wash and scrub. There are proprietary greenhouse cleaning products available. It's also worth cleaning all pots and trays as

this can reduce your exposure to damping off – a disease that will quickly kill off seedlings. Greenhouse-grown crops can also suffer from more pests and diseases in the summer as the pests can thrive in a warm humid environment, away from any natural enemies. Consider using biological controls, which are perfect for using in a greenhouse (see page 217).

Mini greenhouse
A mini greenhouse is perfect for raising seeds in spring. Some will also allow you to remove the shelves and grow tomatoes and other tender crops in the summer.

PART 2: GROWING DIRECTORY

Out of the hundreds of vegetable and salad crops, fruit and nuts in this book, realistically you will be able to grow just a few, at least in your first year. First, pick out the crops you especially like, particularly when picked fresh. Make sure you choose ones that suit your cooking style and your family's tastes too. Second, consider your garden space and the time you have to devote to the crop – grow only those that are likely to succeed in the space you have and the time you can spend caring for your plants.

VEGETABLE AND SALAD CROPS
28

FRUIT CROPS
136

NUTS
188

VEGETABLE AND SALAD CROPS

If you want rewards quickly, vegetable and salad crops are a good place to start. With just a couple of packets of seed, you can be harvesting your first crop of salad leaves within four weeks, and your first radishes in five. And with the multitude of different vegetable and salad crops that can be grown successfully in the garden, with careful planning you can pick fresh food all year round.

ROOT CROPS

Root crops such as potatoes, carrots and onions form the backbone of any vegetable plot. Despite produce being widely available and mostly cheap to buy, there is nothing more rewarding than growing your own. Tasty and fresh, garden-grown carrots and new potatoes can't be beaten. Many root crops can also be stored, giving you access to your harvest for much of the winter too.

Potato

One of the easiest and most productive crops to grow, no kitchen garden should be without a row or two of potatoes.

✪✪✪✪✪ VALUE FOR MONEY
✪✪✪✪✧ MAINTENANCE
✪✪✪✪✪ FREEZE/STORE
CROPPING SEASON: EARLY SUMMER–MID-AUTUMN

Potatoes have been grown by humans for over 7,000 years, and it's not difficult to understand why this American native has become a favourite across the world. In fact, it's the world's most popular vegetable, with an annual production of over 300 million tonnes (330 million tons). Plant a seed potato (one of the tubers from the previous crop) in the spring, and by midsummer, many more will have been produced. Harvest in the autumn, and the potatoes can be used in the kitchen right through the winter. Potatoes are tender plants but can be grown in most parts of the world, as long as there are plentiful amounts of water to help the tubers swell during the summer.

Where to grow Potatoes are a common sight on allotments and in kitchen gardens and often follow on from brassicas on a rotation (see page 22–23), but they'll do well anywhere there are plenty of nutrients. In fact, potatoes are often used on new plots to help break them in, since they do well on all soil types. They are large plants, however, and do require a fair amount of space. If space is short, go for early varieties that don't put on as much growth before they need harvesting. If space is really short, containers are the best option. Potatoes grow very successfully in containers, and many companies exploit this fact by selling special bags or pots to grow potatoes in, but any large container, which holds at least 10 L (2.5 gallons) of compost, will do.

Types and varieties Around 7,000 years of breeding has left us with all manner of potatoes, available in a variety of colours – from cream to blue – as well as a selection of shapes and sizes. However, the most useful variation for the gardener is the speed of growth. While some potatoes are ready for harvesting after as little as 80 days of growing,

Harvesting potatoes
Depending on the variety, you can harvest potatoes from mid- to late summer, then store what you don't need for use through the winter.

others take much longer. This allows the gardener, with one planting, to keep harvesting potatoes from midsummer right through the winter. There are three main groups:

Earlies From a mid-spring planting, these potatoes will be the first to make it onto the kitchen table by midsummer. These young potatoes often command a high premium in the supermarket. Plant earlies 40 cm (16 in) apart in rows 50 cm (20 in) apart. Dig up plants as you need them.

Second earlies These are more likely to be waxy, salad-type potatoes, which will be ready for harvesting around three and a half months after planting – usually in mid- to late

VARIETY SELECTOR

Earlies
• 'Lady Christl', 'Mimi'.
Second earlies
• 'Charlotte', 'Anya'.
Maincrops
• 'King Edward', 'Maris Piper'.

COLOURFUL POTATOES

Potatoes are available in lots of colours, so why not try some more unusual varieties?

- **'Blue Danube'**: fine bright blue tubers, but sadly the flesh is white. Some blight resistance.

- **'Mayan Twilight'**: red and white patched tubers, with a deep yellow, sweet flesh.

- **'Congo'**: dark blue, both inside and out – great for kids' parties.

Colourful potatoes
Potatoes come in many colours – try blue or red for unusually coloured mashed potato!

IN THE KITCHEN

Best for mash
- 'Accent', 'Kestrel'.

Best for roasts
- 'King Edward', 'Maris Piper'.

Best for chips
- 'Golden Wonder', 'Valor'.

Best for baking
- 'Picasso', 'Marfona'.

Best for salads
- 'Charlotte', 'Anya'.

summer. Dig these up as and when you need them. Leave any plants you don't need in the ground. They'll be fine for a couple of months and you can harvest when you need them.

Maincrop The largest harvest usually comes from maincrop varieties. The potatoes need a long growing season, and if you have plenty of storage space, they will stay fresh right through the winter. Space the rows 75 cm (30 in) apart, to give the plants plenty of space to grow. Harvest in one go in the autumn.

In the garden Potatoes will give you a decent yield wherever you grow them, but to maximise your harvest, grow them on rich, deep soil, and if you can, supplement the soil with plenty of homemade compost or other soil improver (see page 220–223). It's also worth adding a balanced granular fertiliser to the soil when you plant.

When you buy your potatoes in winter, they come as tubers, with small 'eyes', which, if left on a cool windowsill, will start to sprout. Potatoes are sensitive to frost, and any growth that emerges can be hit by frosts. Plants will recover from some damage, but if frosts are forecast, cover the stems with fleece, straw or even a layer of compost.

As the plants start to grow, it's worth drawing up soil onto the young shoots, leaving just the young leaves exposed. This can protect the stems from frost and increase the yield.

Pests and diseases Potatoes are susceptible to a variety of pests and diseases, but only a few (some of which are easy to prevent) cause major problems to gardeners. To avoid virus diseases ruining your crop, it's best to buy fresh tubers each year –

GROWING POTATOES IN A CONTAINER

1 Choose an early or second early variety. Fill a large container (10 L or more/2.5 gallons) or potato bag one-third with compost. Place one tuber with the shoots uppermost and cover with 5 cm (2 in) of compost, before watering in well.

2 As the potatoes start to grow, add more compost, covering the stems. Add a slow-release fertiliser, mixing the recommended rate in with the compost.

3 Keep adding compost until just below the rim of the pot.

these will have been produced from virus-free stock.

Common scab Scabby areas develop on the tubers, but can mostly be avoided by ensuring the soil isn't too alkaline. Avoid adding lime to the soil and work in plenty of organic matter.

Blight The most devastating potato disease for gardeners is blight, where brown freckles on the leaves lead to a brownish rot developing in the tubers. The same disease that caused the Irish potato famine over 150 years ago is still causing problems today. There are a number of chemicals that can be sprayed on the crops to prevent the disease taking hold, but for organic gardeners there is little to help. If blight does strike, cut off all the foliage; this will limit the spread of the disease to the tubers. Wait a couple of weeks, then harvest all the potatoes.

Intensive breeding has developed some varieties that are resistant to the disease, but often this resistance lasts only a year or two before the disease mutates and works out how to infect the plant. Recent breeding in Hungary has produced some varieties (usually prefixed with the name 'Sarpo'), which do, for now anyway, keep the disease at bay.

PESTS AND DISEASES

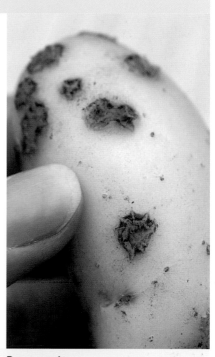

Potato blight
Late blight can ruin your crop, so you'll need to keep a close eye out for it.

Potato scabs
If potato scabs are a problem in your garden, you'll need to improve your soil conditions.

4 Keep watering the potatoes. As the plants start to flower, the potatoes will begin to form.

5 The pot is best kept on a sunny patio. Keep watering your container as this will help the tubers to swell.

6 Try feeling into the pot with your hand, and once you feel decent-sized potatoes, tip the pot out.

Harvesting and storage Harvest earlies and second earlies as they are ready. Dig up a single plant to check the size of the potatoes. One plant should produce more than enough potatoes for a meal. While these types of potatoes don't store too well and should be dug up over the summer as you need them, maincrops will store for much longer. Once lifted in autumn, store in paper or burlap sacks in a cool, dark place. If your potatoes were struck with blight, keep checking the tubers because infection can quickly spread.

In the kitchen Potatoes can be used in all sorts of cuisines – from Asian to European. Potatoes can be harvested all year round and are a versatile crop. Earlies, which you harvest in early summer, work well in warm or cold salads, or just as plain boiled potatoes as they have plenty of flavour. Second earlies are also usually waxy-type potatoes that don't mash well but are great boiled and used in salads. These types of potatoes are also delicious roasted with Mediterranean vegetables or used in soups. The large harvest from your maincrops comes in all shapes, sizes and colours. These can be used for mashing, baking, roasting or chipping. You could also try making your own crisps, adding thinly sliced potatoes to other root vegetables, such as carrots and parsnips.

CALENDAR

EARLY WINTER

Order your seed potatoes and unpack them as soon as they arrive. Leave the tubers in trays in a cool, dry and light spot (but out of direct sunlight). The potatoes will start to "chit" or sprout (see below).

HARVESTING POTATO CROPS

1 Through the early part of the season, draw up the soil around the young stems of potatoes. This will help even more tubers to form. Once the foliage starts to die down, this is a sure sign that your crop is ready. Your potatoes will come to no harm if you leave them in the ground, so you could just dig them when you need them.

2 The best tool for lifting potatoes is a garden fork. Gently push the fork into the ground about 45 cm (18 in) away from the main stems, and ease the potatoes out of the ground. It's impossible to avoid stabbing one or two potatoes, but this method should keep it to a minimum.

3 Collect your potatoes still attached to the plant, but also have a good dig around the area to make sure none are left in the ground. The foliage can go on the compost heap, and the potatoes taken indoors for immediate cooking.

MID-SPRING

Put a sprinkling of fertiliser onto the ground and plant the tubers 15 cm (6 in) deep and 40 cm (16 in) apart. Separate the rows of potatoes by around 50 cm (20 in) (this will depend on the variety).

LATE SPRING

Draw soil from between the rows over the shoots. Keep doing this until you create a ridge of around 30 cm (12 in) in height.

EARLY SUMMER

Water any earlies because the tubers will be swelling now.

MIDSUMMER

Start to harvest your earlies. Use a garden fork to carefully dig out the potatoes. Use immediately.

LATE SUMMER

Your second earlies will start to be ready now. Give the plants a good soaking each week for a few weeks before harvesting. Make sure your maincrops are well watered too, and watch out for blight.

AUTUMN

Maincrops can be lifted through the autumn. These can be stored in paper or burlap sacks.

Sweet potato

This crop can be tricky to grow, but it's well worth it if you're successful.

- ●●●○○ VALUE FOR MONEY
- ●●●●○ MAINTENANCE
- ●●●○○ FREEZE/STORE
- CROPPING SEASON: MID-AUTUMN–LATE AUTUMN

Sweet potatoes naturally grow in sunny climes. They need a long frost-free period and plenty of sun and warmth to grow successfully.

Where to grow For those who have tried growing sweet potatoes and failed, you are not alone. Grown in the soil in your vegetable patch, it's likely that your tubers will be small. To increase the yield, try growing them under black polythene, which helps the soil warm up. A better approach is to grow sweet potatoes in large 10-L (2.5-gallon) containers, either on the patio or in a very warm greenhouse.

In the garden Sweet potatoes come as slips when bought from mail-order vegetable suppliers. Slips are small, unrooted cuttings taken from tubers that have sprouted. When they first arrive, put them in a jar of water to perk them up. If you're growing them in the garden, pot them up in small containers in the greenhouse or on a sunny windowsill and wait until the last frosts before planting outdoors. If you're growing the plants in a pot in a greenhouse or window, plant straight into this.

Pests and diseases Sweet potatoes are trouble free.

Harvesting and storage Tubers should be harvested before any chance of frost. Lift as you would potatoes (see page 34), or if in a tub, just tip them out – but don't expect more than a couple in each pot. Clean off and store as you would potatoes (in paper or burlap sacks in a cool, dark place).

In the kitchen Sweet potatoes can be roasted and served in risottos or on pizzas. You can also make fantastic soups or boil and mash them to serve with Sunday roast.

PLANTING OUT SWEET POTATOES

1 On arrival, place your slips in a jar of water for a day or two. Once perked up, plant deeply in small containers.

2 In the garden, plant out through black plastic sheeting once all risk of frost has passed.

CALENDAR

MID-WINTER
Order your slips from mail-order suppliers.

MID-SPRING
On arrival, pot up slips either into large containers for the greenhouse, or small pots for planting outdoors later.

LATE SPRING
For planting outdoors, dig over the ground well, add some organic matter and plant. Use fleece to protect plants from late frost.

EARLY SUMMER
If growing in pots, keep the plants well watered, and water with a tomato fertiliser.

MIDSUMMER
In the ground, make sure plants don't go short of water, and weed the crop regularly.

LATE SUMMER
Continue watering and feeding your sweet potatoes in containers.

EARLY AUTUMN
You can start to harvest in early autumn, but sweet potatoes get bigger if left longer. Dig up plants or turn out your tubs. Clean off and store in paper or burlap sacks.

MID AUTUMN
In milder areas, harvest now.

LATE AUTUMN
If you like to take a risk, leave your crop in until the beginning of late autumn for larger tubers.

VARIETY SELECTOR

- **'Beauregard Improved'**: a good American variety from Louisiana. These grow to supermarket-sized tubers and have red skins and sweet orange flesh.

- **'Georgia Jet'**: recommended for cooler climates, but it can still be tricky to get a good crop. The bright red skin hides the pale orange flesh.

Carrot

Quick and easy to grow, it's possible to keep your kitchen stocked with fresh garden carrots for most of the year.

- ⬤⬤⬤⬤⬤ VALUE FOR MONEY
- ⬤⬤⬤⬤◯ MAINTENANCE
- ⬤⬤⬤⬤⬤ FREEZE/STORE
- CROPPING SEASON: LATE SPRING–LATE AUTUMN

After potatoes, carrots are probably the most important root crop to gardeners, and for some they're even more rewarding to grow. Spotting the developing orange crowns pushing through the soil and pulling these out is a real joy. Carrots are invaluable in the kitchen — everyone knows how good they taste raw, steamed and roasted, but they can also be used in cakes and puddings. They're rich in carotenoids, which help to protect the body from cancer and heart disease, as well as helping to maintain healthy skin. For some, however, growing carrots can prove very difficult. Carrots are fussy growers, but if your weather or soil doesn't suit them, a container filled with compost will do just as well.

Where to grow Carrots grow best in sandy soil – this way, the carrots can grow undeterred. In stony or heavy soil, carrots can become twisted or forked. If your soil doesn't suit, opt for a container filled with multi-purpose compost.

Types and varieties Like many vegetables today, there is a range of colours to suit all. The traditional orange carrot was developed in the Netherlands in the 17th century – in support of the royal House of Orange. Today, other colours are making a comeback, with cream and even purple carrots available.

Then there are the shapes — most are cylindrical, but one or two varieties are spherical. Of the cylindrical varieties, you can go for shorter, stubby roots or longer, thinner roots. If you're growing in stony or heavy soil, the shorter varieties will prove more successful.

Like potatoes, there are earlies and maincrop types. Earlies tend to grow quicker and can be harvested in as little as 10 weeks

Harvesting carrots
Carrots can be harvested from early summer right into winter, but for the sweetest crop, pick them when they're long and slender.

GROWING CARROTS IN A CONTAINER

1 From early spring onwards, fill large 10-L (2.5-gallon) containers with compost and sprinkle a seed every 2.5 cm (1 in) or so. Cover with a dusting of compost.

2 Water well and continue to water as the plants start to grow. Feeding shouldn't be necessary.

after sowing. Maincrops are slow but steady growers. Harvest these in the autumn.

In the garden Don't add any organic matter to your soil, but dig it over well, then make a shallow drill in which to sow the seed. Water the drill if the soil is dry. Sow in bands (see pages 200–203) and aim for three seeds every 2.5 cm (1 in). If you sow too thickly you can always pull up some baby carrots later to make more space.

You can sow early varieties from mid- to late spring, but the seed is more likely to grow once the soil has warmed up. Late spring is the time to sow your maincrop carrots. Push a garden fork deep into the soil around the carrots, gently easing them out of the ground.

Pests and diseases Carrots are relatively pest-free, except for one major insect: carrot root fly. This pest flies at low heights, smelling out your crop. It lays its eggs on the carrots and the larvae drill into the roots, spoiling the crop. There are no chemicals worth bothering with, but you can outwit this pest. Either put up a low fence of polythene or fine mesh around your crop to a height of 60 cm (2 ft) or cover your crop with fleece.

Alternatively, go for a relatively resistant variety, such as 'Flyaway' or 'Resistafly', or try companion planting (see page 226). Growing in alternate rows with onions has proved to be successful, supposedly because the scent of the onions masks that of the carrots.

Harvesting and storage While early carrots will give you a crop of sweet baby vegetables through the summer, a maincrop variety will keep you going through the winter. As long as the soil doesn't freeze, carrots can be left in the ground and pulled when you need them. If long periods of cold weather are expected, add a layer of straw or compost to protect the crop until needed.

Don't lift or store carrots, as the old methods of storing in clamps or boxes of sand are too much effort for the modern gardener. However, they freeze beautifully: they need to be chopped, blanched and chilled, then frozen.

In the kitchen Young baby carrots can be used in fresh-tasting, warm summer salads. As the season progresses, use maincrop carrots in stews, or slow roast them for sweetness.

CALENDAR

EARLY SPRING
You can start to make sowings now, but germination may be sporadic. Create a 1.5-cm (5⁄8-in) drill and sprinkle seeds along it. Aim for three seeds every 2.5 cm (1 in). Cover the drill with soil.

MID-SPRING
In cooler areas, repeat as above.

LATE SPRING
To be safe, and in cooler conditions, make late spring your main sowing date.

EARLY SUMMER
Start pulling young carrots from the soil, leaving others to grow bigger.

MIDSUMMER
It's not too late to sow another row of carrots – at least 15 cm (6 in) away from your last row.

LATE SUMMER
Keep pulling baby carrots, leaving a plant every 5–10 cm (2–4 in), which will continue to grow right into autumn.

EARLY AUTUMN
Start to harvest your main crop of carrots. They can be left in the ground if you don't need them yet.

3 Leave the containers in a sunny spot on the patio, and as the shoots start to grow, carrots will start forming below ground.

4 Start pulling baby carrots when they're around finger-size, leaving others in the pot to grow bigger.

VARIETY SELECTOR
Earlies
- 'Primo', 'Early Nantes 2'.

Spherical
- 'Parmex'.

Maincrop
- 'Bangor', 'Fall King 2'.

Colourful
- 'Crème de Lite', 'Purple Haze', 'Harlequin'.

For stony soil
- 'Chantenay Red Cored', 'Parmex'.

Parsnip

Once a mainstay of the winter kitchen garden, parsnips can be harvested from summer right through to late winter.

○○○○○ VALUE FOR MONEY
○○○○○ MAINTENANCE
○○○○○ FREEZE/STORE
CROPPING SEASON: EARLY AUTUMN–LATE WINTER

Parsnips are related to carrots, and so many of the techniques used and pests encountered are the same. It's a good idea, therefore, to grow them side by side. Parsnips are renowned for being tricky to germinate; this is mostly due to parsnip seed losing viability quickly with age. If you start with fresh, good-quality seed each time and sow when the soil has started to warm, you should end up with a bumper crop.

Perfect parsnips
A bumper harvest of parsnips will add sweetness to soups and stews right through the winter.

Where to grow Like carrots, parsnips do best in rich, deep soil. Stony or heavy soil will result in the roots forking, making them difficult to clean and prepare in the kitchen. In the garden, grow parsnips alongside other root crops. If your soil doesn't suit parsnips, they can also be grown in containers – follow the advice for carrots (see pages 36–37).

In the garden If you are growing in rows, plant 1 cm (½ in) deep and leave 20–30 cm (8–12 in) between rows. Parsnips can get quite large, so aim for a plant every 15 cm (6 in) along the row. As they can be awkward to germinate successfully, it's best to put in two or three seeds each time, and thin out later. Alternatively, sow a seed every 5 cm (2 in) and thin out baby parsnips in the summer, leaving the others to carry on growing.

Pests and diseases Like carrots, the biggest threat to parsnips is carrot root fly. Prevention is the only way to avoid this dreaded pest, so go for fine meshes, barriers or companion planting (see above, and page 226).

GROWING PARSNIPS

1 Make sure your bed is well weeded – remove any perennial or annual weeds. Dig over well and rake to a fine tilth. Draw out a row with the back of a rake and sow a few seeds every 15 cm (6 in).

2 Seeds should start to germinate in a week or two.

3 If you have more than one plant every 15 cm (6 in), you can thin them out now. If there's more than one plant growing next to each other, be careful when removing the extra seedlings. If you have any gaps, these extra seedlings can be used to fill in.

PROTECTING YOUR PARSNIP CROP

1 Insert canes around your crop in spring, once it is established. Ideally, sow parsnips next to carrots, since they suffer from the same pests and can be protected in the same way.

2 Wrap fine mesh or polythene sheet around the canes up to 60 cm (2 ft) high and secure in place with pegs or wire. Alternatively, you could use fleece (see page 53).

Harvesting and storage You can start harvesting baby parsnips in summer, but the tastiest ones are picked later. Parsnips are renowned for sweetening up after the first frosts, so make sure you leave some for early winter and beyond. They can be left in the ground until required – in very cold areas, cover the row with straw.

In the kitchen Use parsnips to sweeten up stews and soups, or cut lengthways and roast. Parsnips can also be boiled and mashed.

4 After the first frosts, the parsnips should start to sweeten up. These can then be lifted with the aid of a garden fork as and when you need them.

5 The object of the exercise: a bumper harvest of parsnips.

CALENDAR

MID-SPRING
Start seed off in mid- to late spring and sow seeds 1 cm (½ in) deep direct into a well-prepared seedbed.

LATE SPRING
Keep an eye on the seedlings and resow extra seed if any fail to come up.

EARLY SUMMER
Parsnips are slow to get going and can struggle if there are lots of weeds, so ensure you keep weeding your plot.

MIDSUMMER
Water if very dry and start to harvest baby parsnips once the tops are around 5 cm (2 in) in diameter.

LATE SUMMER
Continue weeding.

EARLY AUTUMN
Parsnips should be starting to swell, but leave in the ground for a larger crop.

MID-AUTUMN
Start to harvest your main crop of parsnips. Dig up what you need for each meal, but leave what you don't need in the ground to be harvested at a later date.

VARIETY SELECTOR
Go for F1 varieties as the seed quality is likely to be better.
• 'Countess': very sweet variety.
• 'Gladiator': good choice for baby parsnips.
• 'Albion': smooth-skinned and very white.

Beetroot

This earthy-flavoured vegetable comes in a variety of colours, and is quick and easy to grow.

⬤⬤⬤⬤⬤ VALUE FOR MONEY
⬤⬤⬤⬤⬤ MAINTENANCE
⬤⬤⬤⬤⬤ FREEZE/STORE
CROPPING SEASON: EARLY SUMMER–MID-AUTUMN

Red roots
Bright red beetroot adds colour to your garden and your plate.

This versatile vegetable is a mainstay in any kitchen garden. It is quick-growing, is simple to raise and suffers from few pests and diseases, and best of all, it looks and tastes great.

Baby beetroot can be grown in just nine weeks and so it's a great crop for continuous sowing – from early spring to midsummer.

As well as the traditional purple roots, there are yellow, white and striped versions.

Where to grow Beetroot can be grown in containers, but it is also easy to grow in the ground. It's a good idea to add some general fertiliser to the soil before sowing.

In the garden Beetroot seeds are a type of fruit, each of which contains up to four individual seeds. Therefore, with each seed you sow, you'll probably get a few plants coming up. Let these grow together and they'll naturally push each other apart to form separate beetroot plants. Plant seeds 2.5 cm (1 in) apart and 1.5 cm (⅝ in) deep, with 20–30 cm (8–12 in) between rows.

Pests and diseases Beetroot is pretty trouble free, but the roots can split following periods of drought, so keep the plants watered.

Harvesting and storage Start the harvest early by picking some of the leaves, for salads. Baby beetroot can be pulled up when the roots reach around 5 cm (2 in) in diameter. If you start sowing in early spring and continue until midsummer, you'll have beetroot from late spring to late autumn. Once they're lifted, brush off the soil and twist off foliage – don't cut the root; it will start to bleed.

In the kitchen Slice baby beetroot raw and add to salads. It can be roasted, made into soup, or boiled, then skinned and served with sauces or salads. For pickling, use small ones.

CALENDAR

EARLY SPRING
Start off in early spring on well-cultivated soil. Sow a single row of seeds and repeat this every two to three weeks.

MID-SPRING
Keep sowing beetroot seeds in individual rows every few weeks. If the soil is looking dry, water the drill before adding the seeds. Keep watering until seeds start to emerge.

LATE SPRING
If you really like beetroot and have the space, you can carry on sowing seeds in late spring. You can also harvest some of the young leaves from previous sowings to eat fresh in salads.

EARLY SUMMER
Start to harvest your first baby beetroot. Just pull up by the leaves and twist off. You can keep sowing for a longer supply of beetroot into autumn.

MIDSUMMER
Make this your last sowing. A crop of baby beetroot will be ready in mid-autumn and larger beetroot by late autumn.

VARIETY SELECTOR
Choose colourful varieties to brighten up your kitchen garden.

- **'Boltardy'**: a reliable variety in the more usual dark red colour.
- **'Albina'**: a good white variety.
- **'Burpee's Golden'**: golden flesh.
- **'Chioggia'**: striped (red and white) variety.

GROWING BEETROOT IN A CONTAINER

1 Fill a large container with multi-purpose compost.

2 Scatter seeds over the surface, at least 2.5 cm (1 in) apart.

3 Cover with around 1.5 cm (⅝ in) of compost and then water. Leave in a sunny spot, pulling the beetroot when they are the size of golf balls.

Turnip

Turnips are excellent space fillers and grow in as little as six weeks.

- ●●●●○ VALUE FOR MONEY
- ●●●●○ MAINTENANCE
- ●●●●○ FREEZE/STORE
- CROPPING SEASON: EARLY SUMMER–MID-AUTUMN

Rapid roots
Summer turnips are quicker and easier to grow than most people think.

Another member of the brassica family, turnips can be separated into two groups. Slow-growing or winter types, grown in the same way as swedes (see page 44), will be ready for harvest from autumn. Then there is the more interesting group: the quick-growing or summer varieties. Sow from early spring onwards in succession (see pages 200–203) and small, golf-ball-sized turnips will be available all summer.

Where to grow Summer turnips make a great catch crop. They don't take up much space and can be fitted into gaps in the vegetable garden through summer.

In the garden For winter turnips, sow seeds around 20 cm (8 in) apart in midsummer. You'll be rewarded with large roots that can be left in the ground and harvested through the autumn and winter. From a late spring planting, summer turnips can be ready in as little as six

weeks. This quick turnaround means that summer turnips will also do well in containers with minimum maintenance.

Pests and diseases As with all brassica crops, pests are a problem. Use floating row covers and incorporate (and protect) with your other brassicas. For the slow-growing turnips, grow with your other brassicas, such as swedes and Brussels sprouts.

Harvesting and storage Summer turnips don't keep, so pull them up as you need them. Don't let them get bigger than the size of a golf ball or they will become tough. Leave winter turnips in the ground until mid-winter.

In the kitchen Turnips can be boiled and mashed with carrots and butter. They can also be roasted or even eaten raw, grated in salads.

CALENDAR

EARLY SPRING
You can start to sow summer turnips direct in milder areas. Create a fine seed bed and add some balanced fertiliser. Make drills 1.5 cm (5/8 in) deep and sow seeds thinly.

MID-SPRING
Every couple of weeks sow another row of turnips 15 cm (6 in) away from the last row. As plants grow, they'll push each other apart, but thin them out if they're too dense.

LATE SPRING
Water during dry spells, and keep sowing further rows. Rows of turnips should be ready for pulling in succession.

EARLY SUMMER
Keep pulling up your turnips. If they get any bigger than golf ball size, throw them on the compost heap.

MIDSUMMER
Sow a row or two of winter turnips, plant seeds 20 cm (8 in) apart, around 2 cm ¾ (in) deep.

LATE SUMMER
Keep watering and weeding winter turnips.

EARLY AUTUMN
Start harvesting winter turnips, and leave in the ground and pull up when needed.

VARIETY SELECTOR
Best summer turnips
- 'Snowball', 'Aramis'.

Best winter turnips
- 'Golden Ball'.

GROWING BEST-QUALITY TURNIPS

1 Prepare a seed drill 1.5 cm (⅝ in) deep, and sow turnip seeds 5 cm (2 in) apart. Cover with soil and water in well.

2 Keep watering and pull out turnips when they are the size of golf balls.

Radish

Radishes add spice to salads or can be grown for Asian-inspired cooking. Best of all, they're one of the easiest brassicas to grow.

●●●●●	VALUE FOR MONEY
●●●●●	MAINTENANCE
●●●○○	FREEZE/STORE
CROPPING SEASON: LATE SPRING–LATE AUTUMN	

Wintery morsels
Black-skinned radishes can be a useful crop when there is little else around in winter.

Summer radishes should be sown little and often from early spring onwards. Quick to grow, they take as little as four weeks from sowing to harvest. Best of all, they come in a range of interesting colours: the traditional red, as well as white and purple.

Winter radishes are best known for their use in Asian cusine. One of the best known is the white mooli, but there are red as well as black types too.

Where to grow Grow winter radishes alongside other long-growing cabbage-family crops. Treat summer salad radishes as a catch crop and fit into brassica beds as well as other areas of the garden as space becomes available, but watch out for pests. Sow them little and often to keep a regular supply of salad radishes for your kitchen.

In the garden If you are new to growing food and just can't wait to get started, summer salad radishes are a good place to start. Apart from sprouting seeds and some quick-growing baby-leaf lettuces, radishes will be your first proper crop. To sow them in a pot, aim for a seed every 2.5 cm (1 in), and as they grow, the roots will push each other apart. Alternatively, sow in short rows spaced around 15 cm (6 in) apart, with a seed every 2.5 cm (1 in).

Winter radishes are best in the vegetable bed. You'll need to sow in midsummer and they'll be ready for pulling by mid-autumn.

Pests and diseases As they are members of the brassica family, radishes are susceptible to the same pests and diseases (see page 55).

Harvesting and storage Successional sowing of summer radishes will give you a continual supply of small roots all summer. Pull them as you need them. If any radishes go to flower, allow them to set seed. Their green pods are edible, with a hot and fiery taste. Winter radishes can be left in the ground, but can be damaged by frost. Protect with straw until required.

In the kitchen Keep pulling salad radishes when they reach around 2 cm (¾ in) in diameter. These mild and crunchy roots make a tasty addition to salads. Winter radishes can be very hot and are better cooked. Marinate in soy sauce and add to stir-fries.

GROWING SUMMER RADISHES

1 Make sure your bed is well weeded – remove any perennial or annual weeds. Dig over well and rake to a fine tilth. Draw out a row with the back of a rake.

2 Sow a few seeds every 15 cm (6 in). Seeds should start to germinate in a week or two.

3 Sow short rows every couple of weeks 2.5 cm (1 in) apart and about 1 cm (½ in) deep from early spring onwards.

Peppery roots
Radishes come in a variety of colours and are the quickest vegetable to grow from seed to plate.

CALENDAR

MIDSUMMER
Sow winter radishes now. Make sure your soil is well watered and sow in drills 30 cm (12 in) apart.

LATE SUMMER
Keep watering your seedlings. Thin them to 15 cm (6 in) apart.

EARLY AUTUMN
Make sure your plants don't go short of water and weed regularly.

MID-AUTUMN
Start to harvest your winter radishes when they've reached a decent size and taken on the colour suggested on the seed packet.

LATE AUTUMN
If you haven't harvested all your crop, cover with a layer of straw, or similar, to protect from frosts.

VARIETY SELECTOR
Summer radishes
- 'Cherry Belle': red.
- 'Amethyst': purple.
- 'Albena': white.

Winter radishes
- 'Mino Summer Cross' F_1: white mooli.
- 'Black Spanish Round': black-skinned.
- 'Mantangong': white-skinned, magenta flesh.

4 Cover with fine mesh if pests are a problem.

5 Start to harvest when the radishes start to form.

Swede

A much-forgotten member of the brassica family, these yellow-fleshed roots are worthy of a small spot in your garden.

⬤⬤⬤◯◯	VALUE FOR MONEY
⬤⬤◯◯◯	MAINTENANCE
⬤⬤⬤◯◯	FREEZE/STORE
CROPPING SEASON: MID-AUTUMN–EARLY WINTER	

Versatile vegetable
Swedes are a tricky but rewarding crop to grow.

You rarely see swedes growing in gardens today, but this once-popular crop is worthy of increased interest. It's a slow-growing crop, taking all season to reach maturity, and one that also suffers from the same pests and diseases as other brassicas. So while it's not the easiest to grow, if you provide the right conditions and protect this crop well you'll be rewarded with large, bulbous roots, which can be roasted, boiled or mashed.

Where to grow You'll need a sunny and fertile spot for your swedes. Grow them with your other brassicas such as turnips, radishes and cabbages and move them around your plot each year on a rotation (see pages 22–23).

Pests and diseases Like all brassicas, swedes suffer from a range of pests, most of which can be kept at bay with the use of fine mesh. Swedes can also split in the ground – often caused by an irregular supply of water

– so it's best to water the crops evenly, especially in dry spells. Watch out for slugs and snails (see page 227).

Harvesting and storage After a spring sowing, swedes will start to mature in autumn; however it is worth leaving them until they develop fully. You can leave them in the ground for some time – but don't let them freeze. Once harvested, twist off the leaves at the top and either use in the kitchen immediately, or store for a limited period in a cool place.

In the kitchen Swedes are much milder than other brassicas, such as turnips, but still retain that slight cabbagey flavour. Cutting off the skin will reveal a large yellow root – cut into cubes then boil, mash or roast. Like turnips, try mashing them with carrots, adding plenty of butter for a delicious vegetable accompaniment.

CALENDAR

MID-SPRING
Sow seeds directly in the ground, into a well-prepared seedbed. Place seeds about 1 cm (½ in) deep and 30 cm (12 in) apart. Cover crops with protective fine mesh to prevent pests from attacking them.

LATE SPRING
If you didn't get around sowing seeds in mid-spring, you can still do it now.

EARLY SUMMER
Keep watering your crop – swedes hate to dry out.

MIDSUMMER
Water and weed, check plants for pests.

LATE SUMMER
Keep watering your crop, especially during any dry spells.

EARLY AUTUMN
Pull out of the ground with the top growth intact. Roots will be ready for lifting from late summer to late autumn.

PRODUCING BEST-QUALITY RUTABAGAS

1 Watch out for slugs and use controls such as organic pellets where necessary.

2 Keep flying pests off your crop by using fine mesh over the top.

3 Water your crop in all but the wettest of climates through the summer.

VARIETY SELECTOR
- 'Marian': traditional purple-topped swede with sweet, yellow flesh.
- 'Invitation': large roots, with some resistance to clubroot.

Onion

Onions are one of the most popular vegetables used in the kitchen.

OOOOO VALUE FOR MONEY
OOOOO MAINTENANCE
OOOOO FREEZE/STORE
CROPPING SEASON: EARLY SUMMER–EARLY AUTUMN

Onions come from a group of vegetables and flowering plants called alliums. Used since Egyptian times in cooking, they were then developed by the Romans. Not only were brown-skinned onions used by this time, but red- and white-skinned varieties too. Today there are many varieties available in a selection of shapes, colours and flavours.

There are also a couple of growing methods (by seed or set – see below) as well as some variation in timings (you can plant either in autumn or spring). Select your variety, and harvest and store your onions carefully, to ensure they last you well into the winter.

Where to grow Onions belong to the same group of plants as shallots (see page 48), garlic (see page 49), salad onions (see pages 106–107) and leeks (see pages 104–105), and where possible it's a good idea to grow all of these near to each other. As they suffer from similar pests and diseases, you should rotate them around the garden together too. Use well-cultivated ground for growing onions, preferably with some well-rotted compost added the previous year. Add 35 g (1¼ oz) per square metre of general-purpose fertiliser before you plant. Onions can also be grown successfully in containers; however, they are not the most attractive container vegetable!

Types and varieties Onions are biennial, meaning they take two years to flower and set seed. In the first year they produce a storage organ – the bulb – which is what gets harvested.

Onions can be grown in the garden in two ways. The first is from seed, where seed is sown in pots and transplanted to the garden, or sown direct in the ground. The second is through sets. Sets are small bulbs that have been grown from seed very →

Dry off your onions
Once harvested, onions need to be dried off to ensure they store well through winter. Either leave on the soil surface to dry, or if it's wet, move them to a greenhouse or conservatory.

GROWING ONIONS FROM SEED

1 Sow about six seeds in individual small pots in mid spring.

2 Plant out the whole clump of seedlings four to six weeks later from each pot, about 20 cm (8 in) apart.

3 As the bulbs swell, they'll push each other apart, creating a clump of small onions.

densely by the supplier. Their small size means that in their second year (the year you'll be growing them) they'll continue to grow the bulb rather than setting seed. There are pros and cons to both methods. Growing onions from seed is generally cheaper – there's a larger selection of varieties available and, in theory, they should store better. Sets, on the other hand, are simple to plant and easy for the novice vegetable grower. Growing onions from seed is slightly more tricky, since onion seed is small and fussy. Using sets is generally more expensive than seed and the choice of varieties isn't as great.

Pests and diseases

Onions don't really suffer from pests – their sulphurous compounds seem to put most flying pests off trying to nibble them. However, they do suffer from a couple of diseases:

White rot The most prevalent fungal disease is white rot, which can remain in the soil for many years. You'll see white fluff growing on the bulbs, and the leaves will turn yellow and die. Unfortunately, there is no treatment for white rot, and once it's in the soil you won't be able to grow onions or any other allium in the same patch for at least 10 years. Rotate your crop to another part of the vegetable patch, and if necessary, grow onions in containers.

Downy mildew This is another fungus that affects the leaves, causing oval lesions, which eventually cause the leaves to die. Downy mildew is at its worse in cool, wet summers – remove and destroy any damaged plant material as and when you see it.

Harvesting and storage

When the bulbs have grown and the leaves start to yellow, your onions are almost ready for harvesting. Don't bend the tops over, but do lift the bulbs slightly with a fork. This breaks the roots, encouraging them to ripen and their skins to harden off. You can leave them on the surface of the bed for a couple of weeks, but in a wet summer it's best to move them into a greenhouse to dry off. Be careful when handling onions, as any damage will mean they will rot in storage. Use any damaged onions first. The others can be suspended in braids or bunches and kept in a cool shed or garage. If braiding or bunching your onions, make sure you don't cut off the long stems.

In the kitchen

Onions are used in all sorts of cusines, from Italian to Indian. When chopped finely, they add texture and flavour to a variety of sauces. Brown onions store longest and are best used for cooking, whereas red and white onions are less pungent and sweeter, so are great in salads.

VARIETY SELECTOR

- 'Kamal', 'Red Baron': red.
- 'Setton', 'Turbo': brown.
- 'Spanish Sweet Yellow', 'Snowball': white (sweet).
- 'Brown pickling SY300', 'Paris silverskin': pickling.
- 'Senshyu Semi-globe Yellow': Japanese.

GROWING ONIONS FROM SETS

1 Using sets in either spring or autumn, rather than seed, is a quicker and easier way to grow onions. Whichever season you plant, make sure your soil is fertile and weed free before you begin.

2 Push the sets into the ground, pointed end up, around 10 cm (4 in) apart, with 20 cm (8 in) between rows. Leave just the point sticking out, but watch out for birds that have a habit of pulling the sets out of the ground. You could use a guide as shown to ensure that your rows are straight.

3 By mid- to late summer, the onions should be ready to harvest. Using a garden fork, gently lift them out of the ground.

KNOW YOUR ONIONS

There are lots of types of onion to grow in your garden. Select the varieties that suit your cooking requirements.

BROWN ONIONS

The traditional brown onion is a staple in all kitchens. Tough, shiny skins mean they store well through winter and are best used for cooking.

JAPANESE ONIONS

These are varieties that have been specially bred for autumn planting. They are ready for harvest before your main crop of onions, but don't store well beyond the autumn.

PICKLING ONIONS

These are regular onions sown very densely, resulting in small bulbs. Some onion varieties have been specially bred for pickling, but really any variety will do.

RED ONIONS

Often sweeter and milder than brown onions. The red colour used to be skin deep, but newer varieties have been developed to extend the colour right through. They add colour and a lovely taste to salads.

WHITE ONIONS

Often called sweet or Spanish onions, these are milder and often larger than traditional brown onions. They contain fewer sulphur compounds that make your eyes water and are ideal for eating raw in salads. They do not grow well in cooler climates.

CALENDAR

LATE WINTER

Visit your local garden store and buy your onion sets.

EARLY SPRING

Start to plant onion sets. Push sets into the soil so the tips are just sticking out. Plant sets 10 cm (4 in) apart for decent-sized onions, with at least 20 cm (8 in) between rows.

MID-SPRING

Keep your rows of onions well weeded – no additional watering should be needed.

LATE SPRING

Keep weeding – the plants will look after themselves.

EARLY SUMMER

Plants should start to form large bulbs, but these aren't ready yet.

MIDSUMMER

Maintain your regime of weeding. Some varieties will be ready for harvesting. Lift carefully with a fork, and leave on the ground so the skins dry off.

LATE SUMMER

Most onions will be ready for harvesting in late summer.

EARLY AUTUMN

Order in your autumn sets or Japanese onions.

MID-AUTUMN

Plant autumn sets now, following the advice above, but use a different part of the garden as part of your rotation.

4 Knock the excess soil off the roots, which will encourage the bulbs to dry out.

5 Leave the onions either on the ground (if it's sunny) or move them to a greenhouse until the skins and stem have completely dried. This will encourage the skins to dry off before storing.

Shallot

If you're looking for a more refined cooking onion, you can't go wrong with shallots.

✪✪✪✪✪ VALUE FOR MONEY
✪✪✪✪✪ MAINTENANCE
✪✪✪✪✪ FREEZE/STORE
CROPPING SEASON: LATE SUMMER–MID-AUTUMN

Shallot set
A single shallot set will produce many new, sweet and mildly flavoured shallots in a matter of months.

Shallots are similar to onions in the way they are grown and in the problems you'll face. The rewards, however, are somewhat different. Plant a single bulb in the ground in spring and, unlike onions where you'll just get a single larger bulb in return a few months later, the shallot set will have multiplied into over 10 small oval bulbs.

Where to grow Shallots can be grown with onions and other members of the allium family. Use ground that is reasonably fertile, but preferably not an area that has recently had organic matter added to it because they won't grow as well.

In the garden More often sold as sets (small bulbs), you will now find shallot seed for sale too. Sets can be grown in exactly the same way as onions (see page 45); however, it's better if you space them slightly wider apart – 15 cm (6 in) apart, and 30 cm (12 in) between rows – to allow the multiple bulbs plenty of space.

As with onions, shallots cannot compete against weeds, so it's important to keep your shallot bed well weeded, otherwise your crop won't develop.

Pests and diseases As for onions (see page 46).

Harvesting and storage Shallots will start to ripen up from midsummer. They can be lifted and left to dry off on the soil surface. If the weather is wet, dry them off indoors. There is no need to split the shallots up, as they'll start to break up on their own. Store in net or mesh bags or string together as with onions (see page 46). Stored in a cool, dry place, shallots can keep for up to nine months.

In the kitchen Shallots are well loved by chefs. Their flavour is more subtle than their larger counterparts. Use as you would regular onions, or use whole in stews and casseroles.

CALENDAR

MID-SPRING
Plant your shallot sets individually in rows, 15 cm (6 in) apart, next to your onions. Push individual sets into the ground so their tips are just showing. Use fleece or net to cover the sets until they start to sprout to prevent birds from pulling them out of the ground.

LATE SPRING
Keep your crop well weeded.

EARLY SUMMER
Keep weeding, but additional watering shouldn't be necessary except in the driest of summers.

MIDSUMMER–LATE SUMMER
Gently push a fork underneath the clumps of shallots and lift out of the ground, leaving them on the soil surface for a couple of weeks for the skins to harden, then take in for storage.

GROWING SHALLOTS FROM SEED

1 Ensure your area is well weeded and the soil dug over to create a fine tilth.

2 Using the edge of a rake, draw out a seed drill around 1.5 cm (⅝ in) deep.

3 Place 6 to 8 shallots seeds every 30 cm (12 in), then draw the soil back over with the rake.

VARIETY SELECTOR
- Sets: 'Yellow Moon', 'Topper'.
- Seed: 'Prisma', 'Ambition'.

Garlic

Indispensable in the kitchen, garlic is simple and rewarding to grow.

○○○○○ VALUE FOR MONEY
○○○○○ MAINTENANCE
○○○○○ FREEZE/STORE
CROPPING SEASON: LATE SPRING–EARLY AUTUMN

Ripe garlic bulbs
From a single bulb of garlic you can expect to harvest a dozen or so bulbs. These can be used fresh or dried and used through the winter.

Push a single garlic clove into the soil, and as long as you don't allow weeds to swamp the area, you'll be able to lift a full bulb of garlic from the ground several months later. Garlic is well known for its health benefits and has been used in cooking since ancient times.

Where to grow Grow garlic alongside onions and shallots and rotate them around the garden. Doesn't do well in heavy or wet soils.

In the garden Garlic is a hardy plant and needs a period of cold to succeed (30–60 days below 10°C/ 50°F); many advocate planting garlic in the autumn or early winter. If your winter weather is severe or your soil is wet and heavy though, wait until early spring.

Pests and diseases Fairly trouble-free.

Harvesting and storage Unlike onions, garlic bulbs form well below the soil surface. In midsummer, carefully lift a single bulb of garlic to see if it's ready. If not, leave the others for another couple of weeks. Ease out of the ground, being careful not to bruise the bulbs, and leave on the surface to dry. Make sure all your garlic is lifted by midsummer to avoid the cloves resprouting. You can use fresh garlic immediately, otherwise dry and store it with your onions and shallots in braids (see page 46) or mesh sacks.

In the kitchen Garlic bulbs can be roasted whole, or stuffed into a chicken to add flavour. Use cloves peeled, chopped and fried in Mediterranean, Indian and Asian dishes.

(see page 46)

CALENDAR

EARLY–LATE AUTUMN
Plant now. Break individual cloves from the bulb and plant flat-end down. Push down 3 cm (1¼ in) into the soil.

MID-WINTER–LATE WINTER
Don't plant your cloves during this time – it is too cold and inhospitable.

MID-SPRING
Make sure the plants aren't being smothered by weeds.

LATE SPRING
Continue weeding and water if the weather is dry.

EARLY SUMMER
Bulbs should start to swell and can be harvested from now onward. Check by digging up one plant – if the bulbs are very small, leave for one or two more weeks.

MIDSUMMER
Keep harvesting your bulbs and hang them up to dry.

GROWING GARLIC

1 Break up bulbs and plant garlic, pointed end upwards, as individual cloves direct in the ground.

2 When ready, use a fork to carefully dig up the bulb growing below the ground.

3 Brush off the soil and leave to dry in a greenhouse.

VARIETY SELECTOR

- **'Solent white'**: a tough variety suited to both autumn and spring planting.
- **'Lautrec White'**: originating in France, this white-skinned variety produces deep purple cloves with a smooth and subtle flavour.
- **Elephant garlic**: technically a type of leek, this mild-flavoured garlic lookalike produces bulbs up to 10 cm (4 in) in diameter.

Jerusalem artichoke

An easy vegetable to grow that will reward you year after year with sweet-flavoured, nutritious tubers, perfect for soups and stews.

✪✪✪✪✪	VALUE FOR MONEY
✪✪✪✪✪	MAINTENANCE
✪✪✪✪✪	FREEZE/STORE
CROPPING SEASON: LATE AUTUMN–WINTER	

A native American plant, Jerusalem artichokes grow tall and produce pretty sunflowers, as well as tasty tubers below ground that can be dug up from autumn through to winter. Before you start planting, there is one word of warning: it is extremely difficult to dig up every tuber from the soil and you will find that once planted, Jerusalem artichokes will reappear year after year, so grow this plant only if you know you like the taste, as it's not to everyone's liking. Grow it somewhere out of the way, in an enclosed area so that it can't spread across your borders.

Where to grow
Jerusalem artichokes are tough plants and will do well in all but the most extreme climates.

Jerusalem artichokes are happy growing almost anywhere in the garden, whether in sunny or shady areas. However, they are best positioned out of the way and in a sheltered spot as they can grow to over 3 m (10 ft) tall. Because of their spreading habit, select a bed with enclosed sides. About 2 sq m (21 sq ft) is more than enough to devote to this plant.

Growing in containers is an option as this will prevent plants from spreading. However, they are vigorous growers and will need constant watering in the summer, so consider this option only if you don't mind watering every day or have an automatic irrigation system. Use soil or a soil-based compost for your containers, since this is generally much heavier than multi-purpose compost, which often contains peat or composted bark which, when it dries out, is very light. The heavy soil will help to prevent the plants from toppling over when they grow tall.

Pests and diseases
Jerusalem artichokes are usually trouble free.

Harvesting and storage
Once the foliage is hit by the first frosts, the plants can be cut down to around 5 cm (2 in). Being hardy, the tubers can be left in the ground until they are needed. Work your way along the bed and dig up as many as you need for each meal. This way they'll last throughout the winter. If very hard frosts or snow are likely, cover the ground with a thick layer of straw for protection. The tubers can also be stored in plastic bags in the fridge for a few weeks.

In the kitchen
Similar to potatoes, Jerusalem artichokes can be roasted, baked, fried and boiled, and are harvested from the autumn onwards (harvest as you go).

Winter produce
The knobbly tubers of Jerusalem artichoke can be lifted as you need them right through the winter.

CALENDAR

LATE WINTER–EARLY SPRING
Order your tubers in the winter and plant out 10–15 cm (4–6 in) deep and 30 cm (12 in) apart. For container growing, plant a single tuber.

SPRING–AUTUMN
For the best crop, water in dry weather.

LATE AUTUMN
Cut stems down to 5 cm (2 in) and dig up tubers when required.

WINTER
Either leave a few tubers in the ground or replant a few that you dug up for a crop the following year.

VARIETY SELECTOR
• Many suppliers may just sell Jerusalem artichokes unnamed or called 'Common'. All artichokes are good croppers, but some are more knobbly than others. If you do have a choice, go for 'Feseau' since this named variety is considered to be less knobbly and therefore easier to prepare than other unnamed varieties.

Celeriac

With its distinctive celery-like flavour, celeriac can be used in salads, soups and more.

●●●○○	VALUE FOR MONEY
●●●○○	MAINTENANCE
●●●○○	FREEZE/STORE

CROPPING SEASON: EARLY AUTUMN–LATE WINTER

Delicious, nutritious and from the same family as carrots and celery, celeriac is one of the most underrated vegetables. It is easy to grow, but does need a long growing season and moist soil to allow the roots to swell to the size of a beefsteak tomato by autumn. It can be left in situ and harvested throughout the winter (just like Jerusalem artichokes, opposite).

Where to grow A close relative of celery, celeriac is much easier to grow but requires plenty of water. It thrives in a cool, damp climate with a long, frost-free growing season.

In the garden Favours an open site in the main part of your vegetable patch, reaching 50 cm (20 in) high. It needs plenty of moisture and nutrients, so plant out in rich soil and plenty of organic matter.

Pests and diseases Celeriac is trouble-free.

Harvesting and storage Celeriac can be harvested from early autumn onwards. The leaf stalks will start to rot over the winter so these should be removed – leave the roots in the ground until required. The flavour will improve after a mild frost or two, but a layer of straw may be required to protect it from severe frosts. The colder your climate, the more straw you will need.

In the kitchen Leaves can be picked off celeriac through the summer and used in soups and salads to add a celery flavour. Once harvested, the knobbly roots will need to be scrubbed and peeled. Chop into cubes to use in soups and stews, or slice very finely in salads. Boiled and mashed, it can be eaten alone or mixed with mashed potato.

Tastier than celery
Try the root sliced very finely in salads, or boil and then mash.

VARIETY SELECTOR

There isn't much breeding work on celeriac, and it's likely the varieties on offer will be limited. Look out for these two:

- **'Monarch'**: smooth skins, with a good flavour and texture. Creamy coloured roots.
- **'Brilliant'**: white flesh that doesn't discolour. Also fairly smooth skins.

CALENDAR

LATE WINTER–EARLY SPRING

Buy seed of one of the recommended cultivars. Sow seed into trays or pots. Don't cover the compost with soil as the seed needs light to germinate. Raise in a cool greenhouse or conservatory (around 12°C/54°F or less). Once germinated, prick out the seedlings and grow on individually.

MID-SPRING

Harden plants off in a cold frame or somewhere sheltered outside, then in late spring plant out in their final position, with about 30 cm (12 in) between plants. Protect plants from slugs and snails. Add a layer of organic matter, such as garden compost, to retain moisture, and some granular fertiliser rich in nitrogen. Water well in dry spells.

MID-AUTUMN

Remove dying leaf stalks and start to lift when required in the kitchen.

LEAFY CROPS

Packed full of vitamins and antioxidants, leafy crops such as cabbage, mizuna and spinach make a healthy choice for your kitchen. Their ornamental value, with crops such as lettuce, endive and kale, means they look great in your garden too.

Cabbage

Cabbage is a versatile crop with enough types and varieties to ensure an all-year-round supply.

⦿⦿⦿⦿⦿ VALUE FOR MONEY
⦿⦿⦿⦿⦿ MAINTENANCE
⦿⦿⦿⦿⦿ FREEZE/STORE
CROPPING SEASON: ALL YEAR ROUND

While cabbage may not be your first choice of vegetable to grow, if you are going to grow any brassicas, you should include a row or two of cabbages. As well as cabbages, the brassica family includes other leafy crops, such as sprouts, kale and Chinese cabbage, as well as the root crops turnip and swede and the flower crops broccoli and cauliflower. Most are fairly slow-growing crops and should be rotated around the garden together. If you are growing any of the above, you may as well devote a whole bed to them and grow a wide selection. Brassicas have a few pests and diseases to contend with, so it's worth grouping them together, since your attempts to keep the pests at bay will be most effective when crops are side by side.

Where to grow Cabbages are fairly large, slow-growing crops and don't do particularly well in containers. However, with the ability to grow baby-sized versions and squeeze more plants into a tight space, they are definitely worth trying in a small garden. Clubroot, a common disease (see page 55), can be offset with alkaline soil. If your soil isn't around pH 7, it can be increased to that level with the addition of lime (see page 219).

Types and varieties There is a wide variety of cabbage types, often termed by the season they are harvested. Summer and autumn varieties include some interesting red types; winter varieties include the 'Dutch White' (large coleslaw cabbage), the crinkly green 'Savoy' and red-tinged 'January King'; and spring cabbages are basically ones that give you spring greens and small hearts in the spring and early summer.

In the garden Cabbages like rich, organic soil with plenty of organic matter.

Colourful cabbages
Leafy cabbages are a magnet for pests, but if you manage to keep them off, you'll have a bumper harvest.

INSTALLING INSECT-PROOF FINE MESH

1 Insert pairs of 30-cm (12-in) canes at 90-cm (3-ft) intervals over your vegetable bed.

2 Cut lengths of alkathene water pipe to the desired length using a hacksaw and slip over two canes. Fine mesh can also be draped right over the plants.

3 Drape fine mesh over the top, and either bury the edges or secure with pegs, bricks or lengths of wood to stop pests from getting underneath.

PLANTING CABBAGE FROM SEED

1 Sprinkle a few seeds in a pot of compost, allowing around a finger width between each seed. Cover with a layer of compost and water.

2 Keep the seedlings well watered and under cover until they are strong enough to be planted out.

3 Plant out cabbages once they've grown on. The distance between plants will affect the ultimate size of the cabbages.

4 Cover your crop with insect-proof mesh to deter flying pests.

5 Ensure there is enough space under the fine mesh to allow the young plants to develop.

6 Once the heads are formed, cut carefully at the base of the plant.

They're a greedy crop so it's worth applying a generous amount of balanced fertiliser before planting out. The plants also need to be well watered, particularly during dry spells. Plants are most often raised in small pots before being planted out. Whichever types you are growing, grow them in small pots, then plant out when they've grown on. Sow a single seed in each small pot. Cabbages don't need much heat, so keep them in a cool greenhouse or conservatory. Once the plants have about four leaves, they are ready for planting out. For large cabbages aim for a plant every 50 cm (20 in) or so. If you want to squeeze as much into your space as possible, place them much closer together, up to every 15 cm (6 in). This should produce miniature versions – ideal for a small household. Cover crops with fine insect-control mesh.

Harvesting and storage Spring greens will be ready for harvesting in early spring. Cut the immature heads when required. As they grow they'll start to heart up, so keep cutting for the kitchen until they're all used up. Hopefully by this time your summer cabbages will be ready. Keep cutting as you need them, leaving the others in the garden. For winter cabbages, they too should keep in the garden until needed, but protect them against pigeons. If you do grow 'Dutch White' cabbages, they'll need storing indoors in racks from the start of winter.

In the kitchen With cabbages being available from the garden all year round, you'll need to be inventive to find enough dishes to include them in. Spring greens are fresh and tender and can be steamed like spinach. Other cabbages such as 'Dutch White' and some red cabbages can be used shredded in salads. Other types such as 'Savoy' are fantastic shredded and lightly fried.

Cutting your cabbages
Heads of cabbages can be picked once they're formed.

BRASSICA FAMILY PESTS AND DISEASES

Cabbages, as well as all other brassicas, suffer from a large number of pests and diseases.

This group of diseases can be avoided if you use insect-proof mesh, well secured to keep the pests at bay.

CABBAGE ROOT FLY

The grubs feed on the roots of young plants, stunting and even killing them.

CABBAGE WHITE BUTTERFLIES

 If the butterflies lay their eggs on the leaves, the resulting caterpillars will quickly devour your crop.

FLEA BEETLES

These small beetles feed on the leaves of plants, peppering them with holes. While they can kill very young plants, older plants will survive but will be seriously spoilt.

MEALY CABBAGE APHID

 Grey-green insects that cluster on the undersides of leaves, causing yellowing and distortion.

PIGEONS AND RABBITS

These larger pests love brassicas. While a net will be enough to keep pigeons out, a stouter wire mesh is needed for rabbits.

CLUBROOT

Clubroot affects all members of the cabbage family. It's a disease that causes roots to swell and distort and plants usually wilt and die. Once your soil is infected it's difficult to eradicate. Keep rotating your crop and avoid planting brassicas on soil where you know plants have been affected in the past. Clubroot is less severe in alkaline soils, so if you have this type of soil but still want to grow cabbages, then consider creating a high pH bed, devoted just to brassicas year-on-year.

POWDERY AND DOWNY MILDEW

Both these diseases can affect brassicas. Keep your plot well watered and remove any dead or yellowing leaves. If mildew continues to be a problem, try increasing the spacing between plants.

VARIETY SELECTOR
Summer and autumn varieties
- 'Castello', 'Hispi': green.
- 'Metro', 'Primero': red.

Winter and spring varieties
- 'Dutch White', 'Holland Winter White', 'January King', 'Hardy Late Stock No. 3', 'Savoy', 'Celtic', 'Colorsa', 'Spring Cabbage', 'Durham Early', 'April'.

CALENDAR

EARLY SPRING
If you sowed your cabbages last summer, you should be able to start harvesting them now. Keep harvesting until early summer. Start to sow your summer/autumn varieties in small pots.

MID-SPRING
You can still sow summer and autumn varieties now.

LATE SPRING
Start to sow your winter cabbages in small pots. Plant out your summer/autumn varieties in the garden.

EARLY SUMMER
Plant out the winter varieties you sowed six or so weeks ago. Start harvesting summer varieties.

MIDSUMMER
Watch out for pests, water well and keep harvesting your summer cabbages. Sow spring cabbages in pots.

LATE SUMMER
Keep plants well watered.

EARLY AUTUMN
Plant out spring cabbages. Harvest autumn cabbages.

MID-AUTUMN
Keep harvesting.

LATE AUTUMN
Check over your spring cabbages, and keep them protected from birds pecking and destroying your crop.

EARLY WINTER
Finish harvesting autumn cabbages and start harvesting winter cabbages.

Brussels sprouts

Make sure you have room in the vegetable garden as this relative giant takes up lots of space!

○○○○○ VALUE FOR MONEY
○○○○○ MAINTENANCE
○○○○○ FREEZE/STORE
CROPPING SEASON: MID-AUTUMN–LATE WINTER

This hardy winter vegetable is a member of the cabbage family. It has been bred to produce tight, leafy buds up its tall stem. Picked over winter, sprouts have a spicy, pungent flavour. The plants need a sizeable area of space to allow them to reach their full potential, growing to around 50 cm (20 in) wide and up to 75 cm (30 in) tall.

Where to grow Grow Brussels sprouts alongside other brassicas, such as cabbages and swede. They need a long growing season, plenty of space and fertile soil in a reasonably sunny spot. Avoid adding organic matter just before planting.

In the garden Because plants grow tall and become very bulky, they're liable to fall over, so it's a good idea not to dig over the soil before you plant your sprouts, maintaining a firm soil bed. It may also be necessary to push in canes and tie the plants to the cane to provide additional support. Sprouts are best planted out on a bed that has had beans in the previous year or a limed brassica bed (see pages 22–23 for more on crop rotation). Add 100 g (3½ oz) per square metre of general-purpose fertiliser when you plant.

Pests and diseases As with cabbage (see page 55).

Harvesting and storage Early varieties such as 'Peer Gynt' can be ready for picking as early as late summer. Others, such as 'Trafalgar', will be ready by autumn. Check the plants and wait until the buds are tightly formed. Leave sprouts on the plants and pick from the bottom up. Sprouts are reputed to taste sweeter after the first frosts but if you

Ripe for the picking
Tight buds of Brussels sprouts will be ready to be picked from autumn right through the winter.

have very cold winters, pull out the whole plant and hang in a frost-free but cool shed.

In the kitchen A traditional choice for Christmas dinner, sprouts can be steamed and sautéed with chestnuts. You can also make hearty soups with sprouts, adding other winter vegetables from the garden.

VARIETY SELECTOR
• 'Braveheart': tall variety producing small, sweet sprouts.
• 'Peer Gynt': an old favourite that starts to crop early.
• 'Trafalgar': a good choice for sprouts at Christmas.
• 'Falstaff': produces red leaves, and sprouts. Sadly, the colour disappears on cooking.

CALENDAR

MID SPRING
Sow a single seed in individual small pots. These can be left outside in a sheltered spot. You'll probably want half a dozen plants at most.

LATE SPRING
When plants are 15 cm (6 in) high, plant out, leaving around 90 cm (3 ft) between each plant. Draw soil around the stems and firm down. Water the plants well, protect from slugs and snails and cover with fine mesh.

MIDSUMMER
Stake plants when they get too tall. It's a good idea to add another dose of general fertiliser.

AUTUMN ONWARDS
Start picking from the bottom upwards.

Kale

An old favourite in the kitchen garden. With its architectural appearance, kale is now making a comeback in the home garden.

●●●●● VALUE FOR MONEY
●●●●○ MAINTENANCE
●●○○○ FREEZE/STORE
CROPPING SEASON: EARLY AUTUMN–LATE WINTER

Kale, or borecole as it used to be referred to, is another leafy brassica. Traditionally grown from spring for an autumn and late winter crop, you can also grow it as a salad crop from late summer onwards, similar to mizuna (see pages 58–59). Some of the prettier varieties, such as 'Cavolo Nero', are also popularly grown in ornamental gardens and make an enjoyable snack while you're working in the winter garden.

Where to grow Kale fits in with other brassicas and should be grown alongside them so pest protection can be applied easily to all. If you are after a crop of cut-and-come-again salad, consider growing kale in a pot or any area of the garden where you have space.

Types and varieties The traditional varieties of kale include curly kale varieties that produce crinkly leaves. Most are green but there are also some attractive red varieties. Making a comeback are the strap-shaped leaves of the black kales or 'Cavolo Nero', widely grown in Italy. They can reach over 2 m (6 ft 5 in) tall.

In the garden Kale requires the same soil and site as Brussels sprouts and other brassicas. It is normally grown as a winter vegetable (see calendar) but can be grown as a salad too. For a cut-and-come-again crop of salad leaves, seeds can be sown direct in the ground in rows spaced about 20 cm (8 in) apart, or alternatively every 2.5 cm (1 in) in a 30-cm (12-in) diameter container. Sowings can be made all year round, but perhaps the best will be in late autumn, which should provide you with a crop throughout the winter. You should be able to start cutting the young leaves at the base of the plant after around six to 10 weeks. They should resprout a couple of times, but won't be as good as the first harvest.

Pests and diseases As for cabbage (see page 55). Protect with your other brassicas. Late-autumn sowings of kale for a winter crop of salad should remian more pest-free, but a fine mesh or fleece will help to keep any pests off.

Harvesting and storage Tender leaves grown as a cut-and-come-again crop should be cut as required. Later, the main crop of kale should be ready to start harvesting. Pick individual leaves as you need them. Plants will continue to grow into the spring.

In the kitchen Packed with iron and vitamin C, young leaves can be used in salads. The slightly tougher leaves can be stir-fried or steamed like Chinese vegetables. Kale can simply be steamed with a little butter added for a delicious vegetable accompaniment.

VARIETY SELECTOR

- 'Darkibor': traditional green variety of curly kale.
- 'Redbor': unusual and attractive red-coloured curly kale.
- 'Black Tuscany': traditional black kale variety.

Statuesque vegetable
'Cavolo Nero' (black kale) can bring colour and structure to your garden in winter, as well as useful leaves for your kitchen.

CALENDAR

MID-SPRING
Plant a couple of seeds in small pots, weeding out the smaller one if both come up. Leave to grow in a cool greenhouse or sheltered spot in the garden.

EARLY SUMMER
Carry on growing in the pot. Leave in a sheltered spot, but watch out for pests nibbling your plants. Cover with fine mesh for added protection if necessary.

MIDSUMMER
Plant out into the garden, 45 cm (18 in) apart. Keep well watered and protect from slugs and snails.

AUTUMN ONWARDS
Start to pick leaves as you need them. Leave crops through the winter as they'll continue to grow, if somewhat slowly.

Mizuna and Mibuna

This group of Japanese plants from the cabbage family provides a welcome addition to the salad bowl throughout the winter.

⬡⬡⬡⬢⬢ VALUE FOR MONEY
⬡⬡⬡⬢⬢ MAINTENANCE
⬡⬡⬢⬢⬢ FREEZE/STORE
CROPPING SEASON: MIDSUMMER–MID-WINTER

Fast-growing and delicious, mizuna and mibuna produce highly attractive spiky and serrated leaves in huge quantities. If you want to keep your salad bowl well stocked in winter, these should be two of your regular crops. They are fairly hardy and will survive outside throughout the winter. If you keep your crop covered with mesh or fleece, the leaves will remain undamaged and perfect for the kitchen.

Where to grow These greens can cope with a fairly wide range of soils, but they prefer rich, fertile soil – much like other brassicas – and can cope with light shade. They will do well in a pot, hanging basket or window box.

Types and varieties Often sold just as mizuna and mibuna, there has been some recent breeding, with a few new varieties available. All are fairly hardy and productive.

Other winter salads Mizuna or mibuna is a great winter salad and is perfect to keep you in fresh leaves through the winter – if you're growing under a cloche or fine mesh, or in a greenhouse.

However there are other winter salads that can also be grown in the winter. Aim to sow all of these in early autumn and they should start to crop through the winter.

Mustard 'Red Frills' This crops from early winter right into early spring. This variety is particularly fine-leafed – other varieties can be much coarser. Growing in the winter means that the usual brassica pests aren't around to cause it any trouble, but it does do better with some protection, such as fine mesh. It will start to run to seed in the spring.

Corn salad 'Cavallo' This is a great salad for padding out the winter salad bowl. Also known as lamb's lettuce, its flavour is very mild, but the leaves are soft and tender. It forms rosettes of round leaves that can be picked right through mid-winter and into spring. Again, since the weather is cold, it should be untroubled by diseases and pests such as slugs and snails.

Claytonia Also known as miner's lettuce, this salad produces lots of small leaves on long stalks. Again, it's a good filler to your salad bowl, but useful if you find the leaves of mizuna and mustard quite spicy. It should crop from mid-winter right into spring.

In the garden Mizuna and mibuna can be grown throughout the summer, but with so many other vegetables and salads available at that time of year, it's best to wait until the

GROWING MIZUNA

1 When leaves reach a decent size, cut them down around 2 cm (¾ in) from the base and enjoy the leaves.

2 Make sure the soil is kept moist, and water with a general-purpose fertiliser.

3 Recut the leaves when they've regrown. Mizuna leaves can be cut down up to three times.

Winter leaves
The spicy leaves of mizuna make an interesting addition to the winter salad bowl.

CALENDAR

EARLY AUTUMN
Sow in rows, sprinkling seed every 2.5 cm (1 in) with 40 cm (16 in) between rows. Cover with soil, water and sprinkle with organic slug pellets.

MID-AUTUMN
As plants appear, cover with a protective cover, such as a cloche, fine mesh or polythene tunnel.

LATE AUTUMN ONWARDS
Cut leaves as required.

autumn. When most other vegetables start tailing off, it's time to sow your mizuna and mibuna. Given some protection, it will happily sit in your kitchen garden throughout the winter just waiting to be picked.

Pests and diseases As with other brassicas (see page 55), but less likely to be affected through the winter. A crop cover – cloche, tunnel or fleece – over the top of the plants will help prevent the leaves becoming too tough and nibbled.

Harvesting and storage Cut leaves off at the base as you need them. Leaves should be ready for harvesting in as little as six weeks. Cut stems may resprout in mild areas. Leave the plants in the ground throughout the winter, since they can survive temperatures down to -10˚C (14˚F).

In the kitchen These spicy leaves can be used to pep up a winter salad. Alternatively,

they can be wilted and added to tomato sauces and spooned onto pasta. They can also be used in stir-fries, steamed and in soups in Asian cooking.

Miner's lettuce
Like mizuna, Claytonia is a winter lettuce, but it has a milder flavour.

VARIETY SELECTOR
Often sold as mizuna, or even as part of a spicy salad mix. However, you may have some luck finding specific varieties such as the following:

• 'Early Mizuna': has serrated leaves.

• 'Tokyo Belle': mizuna variety that has broader leaves.

Chinese cabbage and pak choi

Chinese cabbage and pak choi will make
a rewarding harvest.

✿✿✿✿✿ VALUE FOR MONEY
✿✿✿✿✿ MAINTENANCE
✿✿✿✿✿ FREEZE/STORE
CROPPING SEASON: LATE SUMMER–EARLY WINTER

A common problem with Asian vegetables
is bolting (running). Bolting is exacerbated in
hot and dry conditions and long days. Some
modern varieties claim to resist the urge to
bolt. As with other members of the brassica
family, Chinese cabbage and pak choi suffer
from slug attacks as well as flying pests. But
these tasty, tender leaves and stems will allow
you to create some authentic Asian dishes. If
you struggle with bolting, plants can be grown
as cut-and-come-again crops – follow the
advice for mizuna (see page 58).

Where to grow A late summer planting
can follow on from early potatoes or broad
beans (see page 72). Alternatively, these
crops do well in containers if protected
from pests. They are quick-growing vegetables,
but need a good supply of water to keep
them growing fast. Use an area of good-
quality ground.

Types and varieties Chinese cabbages
are much faster growing than the Western
types of cabbage, and are usually white and
light green in colour with a pungent brassica
flavour. The hearted Chinese cabbages – often
known as Chinese leaves or Napa cabbage –
form crisp hearts of tightly folded leaves. Pak
choi produces broad leaves, either green or
red depending on the variety, as well as broad
white edible stalks that widen at the base.

In the garden To prevent plants bolting,
the best chance of success is to sow in the
summer. Add a handful of general fertiliser to
the soil prior to planting out. It's a good idea
to mulch the plants with compost after

VARIETY SELECTOR
Chinese cabbage

- 'Kasumi', 'Yakimo': form
  barrel-shaped heads and have
  some resistance to bolting/
- 'Jade Pagoda', 'Green Tower':
  taller plants, forming cylinders of
  tightly curled leaves.
- 'Ruffles': an unusual variety, forms
  many heads of loose, fluffy leaves.

Pak choi

- 'Joi Choi': large white stems and
  dark green leaves. Good bolting
  resistance.
- 'Canton Dwarf': a smaller type
  with small heads.

GROWING PAK CHOI IN CONTAINERS IN SUMMER

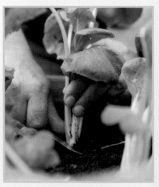

1 Plant up to six seeds, equally
spaced, in a large container.
Cover with a dusting of potting soil
and sprinkle with a few organic
slug pellets.

2 Protect the container from
flying pests by covering it with
fline mesh.

3 Keep watering and feeding
with a general-purpose
liquid fertiliser.

4 Crops should be ready to
harvest in eight weeks.

Stir-fry perfection
The bolt-resistant Chinese cabbage 'Mei Qing Choi' has vigorous growth and crisp, tender leaves.

CALENDAR

EARLY–MIDSUMMER

Add a general-purpose fertiliser or one high in nitrogen. Sow in the ground. Aim for a Chinese cabbage every 30 cm (12 in) or pak choi every 20 cm (8 in). If you sow more than this, you can thin seedlings later. Alternatively, sow individual seeds in small pots.

LATE SUMMER

Transplant pot-sown plants once they have grown to a reasonable size. Carefully remove plants from the pots and space as above, leaving 30 cm (12 in) between rows. Mulch plants with compost and water every week.

EARLY–MID-AUTUMN

If plants are looking weak, water with a liquid fertiliser. Start to harvest. Cut Chinese cabbage around 2.5 cm (1 in) above the base to encourage reshooting.

LATE AUTUMN

Cut the remaining crop. Start picking the re-shooted stumps of Chinese cabbage.

EARLY–LATE SPRING

Plants will survive the winter and start producing flowers. Cut these like broccoli.

MORE ASIAN GREENS

As well as Chinese cabbage and pak choi, there are a range of other Asian vegetables that form loose heads and are suitable for stir-fries or steaming. Grow in exactly the same way as above.

• 'Tatsoi': produces dark-green, rounded leaves that form rosettes (often called rosette pak choi). Look for 'Ryokusai' and 'Yukina Savoy'.

planting, helping to keep them weed-free and retain moisture. The shallow roots benefit from watering little and often.

Pests and diseases Growing in containers helps to reduce slug damage, but you may still need to apply controls as any damage can spoil the crop. Using a fine mesh generally prevents all the common brassica pests (see page 55).

Harvesting and storage Crops can be ready in as little as 10 to 12 weeks. However, if you time your plants to harvest in late autumn and cover them with fleece to protect from light frosts, they should remain intact for several more weeks. If heavier frosts are forecast, then the heads can be removed and stored for several weeks in the fridge. Cut the vegetables at the base, which should resprout and produce a fresh flush of leaves.

In the kitchen Young leaves can be used in salads and are commonly used in Asian cooking, steaming or stir-frying.

Spinach

A much-loved, leafy vegetable. Sow close and pick young for salads or sow further apart for fresh leaf spinach for cooking.

⬤⬤⬤⬤⬤	VALUE FOR MONEY
⬤⬤⬤⬤⬤	MAINTENANCE
⬤⬤⬤⬤⬤	FREEZE/STORE

CROPPING SEASON: EARLY SUMMER–MID-AUTUMN

Famous for its health benefits, spinach is an often-forgotten crop. However, it's useful in the garden as it will fit into the smallest of spaces, and for a salad crop, will be ready for harvesting just a few weeks after sowing. However, spinach can be quite a difficult crop to get right – too dry or too hot and it will run to seed. An easier, but similar crop is perpetual spinach and chard (see opposite). However, for the smallest and freshest salad leaves, spinach is difficult to beat.

Where to grow Best grown as a quick-growing salad, spinach will do well in containers or in the ground. It isn't too fussy, as long as the soil is reasonably fertile and well drained. Quick-growing spinach can be squeezed in between other crops that are slower growing, such as corn or brassicas.

Types and varieties Spinach varies little in taste between varieties. However, some claim to be hardier than others, and they are often separated into summer and winter varieties. Select a variety that suits the time of year you intend to grow it.

In the garden Spinach can be sown from early spring to early summer. Spinach doesn't do well when the weather is really warm, but sowing can start again in late summer. Spinach does well in containers because leaves can be picked when they reach just 5 cm (2 in) across. Fill a large container with compost, sprinkle seeds every 5 cm (2 in) or so, and cover with a dusting of compost and water.

Pests and diseases Generally trouble-free, spinach is sometimes troubled by aphids (see page 227) and downy mildew but some varieties claim resistance to this disease. Slugs also need to be controlled.

Harvesting and storage Repeated sowings of spinach will provide a crop intermittently throughout the year. Pick when young for salads, or allow to grow on for use in cooked dishes. Spinach is liable to bolt, and if this happens, just pull up the unwanted plants.

In the kitchen Use small leaves in salads. Larger leaves should be washed and cooked in a pan (water not necessary) and wilted.

VARIETY SELECTOR

- 'Bordeaux': good choice for baby-leaf spinach.
- 'Lazio': claims to be resistant to bolting and downy mildew.
- 'Polar Bear': slow to bolt and a good winter survivor.

Crisp and fresh
Spinach is an elegant-looking and healthy vegetable that can be used in the same way as Swiss chard.

CALENDAR

EARLY SPRING
Make your first sowing of seed, 1 cm (½ in) deep, in rows 30 cm (12 in) apart. Cover with cloches or fine mesh if the weather is still cold.

MID–LATE SPRING
Keep sowing rows of spinach every few weeks for a continuous supply of salad leaves. If you leave a plant every 15 cm (6 in), this can be left to grow on.

EARLY–MIDSUMMER
Keep watering your spinach during dry spells and harvest as required.

LATE SUMMER
Sow winter-hardy spinach for an early crop next spring, 1 cm (½ in) deep, in rows 30 cm (12 in) apart. Aim for a plant every 20 cm (8 in).

Perpetual spinach and Swiss chard

Providing alternatives to spinach, New Zealand spinach and chard taste great and make attractive ornamental plants.

○○○○○ VALUE FOR MONEY
○○○○○ MAINTENANCE
○○○○○ FREEZE/STORE
CROPPING SEASON: EARLY SPRING–LATE AUTUMN

Perpetual spinach, or leaf beet, is easier to grow than true spinach (see opposite) because it is unlikely to bolt. The leaves look and taste very similar, but they are usually much larger.

Swiss chard grows bigger still, when stalks and leaves are best separated prior to cooking. Some varieties are brightly coloured and will liven up both the garden and the plate.

GROWING SWISS CHARD IN CONTAINERS

1 Fill a large pot with multi-purpose compost. Sow six to eight seeds and cover with a sprinkling of compost.

2 Keep your pot well watered and cut stems as required in the kitchen.

Where to grow These leaves prefer rich, moisture-retentive soil. Add extra organic matter if you have any. Plants should cope with some shade.

Types and varieties As members of the beetroot family, Swiss chard and perpetual spinach are biennials, meaning that they shouldn't flower in their first year.

Perpetual spinach is thin-stemmed, with slightly thicker leaves than spinach, but taste-wise, there is little difference between them.

Swiss chard is a much larger plant, reaching up to 45 cm (18 in) high. Leaves can be picked young, but leave it to grow and the plant will produce thick stems in a range of bright colours.

In the garden Perpetual spinach and Swiss chard are very easy to grow. Sow once and they will keep growing all year. Sow twice and they'll crop well into the next year too. Fast-growing and thirsty, they do prefer a rich, moisture-retentive soil, but will do well in a container. The bright colours of chard stems are often used in containers and in ornamental borders for their colour alone.

Pests and diseases Relatively trouble-free, but can be affected by downy mildew, as with spinach (see opposite).

Harvesting and storage The outer leaves can be picked regularly for a continuous supply. Alternatively, cut whole plants down to 2 cm (¾ in) above soil level and they should resprout. Leave the plants growing throughout the year and harvest as required.

In the kitchen Use perpetaul spinach in the same way as regular spinach. Young chard leaves can be used in the same way too, but on mature plants the stems become much thicker. Separate the stems and leaves, steaming or using both in stir-fries.

CALENDAR

MID-SPRING
Make a single sowing of New Zealand spinach and Swiss chard. Raise in small pots and plant out later or sow direct, 1.5 cm (⅝ in) deep in rows 30 cm (12 in) apart.

LATE SPRING
Thin out seedlings to around 30 cm (12 in) between plants. Spacing can be greater for Swiss chard to allow the stems to be displayed.

EARLY SUMMER
Start to pick outer leaves, or cut whole plants as required.

MIDSUMMER
Sprinkle over a general-purpose fertiliser and keep well watered. Sow some more seed now, as above, for a crop well into next year.

LATE SUMMER
Keep picking leaves for use in the kitchen from now right into winter.

VARIETY SELECTOR
Perpetual spinach
• No named varieties.

Swiss chard
• 'Bright Lights': red, yellow, gold, and white stems.
• 'Rhubarb Vulcan': very bright red stems and green leaves.

Lettuce

Dating back to Egyptian times, lettuce has always been a popular food.

✪✪✪✪✪	VALUE FOR MONEY
✪✪✪✪✪	MAINTENANCE
✪✪✪✪✪	FREEZE/STORE

CROPPING SEASON: EARLY SUMMER–LATE AUTUMN

The first lettuces were grown for their oil-rich seeds, but it was probably the Romans who popularised eating the leaves, which were bred to be palatable and sweeter than plants found in the wild. Now, after many centuries of intensive breeding, there is a wide range of lettuce varieties. A staple crop of our salad bowls, there are crispy and soft, or buttery-leafed types, as well as more colourful varieties.

Recent developments in growing methods have introduced the idea of baby-leaf salads and cut-and-come-again leaves. Here, lettuce makes a great quick-growing salad crop that can make it from the seed packet to your plate in a matter of a few weeks.

Where to grow Lettuce can be squeezed into the smallest of spots. It is happy in a slightly shady bed and prefers good, rich soil with plenty of organic matter. Because it's a quick-growing crop, you can plant it in between other slower-growing vegetables, such as sweetcorn or brassicas, earlier in the year. You can also plant it into gaps when other vegetables, such as peas and broad beans, are pulled out. However, you should also bear in mind that it is best to rotate lettuces around the garden to avoid pests and diseases.

Lettuce can be grown throughout the year in containers. Plant during the growing season for a decent crop from your garden, or sow in the greenhouse both early and late in the year for a late-autumn, winter and early-spring supply.

Types and varieties Lettuces can be broadly separated into two groups – lettuces that form hearts (hearting varieties), and ones that do not, often called loose-leaf types. *Hearting types* Hearting types can be further broken down. Firstly, there are the butterheads. Usually with fairly thick leaves,

butterheads are soft and flavoursome, but leaves do wilt quickly after picking. The second type, the crispheads, are generally not as popular as they don't work as well in the salad bowl. These crispy, hearting lettuce varieties can be further separated into cos or romaine types, extremely popular in the kitchen. Sweet, crispy and flavoursome, they come in a wide range of sizes from the little gems to the larger, sweeter romaines. Then there are the icebergs, best known for their use in fast-food outlets and sandwich bars. Their leaves remain crisp, but lack flavour. Finally, there are the Batavian types, which are more of a cross between a cos and a butterhead, often with good flavour.

Loose-leaf types The loose-leaf types don't form any sort of heart. They are particularly good, therefore, for use as a cut-and-come-again lettuce. The red and green lollo rosso types are well known and often frilly, but unfortunately, they don't taste as good as they look. Better tasting are the oak-leafed types, with thicker, juicy, sweet leaves.

Pests and diseases Lettuce suffers from a few pests and diseases. If slugs are a problem, one way to avoid them is to grow in a container. Alternatively, cut-and-come-again crops grow so quickly that often the pests and diseases don't have time to take hold.

GROWING CUT-AND-COME-AGAIN LETTUCES

1 You don't need a deep pot – a shallow, wide one would do fine. Fill it with multi-purpose compost.

2 Sprinkle seeds across the surface, aiming for a seed every 1.5 cm (⅝ in). Cover with a dusting of compost.

Crisp leaves
Grown in the garden, lettuce can provide the kitchen with a regular supply of leaves right through spring and into autumn.

While lettuce can be sown direct, slugs will often eat the seedlings before they make it above ground. It is better to plant out larger plants and protect them from slugs and snails. Aphids such as greenfly are a problem too, and once on the leaves they are difficult to clean off. If the problem gets worse, reach for an organic trigger spray. Root aphids can also damage plants, making them wilt. Downy mildew is a disease that affects lettuce, causing yellowing leaves and mould growth – worse in cool, damp conditions. Avoid getting the plants wet and don't plant them too closely together. If plants are badly affected, pull up and discard.

Harvesting and storage Lettuce should be harvested as you need it and depending on the type, when it's ready. Store in the fridge and use within a week.

In the kitchen Lettuce is the most widely grown salad crop. Its sweet, fairly

Red lettuce
Red leaves make a colourful addition to the salad bowl.

bland flavour makes it an excellent basis for all sorts of salads. Mix with more spicy leaves of rocket or mizuna, or combine with the bitter leaves of endive and chicory to spice up salads. Crispy varieties are used in Caesar salad, or go for a soft butterhead type to fill out sandwiches.

VARIETY SELECTOR
Hearting types
• 'Butterhead'.
• 'Tom Thumb': quick growing.
• 'Clarion': soft, buttery leaves.
Crispheads
• 'Cos'/'Romaine'.
• 'Chatsworth': sweet and crisp.
• 'Winter Density': for winter sowing.
• 'Little Gem Delight': small, sweet.
• 'Batavian'.
• 'Giardina': red serrated outer leaves, green heart.
Icebergs
• 'Set': easy to grow, crisp and green.

CALENDAR

LATE WINTER
Start sowing seeds in small containers. Keep the pots out of direct sun and well watered.

MID-SPRING–SUMMER
Keep sowing batches of seed, planting out into the garden when large enough to handle – this way you'll have a constant supply of leaves through the season.

MIDSUMMER
Stop sowing now as lettuce seeds don't germinate well when it's hot.

LATE SUMMER
Another sowing now will provide leaves into autumn. Keep harvesting your earlier sowings. Pick leaves off the loose heads or cut whole crispheads at the base.

AUTUMN
If you have a greenhouse, sow a variety such as 'Winter Density', and plant out in the greenhouse border or growing bag.

WINTER–SPRING
Harvest your greenhouse-grown lettuce.

3 Water the plants, and after four weeks they should be ready for cutting. Snip off 2.5 cm (1 in) from the base.

4 Keep watering and they should resprout. You should be able to get three cuts from one container.

Chicory and Endive

You either love or hate the slightly bitter leaves of chicory and endive – if you enjoy them, they're definitely worth growing.

○○○○○ VALUE FOR MONEY
○○○○○ MAINTENANCE
○○○○○ FREEZE/STORE
CROPPING SEASON: MIDSUMMER–EARLY WINTER

As easy to grow as lettuces, chicory and endive are their slightly bitter cousins. Popular in France and Italy, they're a staple ingredient in supermarket salad bags. Many people blanch the leaves by covering the plants with a pot to exclude the light a week or two before picking. This tempers their slightly bitter flavour.

Where to grow Can be grown in a container as a cut-and-come-again crop, as with lettuce. Alternatively, grow in rows in your vegetable garden. The crinkly leaves of endive and the bright colours of radicchio endive will brighten up any space.

Types and varieties You can get green or red chicory, but it's the red variety that is most popular (often known as radicchio, it forms dense heads of bitter red leaves). Certain types of chicory can be forced into chicons – tightly packed blanched shoots often seen in supermarkets.

The most popular endives are the curly types, with heads of finely divided, crinkly leaves. They are often dark green, but blanching them can turn them yellow.

In the garden Chicory and endive can be sown throughout the spring and summer to keep the crop coming right into winter.

Pests and diseases Chicory and endive tend to suffer from the same problems as lettuce (see page 64).

Harvesting and storage Pick as required. Plants are fairly hardy so can last throughout the winter.

In the kitchen Use raw in salads. Forced chicory or radicchio can be grilled and used in warm salads and starters.

CALENDAR

EARLY–MID-SPRING
Sow in small pots as with lettuce. Plant out in rows 30 cm (12 in) apart when at a reasonable size.

LATE SPRING
You can still sow now as above.

EARLY SUMMER
This is the last chance to make your spring and early summer sowing.

MIDSUMMER
When endive plants are large enough to be picked, blanch by placing a plate over the leaves for a week or two before picking. Resow another batch of seed for a winter crop.

LATE SUMMER
Plant out small plants sown last month 30 cm (12 in) apart for a crop throughout the winter. Cover with fleece in cold areas in the autumn.

EARLY AUTUMN
Keep harvesting plants as they become ready.

FORCING CHICORY

1 Once you've grown the plant outside, you'll need to lift the roots in late autumn after cutting off all the foliage. Alternatively, try growing them in a pot.

2 Plant several roots in pots filled with multi-purpose compost. If you've grown them in a pot, just leave them in situ.

3 Cover the plants to exclude the light. Place somewhere warm with a minimum temperature of 10°C (50°F). In a few weeks, a chicon should have grown from each root. Cut off just above the base.

Rocket

Hot and peppery, rocket is a firm favourite in the kitchen – and it's easy to grow!

✪✪✪✪✪ VALUE FOR MONEY
✪✪✪✪✪ MAINTENANCE
✪✪✪✪✪ FREEZE/STORE
CROPPING SEASON: LATE SPRING–MID-AUTUMN

Once seen only in Italian cuisine, rocket has become a firm favourite on dinner plates all over the world. It adds spiciness to salads and is even used in pasta sauces and on top of pizzas. Rocket can be grown easily throughout the year.

Where to grow As it is fast-growing, rocket can be grown in with other brassica crops to keep the rotation together. Rocket can be ready for harvesting in as little as six weeks, so if you're using fine mesh on your other brassicas it's worth sowing some rocket in the gaps early and late in the year. In fact, rocket doesn't do well in the middle of summer because it tends to bolt (run to seed).

Easy to grow in containers too, a sprinkling of rocket seeds will provide you with a quick supply of leaves. Cut them down and they should resprout, at least once, to give you a double crop.

VARIETY SELECTOR

Wild rocket
• 'Fairway', 'Grazia'.

Salad rocket
• 'Victoria', 'Voyager'.

Cut and come again
Cut rocket at the base to encourage it to produce more edible leaves.

Types and varieties Until a few years ago, only wild rocket was available. It has deeply serrated leaves, and is slightly tough and chewy, and very peppery. Nowadays, many more salad rocket varieties are available – these have much larger, less-serrated leaves that are softer and not as peppery.

Pests and diseases Usually the only pest with this quick-growing crop is flea beetle, which peppers the leaves with small holes. Early and later crops may avoid flea beetle, or use a fine mesh to protect the crop.

Harvesting and storage Snip off as many leaves as you need. If you have sown successional batches of seed, rocket should be available for most of the spring, summer and autumn.

In the kitchen Sprinkle into salads, pasta sauces, and on top of pizzas.

CALENDAR

MID-SPRING
Don't start rocket off too early – mid-spring should be fine. Either sow direct in rows, aiming for a seed every 1 cm (½ in), or sprinkle into a large but shallow container filled with multi-purpose compost.

LATE SPRING
Start to harvest the first leaves – pick them off or cut down plants 2.5 cm (1 in) from the base.

EARLY SUMMER
Continue sowing a pot or a row of rocket every month. This way your salad will be perfect for picking when you need it.

EARLY AUTUMN
Make this your last sowing of rocket as it doesn't do so well during the winter. Switch to mizuna (see pages 58–59) for peppery leaves throughout the winter.

SEED AND FRUIT CROPS

If you think peas and beans can easily be bought in the supermarket, you've obviously never tasted their freshly picked garden flavour. Easy to grow too, both the climbing and dwarf varieties are worth finding a space for.

Also included here are the curcubits, from courgettes to cucumbers, all of which are straightforward to grow and very bountiful.

Climbing beans

If you want a productive, easy-to-grow crop, then climbing beans come top of the list.

OOOOO VALUE FOR MONEY
OOOOO MAINTENANCE
OOOOO FREEZE/STORE
CROPPING SEASON: EARLY SUMMER–MID-AUTUMN

The legume family of crops are grown worldwide and include all beans and peas. Climbing beans are those that twist themselves around supports as they climb upwards. They're tender crops, but are quick to reach maturity so from a spring sowing, beans can be ready for picking as early as midsummer. The best thing about beans is that the more you pick, the more they produce. They just keep on growing until the first frosts.

Peas and beans are also known for their ability to fix nitrogen from the atmosphere and use it as a nutrient. In fact, this process is possible because of certain species of bacteria that reside in their roots, but still, this means the plants need little in the way of additional fertiliser.

Where to grow All climbing beans need supports and plenty of space to allow them to grow upwards. Peas and beans should be fitted into your rotation (see pages 22–23) and grown as a group.

They often follow on from brassicas, which are greedy crops, and will have used up much of the fertility of the soil. Because of the amount of foliage they produce, climbing beans need a plentiful supply of water, so grow in rich, moisture-retentive soil and add lots of compost. They can cope with some shade but prefer a sunny spot.

Types and varieties Runner beans, which are extremely productive, produce tough, stringy beans. Also, runner beans are pollinated by insects and sometimes suffer from pollination problems early in the season.

For a much earlier crop, go for climbing French beans, that come in a wide number of colours and shapes – flat and cylindrical pods, as well as green, yellow and purple pods. All should be picked over

Bountiful beans
Climbing beans will provide you with a long supply of tasty beans right up to the first frosts.

regularly, taking off pods when they're still fairly small and tender.

A similar type is the Italian borlotti bean with green and red pods. These are best left on the plant, picked when mature, then shelled and dried. They can then be used through the winter as a dried bean.

Pests and diseases Blackfly can be a problem – use an organic spray.

Harvesting and storage In the height of the season, pick the beans every few days. If you leave it longer, they will become tough and stringy. Be careful not to damage the remaining beans when pulling the pods off the plant.

Excess beans can be blanched in boiling water and frozen. Beans saved for drying should be left to dry, shelled and stored in an airtight container.

In the kitchen Fresh beans can be used throughout the summer – they are best steamed. Dried beans can be incorporated into soups and stews throughout the winter.

VARIETY SELECTOR

Runner bean
• **'Red flame'**: red flowers.
• **'White Lady'**: white flowers.

Climbing French bean
• **'Blue Lake', 'Fasold'**: cylindrical green pods.
• **'Violet Podded'**: flat, purple pods.
• **'Goldfield'**: flat, pale yellow pods.

Borlotti bean
• **'Barlotta Lingua di Fuoco'**: green and red flattish pods.

MAKING A SUPPORT FOR CLIMBING BEANS

1 Choose a sunny site, but an area that won't cast shade on your other plants. In early spring, make a bean trench and dig in as much compost as you can spare.

2 Select canes 2 m (6 ft. 5 in) high, and push six to 10 of them positioned at least 15 cm (6 in) apart into the ground to form a wigwam shape.

3 Tie the canes securely at the top with string.

4 When planting your beans (one plant per cane), guide them around the canes to encourage them to climb.

CALENDAR

MID–LATE SPRING
Don't sow beans too early because they are a tender and fast-growing crop. Plant beans singly in small pots filled with multi-purpose compost.

EARLY SUMMER
When all threat of frost has passed, plant out beans along your supports. If you have more plants than supports, plant a couple of plants at the base of each support.

MIDSUMMER
Climbing French beans should be ready for picking, but runner beans may take a little longer. Pick your beans every few days. Water in dry spells.

LATE AUTUMN
Pick beans left on the plant for drying. Leave them somewhere cool and dry, such as a garage or greenhouse, and wait until the pods have dried. Remove the beans from the pods and store in a paper bag until next spring.

TIP
Before you go on holiday, make sure you pick off every bean you can find – this will ensure the plants carry on producing beans when you return.

Dwarf beans

If you are short on space but love beans, select a dwarf variety, ideal for containers and hanging baskets.

○○○○○ VALUE FOR MONEY
○○○○○ MAINTENANCE
○○○○○ FREEZE/STORE
CROPPING SEASON: EARLY SUMMER–MID-AUTUMN

Crunchy pods
Stringless, tender dwarf beans are easy to raise from seed, require very little maintenance and provide a huge harvest.

Like their larger, climbing cousins, dwarf beans come in a wide range of colours and shapes. There are also some varieties that are perfect for drying. You have a choice of two types of dwarf beans: runner beans or French beans. There are not that many varieties of runner beans available, but there are lots of French beans, and generally these are more popular.

All dwarf beans are easy to grow and are generally free from pests and diseases. While runner beans need insects to pollinate their flowers, French beans do not, meaning there is usually no problem with the beans setting, even if you are growing them in a greenhouse, or growing them slightly out of season.

Where to grow Similar to climbing beans, dwarf beans are tender, so need to be grown in a frost-free place. They also like rich soil and will do fine in a slightly shady spot, but full sun would produce the highest yields.

If you have plenty of space, grow them in the garden, with other peas and beans, and rotate each year to prevent pest problems building up. They prefer light but moisture-retentive soil.

If you are short on space, a pot or hanging basket is ideal. They're attractive plants too,

especially when in flower or when the colourful beans have set. If you have a greenhouse, you can grow dwarf beans in the soil border or in containers either for an earlier or later crop than you would get outdoors.

Types and varieties There are only a few dwarf runner bean varieties and all look attractive, reaching about 45 cm (1½ ft) high. They're a good choice if you have only a small space and prefer fewer beans than are produced by their climbing cousins.

The choice of dwarf French beans is much greater. Filet types produce very fine, pencil-thin pods. Standard French beans produce cylindrical green, yellow or dark purple pods.

Pests and diseases Blackfly. As with climbing beans, use an organic spray if the problem worsens. Alternatively, encourage natural predators such as ladybirds and lacewings.

Harvesting and storage Start picking pods when they're about 10–15 cm (4–6 in) long. Picking can damage the plant so don't pull the plant too hard. Blanch excess beans and freeze.

In the kitchen As with climbing beans, dwarf beans are best steamed and served with butter. The most tender beans taste just as good as asparagus!

VARIETY SELECTOR

Dwarf runner bean
• 'Hestia': red and white flowers.

Dwarf French bean
• 'Purple Teepee': dark purple.
• 'Sungold': bright yellow.
• 'Capitole': green.

CALENDAR

MID-SPRING
Dwarf beans are sensitive to frost, so sow in small pots about four weeks before the last frosts. In milder areas, sow direct into the soil. Separate rows by around 30 cm (12 in), and place one seed every 5 cm (2 in), 2 cm (¾ in) deep.

LATE SPRING
In colder areas, start sowing now, ready to plant out in early summer.

EARLY SUMMER
Keep watering your plants when beans start to form to encourage pods to fill out. Start picking when beans are 10 cm (4 in) long.

MIDSUMMER
Sow another crop of beans direct into the soil, as above. Beans should start cropping in early autumn, when the earlier beans have finished.

LATE SUMMER
Keep watering and picking your beans.

Broad beans

Broad beans are delicious and
easy to grow too.

✪✪✪✪✪	VALUE FOR MONEY
✪✪✪✪✪	MAINTENANCE
✪✪✪✪✪	FREEZE/STORE

CROPPING SEASON: EARLY SUMMER–LATE SUMMER

Expensive in the supermarkets and often not
as sweet as you'd like, fortunately broad beans
are an easy crop to grow, and unlike French
and runner beans, are hardy. Often they're
planted in the autumn, to give one of the
earliest crops in the spring. From a further
spring sowing, you can extend the harvest from
around four weeks to seven or eight weeks.
In the kitchen, they combine well with early
summer vegetables, such as young carrots,
peas and asparagus. If you're feeling
adventurous, pick them young and eat them
whole – pods and all!

Perfect for picking
Whether you sow in spring or autumn, it's important to pick broad beans when
they're still young to ensure you get great-tasting, tender beans.

Where to grow Broad beans fit with
other beans in a rotation (see pages 22–23).
They take up a fair amount of space, and
each plant will produce only a couple of
handfuls of beans, so they are not ideal for
growing in pots. They're best grown in blocks
or as a series of rows. Broad beans can get
fairly tall too, and if you do grow them in a
block, there is a simple way to help the beans
stand upright (see right).

Types and varieties Often, broad
beans are categorised into spring-sowing
varieties and autumn-sowing varieties. In reality,
they are all hardy, and so all varieties will grow
in the autumn too. More recent breeding has
produced many small-podded broad beans,
which are easier for agricultural machines to
pick. Generally, these are meant to be sweeter
than some of the older varieties and they can
be picked young and eaten whole.

Pests and diseases Broad beans are
fairly trouble-free, except for black bean aphid.
These cluster around the growing tip – nipping
these out in early summer will help to control
the pests. You could try spraying with an
organic pesticide if the pests persist.

Mice can also be a problem if you sow direct
into the soil – if they are eating your seeds,
consider starting the beans off in pots and plant
out after a few weeks.

Harvesting and storage Pick over
the beans each week, selecting those that have
filled out the pods.

You can pick beans when they're very
young and tender, or just 5 cm (2 in) or so
long. These can be eaten whole, including
the pods. They are best eaten fresh from
the garden.

In the kitchen The skins, which can be
tough, are easily slipped off. Broad beans are

SUPPORTING BROAD BEANS

1 When the plants reach a height of
30 cm (12 in), they can be damaged
in strong winds.

2 Insert canes around the edge of
the crop.

CONTROLLING BLACK BEAN APHID

1 Keep an eye out for aphids on the tips of your beans. If left, they'll spread down the plant and spoil your crop.

2 Nipping out the growing tips of broad beans helps minimise the damage caused by aphids. Pinch out the top 10 cm (4 in) or so.

fantastic lightly steamed with other early-summer vegetables. If you're eating the beans and the pods, steam lightly and add butter.

VARIETY SELECTOR

- 'Witkiem Manita': can be sown in both autumn and spring.
- 'Red Epicure': pretty red flowers and pink beans.
- 'Stereo': decent small-podded type.

3 Tie string around the canes, keeping the beans inside the support.

CALENDAR

LATE AUTUMN
In mild winter areas, sow blocks of beans 5 cm (2 in) deep, with 20 cm (8 in) between seeds. Sow a short row of extra beans close together that you can use to fill any gaps.

EARLY WINTER
Order more beans now for planting in the spring.

EARLY SPRING
Provide supports to growing crop (see opposite).

MID-SPRING
Sow another block of seed now, which will produce a harvest later in the summer.

LATE SPRING
Watch out for black bean aphid and pick off the tips of plants where they congregate.

EARLY SUMMER
Provide supports to your spring-sown crop.

MIDSUMMER
Your autumn crop should be ready for picking. Pick over the crop each week, squeezing the beans to see if they've filled out.

LATE SUMMER
Check the spring-sown crop. Pick when ready.

EARLY AUTUMN
Clear away your spent plants and place on the compost heap.

Peas

Universally popular, fresh, super-sweet peas rarely make it from garden to kitchen without a few being podded on the way.

○○○○○ VALUE FOR MONEY
○○○○○ MAINTENANCE
○○○○○ FREEZE/STORE
CROPPING SEASON: LATE SPRING–MID-AUTUMN

One of the earliest crops to sow, peas are quick and easy to grow. Provide them with a little support and they'll scramble up some strategically placed twigs or net, and produce a welcome crop in midsummer. Peas have been bred to be so tender and sweet that it isn't really necessary to cook them any more. In fact, if you have children, you'll be lucky to see any at all!

Where to grow Peas fit in with the other peas and beans, and should be part of your crop rotation (see pages 22–23). Like broad beans, they take up a fair amount of room, so you need to make sure your garden can accommodate them. Best sown in rows, most require some support as they can reach well over 1 m (3 ft 2 in) high.

Types and varieties Peas are often separated into earlies and maincrops. However, you'll be just as successful sticking to one variety but sowing it every couple of weeks.

In the garden Peas are generally sown in late winter before the last spring frost date. From a single sowing you'll get around a month when peas can be picked. If you sow every fortnight right through early and mid-spring,

then the supply of peas for the kitchen will be much greater and more sustained.

Pests and diseases Pea moths can lay eggs inside the pods, allowing larvae to feed on the developing peas. Pea moth is only around for a certain period – sow successionally, and you may avoid it.

Plants can suffer from powdery mildew too – keeping plants well mulched and watered during dry spells should help.

GERMINATING PEAS

1 Buy (or scavenge) some plastic guttering and cut it into 1-m (3 ft 2-in) lengths (or the length of your rows).

2 Block the ends with a brick or any other suitably sized object and fill with multi-purpose compost.

3 Sow the seeds about 5 cm (2 in) apart (you'll get a couple of rows). Cover the seed with a dusting of compost.

STAR PLANT
SWEET TASTE
SUMMER CROP

Sweet treats
There is nothing more rewarding than picking fresh peas from your garden. Make sure you keep picking every few days to ensure your crop is especially sweet.

CALENDAR

LATE WINTER
Make your first sowing towards the end of winter. Peas tolerate frost and snow. Create a trench and sow a double row 2.5 cm (1 in) deep and around 5–10 cm (2–4 in) apart.

EARLY SPRING–LATE SPRING
Keep sowing rows every fortnight. Create some supports for your peas, either using sticks from the garden or canes and netting.

MIDSUMMER
Keep watering plants. Start harvesting now.

Harvesting and storage When the pods start to fill out, pick a few peas. If they're not quite ready, leave them a few more days. You'll need to pick over your peas every few days to avoid the peas over-maturing and becoming dry and tough.

In the kitchen Fresh peas can be eaten raw, straight from the pod. Steam lightly and add butter – they'll be so much tastier than the frozen versions.

VARIETY SELECTOR
• **'Misty'**: short variety, reaching just 70 cm (28 in) high.
• **'Saturn'**: a heavy cropper of sweet peas.
• **'Endeavour'**: produces masses of tendrils at the expense of leaves – a good climber.

4 Water and leave to grow in a sheltered spot, such as a greenhouse, a polytunnel, or even in the shelter of a wall or fence.

5 When plants have germinated, create a shallow trench in your plot and carefully push the peas out of the guttering and into the trench.

6 Once the peas are planted, water them in well and use twiggy stems or a series of canes and netting to support the peas as they grow.

Mangetout and Sugar-snap peas

If you tire of shelling peas but love the flavour, these two alternatives fit the bill perfectly.

✪✪✪✪✪ VALUE FOR MONEY
✪✪✪✪✪ MAINTENANCE
✪✪✪✪✪ FREEZE/STORE
CROPPING SEASON: LATE SPRING–MID-AUTUMN

Time your harvest
Pick mangetout as soon as the pods are formed, since these will provide the sweetest pods.

Young pods taste as sweet and juicy as the peas themselves. Mangetout produce flat pods, while sugar-snaps are rounded, often with peas just starting to grow inside. At the supermarket, both command premium prices. At home, they're just as easy to grow as peas, and as you eat both the peas and pods you'll get even more edible crop for the same amount of space. In fact, from a 1-m (3 ft 2-in) row of either mangetout or sugar-snap peas, you can expect to harvest around 2 kg (4½ lb) of good-quality pods – if you manage to keep up with the picking, that is. In the kitchen, both can be used fresh, in stir-fries or lightly cooked as a summer vegetable.

Where to grow Just like peas, varieties of mangetout and sugar-snaps differ in height. Some shorter varieties can be self-supporting, while others definitely need support for their tendrils to cling on to. Grow them alongside other peas and beans, but as with peas, a few

PEA TENDRILS

One other part of the pea plant is perfectly edible and tasty – the tendrils. They can be picked and eaten in salads. There are semi-leafless types of peas, which produce more tendrils than most. A good semi-leafless variety of manetout is 'Sugar Crystal'. Start picking the tendrils when the plant is young, but be sure to leave enough to allow the plant to cling while it climbs.

VARIETY SELECTOR

Mangetout

- **'Carouby de Maussane'**: a tall variety, with high yields. Pretty purple flowers give way to pale green pods.

Sugar-snap

- **'Delikett'**: dark green pods with decent yields.

- **'Sugar Gem'**: deep green stringless pods.

sowings through late winter and early spring will provide a continual supply of pods through early summer.

All peas prefer an open site, with fertile soil that has plenty of organic matter dug in. The soil also needs to drain freely. As with other vegetables, it's a good idea to work over the soil before sowing direct. This way, you remove any unwanted weeds and allow the seeds to get off to a good start. If you struggle to get peas germinated in the soil direct, consider sowing in pots. Place two or three seeds in each small pot, and keep in a cool greenhouse or on a sunny windowsill until big enough to plant out. Plant out in their clumps around a wigwam or other support. Once the peas start to flower, it's a good idea to make sure they don't go short of water. Watering at this stage will really boost your harvest.

Pests and diseases As with peas (see page 74).

Harvesting and storage You can start to pick mangetout as soon as they form on the plant. If left too long they can become stringy, tough and bitter – it's a good idea to pick the pods a couple of times a week during the harvest period. Sugar-snaps are generally sweeter than mangetout and will need to be harvested when mature. Pick as soon as they plump out – pods make a characteristically pleasing snap when bent.

In the kitchen Both can be used raw in salads or very lightly steamed or stir-fried. If left to mature, they can be shelled like ordinary peas, but often the taste is dry and unpleasant so eat fresh for best results.

CALENDAR

LATE WINTER
Make your first sowing now. If still cold, either plant under cloches or start off in pots in a cool greenhouse or on a sunny windowsill.

EARLY–MID-SPRING
Continue sowing outside. Sow 5 cm (2 in) deep and about 10 cm (4 in) apart. You can sow in bands – double rows – as shown on page 74 when sowing into guttering.

LATE SPRING
Insert supports around the plants to allow the peas to climb.

EARLY SUMMER
Pick over peas regularly. Be sure to pick over-mature peas, even if you are not going to eat them.

MAKING PLANT SUPPORTS FOR PEAS

PEA STICKS
Use pea sticks – twiggy sticks scavenged from around the garden. They can be used on their own for shorter varieties to clamber up, or used on a wigwam to give young plants a head start.

WIGWAMS
These are a series of canes tied at the top to create a wigwam shape. Either tie string around or use large-gauge netting to provide support for the peas.

PLANTING PEAS
Wherever you plant, give the peas a helping hand and encourage them to grow up the supports.

Courgette

Just one or two courgette plants will provide plenty of courgettes through summer and into autumn.

○○○○○ VALUE FOR MONEY
○○○○○ MAINTENANCE
○○○○○ FREEZE/STORE
CROPPING SEASON: EARLY SUMMER–MID-AUTUMN

Courgettes are tender plants, but as they are such quick growers, they'll be successful in all but the coldest of climates. They crop readily too: in midsummer you'll need to pick over your plants every other day to keep up with production. Left on the plant, a courgette fruit will just keep on growing at the expense of any other courgette, so it's worth picking them even if you're not going to eat them. With a courgette produced every other day, just one or two plants are plenty for any household. While the green, long courgettes are most widely grown, it's also worth trying a more colourful yellow variety, or even one of the unusual-shaped summer squashes. These are grown and cooked in the same way as courgettes and should also be picked regularly.

Where to grow Courgettes are attractive plants with broad green leaves. They grow as a small bush, so even though they get pretty big, they don't get out of control. You'll need around 1 sq m (10 sq ft) for each plant in the ground, or alternatively, an individual plant can be grown in a large container – one that holds at least 30 L (8 gallons) of compost.

Because they're tender plants, courgettes tend to be germinated in a greenhouse or on a windowsill, and only planted out when the last chance of frost has passed. Once in the ground, they grow rapidly and are greedy feeders, and require deep, fertile and moisture-retentive soil, so it's worth digging in plenty of organic matter before you plant. Courgettes are part of the cucumber – or curcurbit – family, which also includes pumpkins and cucumbers. It's best to keep all of these plants together in the garden and rotate them with your potatoes and onions (see pages 22–23).

PREPARING FOR AND PLANTING COURGETTES

1 Before planting, dig in plenty of organic matter and create a small mound.

2 To prevent the stem rotting off, push down a piece of tubing next to where the plant will go. Water once a week down the tubing to get the water straight to the roots.

Patty pan squash
As well as traditionally shaped courgettes, why not try growing some of the more unusual patty pans, such as the kind that carry "flying-saucer" fruits.

The mighty courgette
Courgettes grow into huge plants. They're productive too, so you'll only need a couple of plants to keep your family in good supply.

Types and varieties The most popular and well-known courgettes are the long, green varieties. More recently, spherical green courgettes have been developed, but the yields aren't as great. The yellow varieties are a colourful choice, producing bright yellow fruit.

Similar to the courgette is the summer squash. Like courgette, it doesn't store well, so should be used as close to picking as possible. There are some unusual-looking squashes, such as the knobbly crooknecks or the patty pan squashes which look attractive in the garden as well as on the plate.

Pests and diseases Courgettes need plenty of water. When the soil runs dry, a powdery mildew can develop, forming white patches across the leaves, which weakens and can even kill plants. Pick off the leaves where it develops. Prevent mildew by keeping plants well watered.

Courgettes can also succumb to mosaic virus, which is spread by aphids. The leaves turn yellow and the plants weaken. Where this happens, dig up and discard the affected plants.

Harvesting and storage Courgettes grow prolifically given a decent summer and plenty of water. Pick over plants every other day – small courgettes are definitely tastier than if left to grow too big. Flowers can be picked and eaten too. Pick them just as they're about to open and before any fruit has developed. If you're going away for a few days, it's a good idea to pick over any developing flower buds and young fruit to prevent massive courgettes developing while you're away.

In the kitchen Flowers can be dipped in batter and deep-fried as a delicacy. Young courgettes are delicious and can be grated or chopped and eaten raw in salads. Larger courgettes are best cooked. For best results, fry in a pan or on a griddle to take on a slightly smoky flavour, and add to Mediterranean-style dishes.

VARIETY SELECTOR

Best green courgette variety
• 'Patriot'.

Best yellow courgette variety
• 'Soleil'.

Best spherical courgette variety
• 'One Ball (yellow)'.

Crookneck squash
• 'Early Golden Crookneck'.

Patty pan squash
• 'Scallop Mixed'.

CALENDAR

LATE SPRING
There is no point starting any earlier than this as courgettes are rapid growers but sensitive to frost. Start off seeds in individual small pots. Place the seeds on their side and cover with 1 cm (½ in) of compost. Plants need a temperature of around 18°C (65°F), but at this time of year seeds will quickly grow in a greenhouse or on a windowsill.

EARLY SUMMER
Keep plants well watered, and when the threat of frost has passed, plant out in the garden, giving each plant at least 1 sq m (10 sq ft).

You can also plant individually in large 30-L (8-gallon) containers filled with multi-purpose compost and slow-release fertiliser.

MIDSUMMER
Start picking fruit once they start to form. Keep plants well watered.

LATE SUMMER
Remove any leaves that look affected by powdery mildew. Keep watering plants if the weather is dry, and keep picking the fruit.

EARLY AUTUMN
Plants should continue producing fruit.

3 Plant an individual courgette plant on top of each mound. While they like plenty of moisture, this will prevent the stem from rotting off.

Squash and Pumpkin

If you've got plenty of space but not much time, low-maintenance winter squashes and pumpkins are rewarding crops to grow.

○○○○○ VALUE FOR MONEY
○○○○○ MAINTENANCE
○○○○○ FREEZE/STORE
CROPPING SEASON: MIDSUMMER–MID AUTUMN

Winter squashes are different from summer squashes in that they take all summer to grow and are ready for harvest at the beginning of winter. The same is true of pumpkins, but while the flesh of pumpkin is wetter and less tasty than that of winter squash, they can't be beaten for Halloween!

The only downside to winter squashes and pumpkins is the space they require. They grow into huge trailing plants, each plant easily covering several square metres. Each plant will give only a handful of fruit at most. Winter squashes do store well, right through the winter, but pumpkins with their thinner skins don't last much beyond Christmas.

Halloween treats
Orange pumpkins are great for carving, but if you select your variety carefully, winter squashes and pumpkins can also be extremely productive for the kitchen.

Where to grow If you have a very large garden it would be sensible to rotate your winter squashes and pumpkins around it (see pages 22–23). If you've also decided to grow melons, outdoor cucumbers and courgettes, it's best to try to keep them all together. In reality, since they take up so much space, they may not fit into your vegetable-growing plot, and you may need to find a corner of the garden in which to grow a couple. Many people plant direct into an old compost heap because they like plenty of nutrients and moisture. Otherwise, you'll need to enrich the soil with organic matter and select a sunny spot. Because they take up a lot of ground space, many people interplant (see page 226).

Types and varieties The large, orange winter pumpkins are an obvious choice to grow, but they don't taste that great. For eating, it's best to stick to winter squashes. Winter squashes come in all shapes and sizes – many are incredibly beautiful with their bumps and nobbles. There is also a wonderful diversity of colours, ranging from orange and yellow, to green, multi-coloured and even blue!

GROWING SQUASH AND PUMPKIN

1 Dig in plenty of organic matter. Plant young plants once all threat of frost has passed. Plant an inverted large plastic bottle with the end cut off next to the squash.

2 During the summer, the bottle can be topped up with water – an easy way to make sure water reaches the roots.

One very popular sort of squash available at supermarkets is butternut squash. While squashes need a fairly long season to grow and ripen, recent breeding means that even in the coolest of climates you should be able to grow a butternut squash to maturity in a single year outdoors.

Pests and diseases Squashes and pumpkins are generally trouble-free.

Harvesting and storage Pumpkin and squash fruits should be left outside until they take on their full colour. If the weather is fine, leave them outside. But as soon as frost is forecast, bring them inside. Leave the skins to harden and the stalks to dry to prolong the storage period (this is known as 'curing').

Pumpkins don't store so well, so it's best to carve by Halloween or eat by Christmas.

Squashes, however, can last much longer and since they're generally tastier can last right into the new year. Store them in a cold, dry and light place such as a garden shed or greenhouse.

In the kitchen Once peeled and the seeds removed, the flesh can be roasted with other winter vegetables. It is also fantastic puréed and made into hearty winter soups. The seeds are edible and can be roasted.

The prince of pumpkins
Varieties such as 'Crown Prince' (left) and butternut squashes can be harvested in late autumn and stored for use right through the winter.

VARIETY SELECTOR

Orange pumpkins
- 'Atlantic Giant' or the slightly smaller 'Halloween' (a.k.a. 'Sunny').

Winter squash
- For a heavy crop of winter squash, go for 'Geode'.
- An excellent-tasting winter squash is 'Bonbon'. Another great-tasting squash, and one which keeps well is 'Crown Prince'.

For butternut squash, look out for new varieties. Good examples include 'Hunter' and 'Metro'.

CALENDAR

MID-SPRING
Sow seeds individually in small pots. Place the flat seed on its side and cover with 1 cm (½ in) of compost. Keep in a well-lit and warm place (above 18°C/ 65°F).

LATE SPRING
Pot on into larger pots if frosts are still likely. When all chance of frost has passed, plant outside with at least 1 m (3 ft 2 in) between plants.

EARLY SUMMER
Keep unruly plants under control by moving their long, winding stems back into their allotted space.

MIDSUMMER
Water if very dry – a couple of really good soaks should do.

LATE SUMMER
Fruit should be set and starting to ripen.

EARLY AUTUMN
Once fruits start to ripen and reach their full size, start to harvest from now on.

Marrow

Too large to be a courgette and not sweet enough for a squash, marrows make attractive plants and provide plenty of fruit for the kitchen.

✪✪✪✪✪ VALUE FOR MONEY
✪✪✪✪✪ MAINTENANCE
✪✪✪✪✪ FREEZE/STORE
CROPPING SEASON: MIDSUMMER–MID-AUTUMN

Marrows may look just like large courgette, but they are in fact a vegetable in their own right. The fruit grow much bigger than courgettes and often have an unusual stripy appearance. They are similar to courgettes in that they produce fruit throughout the summer, which you can pick as they grow. However, the last fruits of the year, harvested just before the first frosts, should store for several months.

Where to grow Grow marrows with your other courgettes and squashes. Marrows either come as bush varieties – making growing in a relatively small space possible – or as trailing varieties – more like the squashes that send out long shoots reaching well beyond their original space.

Bush varieties are good for small spaces but trailing varieties can be trained – when tied into a wigwam or trellis, they look attractive when the fruits form and hang down.

Types and varieties Mainly split into bush or trailing types; some types store better than others.

Pests and diseases As with courgettes (see page 79).

Harvesting and storage Fruits can be picked throughout the summer when they reach the size suggested on the seed packet – usually around 30 cm (12 in). Keep picking until the first frosts. These last fruits should be left outside (or in a greenhouse) to cure and for the skins to harden, but make sure all are collected before any severe frosts.

Store in a dry, cool place – a shed or garage is fine. Either store individually in boxes or hang in nets to allow air to circulate.

In the kitchen Marrow can be used like courgette. Once the skins have gone hard, peel

Mammoth marrow
An overlooked vegetable, the humble marrow doesn't store well and can lack flavour. However, it can look impressive when the large fruit forms in the summer and autumn.

or cut the flesh lengthways. They can then be stuffed and roasted.

CALENDAR

LATE SPRING
Sow seeds individually on their side in small pots. Cover with 1 cm (½ in) of compost. Keep somewhere bright and warm (at least 18°C/ 65°F).

EARLY SUMMER
Wait until any threat of frost has passed and plant out into rich, fertile soil with plenty of organic matter. Allow 1 sq m (10 sq ft) for each plant.

MIDSUMMER
Water the plants during dry spells – a couple of really good soaks. Fruits can be protected from damp by placing an old plate, brick or tile underneath them as they form.

LATE SUMMER
Keep picking fruit.

EARLY AUTUMN
At the first sign of frosts, the mature fruit can be picked, cured and put into storage.

TRAINING A CLIMBING MARROW

1 Plant against a sunny trellis.

2 As the plant grows, tie in stems up the trellis. Ensure plants are well supported when large fruits form.

Cucumber

This summer salad mainstay is easy to grow outdoors and under cover.

⬤⬤⬤⬤⬤	VALUE FOR MONEY
⬤⬤⬤⬤◯	MAINTENANCE
⬤⬤◯◯◯	FREEZE/STORE

CROPPING SEASON: MIDSUMMER–MID-AUTUMN

Cucumbers are one of the most popular salad crops, and they're also one of the easiest to grow. You don't need too many plants as just one can produce over 10 kg (22 lb) of cucumbers – more than enough to feed a family every week throughout the summer months. In cooler climates, if you have a greenhouse, you'll probably opt for a variety that has been bred specifically for growing under glass, in the same way as a cordon tomato. If you don't have a greenhouse, some cucumbers (and gherkins) can easily be grown outside. If they are left to trail over the ground, much like squashes and melons, you'll have to hunt for the cucumbers under the plants' large, hairy leaves.

Prolific croppers
Cucumbers can be extremely productive – expect a couple every day during the summer months.

GROWING CUCUMBERS IN GROWING BAGS

1 Place a pot over the growing bag and cut out a circular hole the size of the pot.

2 Repeat this twice more, so that the holes are spaced evenly along the length of the bag.

3 Once all threat of frost has passed, gently remove your young cucumber from the small container it has been raised in.

4 Plant one cucumber into each hole, making sure the plant is level with the growing bag. Water well.

Where to grow In the greenhouse, it is best to grow cucumbers in either growing bags or 15-L (4-gallon) pots filled with multi-purpose compost. Plants grow very large and require lots of watering and feeding in the summer. This is ideal if you have a greenhouse packed with tomatoes, aubergines and peppers, since they can be cared for together.

Outside, cucumbers need a sunny spot and rich, fertile soil. It's worth adding some homemade compost to the soil before you plant. Grow in an area with your other curcurbits – squashes, pumpkins and courgettes – rotating around the garden each year (see pages 22–23).

All cucumbers are sensitive to frost, so you'll need to be careful when planting outside, waiting until late spring or early summer in most parts. Even in the greenhouse it's not worth starting seeds too early, unless your greenhouse is heated – greenhouse cucumbers like a temperature of around 20°C (68°F).

Types and varieties Cucumbers are mainly separated according to where they are grown.

Outdoor cucumbers
Growing cucumbers outside is really easy, and recent breeding has meant that these new varieties can be just as sweet and tender as greenhouse varieties.

Greenhouse types Cucumbers grown under glass generally have very smooth skins and are similar to the ones found in the supermarkets. Their taste, however, fresh from the greenhouse, far surpasses anything you'll find wrapped in plastic at your local greengrocer's. Modern greenhouse varieties are bred to produce only female flowers and don't need to be pollinated to set fruit. You'll need to train this type up a cane or string. As they produce only female flowers, their seeds cannot be kept to produce new plants each year because there are no male flowers to pollinate them.
Outdoor types Cucumbers grown outdoors are often called 'ridge types' because

traditionally they were grown on ridges to improve drainage. This isn't necessary anymore and intense breeding has ensured that there are lots of varieties that will succeed outdoors. Typically, ridge types were renowned for having thicker skins and spikes or prickles, as well as a more bitter flavour. Now, breeding has ensured you can get fairly smooth-skinned, sweet-tasting cucumbers outside too.

Typical cucumbers reach about 40 cm (16 in) in length but there are lots of smaller-fruiting varieties that reach about half that size. More recent breeding has developed varieties that produce fruit that measure just 10 cm (4 in) – perfect for snacking on.

TRAINING GREENHOUSE CUCUMBERS

1 Position a supporting cane or string attached to a high horizontal wire down next to the plant.

2 Wind the plant around the support as it grows. Tie in loosely a couple of times.

3 Shoots that appear from the leaf joint of the main stem need to be removed on a regular basis to create a thin cordon plant. These can be nipped out with the fingertips, leaving just the main stem growing.

4 When the leading shoot reaches the top of the support, tie it in. Pinch out the growing tip and allow the last two side shoots to hang down.

Pests and diseases Cucumbers can succumb to the typical greenhouse pests of spider mites and whitefly. Try an organic pesticide on outdoor crops, or alternatively go for a biological control – but this will only work for greenhouse crops because the insects released to devour the spider mite and whitefly will be lost if placed outdoors. Keeping a greenhouse humid will also help to deter spider mite – try 'damping down', which is basically watering the floor of your greenhouse every day during the summer to allow a humid atmosphere to develop.

Powdery mildew also affects cucumbers. In hot, dry conditions, white powdery patches develop across the leaves. The best way to avoid powdery mildew outdoors is to ensure the soil is rich, fertile, and moisture-retentive, and water (at the base of the plant, not on the leaves) when the weather is dry. Planting through black polythene or any other type of mulch is also said to help. In the greenhouse, you just need to ensure your plants don't dry out and keep the windows open on hot days.

Harvesting and storage Cucumbers are ready for harvesting towards the end of midsummer, and in a good year should continue through late summer and well into early autumn. Check your plants as cucumbers can easily blend in with their surroundings or hide behind large leaves! You'll need to pick cucumbers at least twice a week. They should keep for a week or so in the fridge.

In the kitchen Well loved in salads and sandwiches, cucumbers, particularly the smaller varieties, are a good choice for children, who can munch on them whole.

CALENDAR

GREENHOUSE CUCUMBERS

MID-SPRING
Sow seeds singly in small pots. Keep pots somewhere warm – preferably around 25°C (77°F). They should germinate quickly and grow rapidly. Pot seedlings into larger pots after a couple of weeks.

LATE SPRING
Plant up in a growing bag – three per bag – or in large containers filled with multi-purpose compost. Place in the greenhouse.

EARLY SUMMER
In colder areas, plant in your greenhouse now, as above. You'll need to start training the plants up a support (see opposite). Keep watering.

MIDSUMMER
Water well, and when the first fruits start to form, also start watering with a tomato fertiliser. You'll need to water every day during this time. Start picking your first cucumbers.

LATE SUMMER
Keep watering and feeding, as well as damping down the greenhouse floor to deter spider mite.

EARLY AUTUMN
Cucumbers should still be producing. Pick over twice a week at least, even if you're not going to eat them all – the plant will stop fruiting otherwise.

OUTDOOR CUCUMBERS

MID-SPRING
Sow in small individual pots about 1 cm (½ in) deep, keeping the pots in a warm place – preferably a heated propagator, or outdoors if the chance of frost is past.

LATE SPRING
Pot plants on into larger pots, but don't consider planting outside until all threat of frost has passed.

EARLY SUMMER
It should now be safe to plant outdoors. Give each plant at least 1 sq m (1 sq yd) of enriched fertile soil to grow in. If possible cover the ground with black polythene, burying the edges – cut a slit in the middle and plant through.

MIDSUMMER
Water the plants and feed regularly with a tomato fertiliser once plants start to flower. Fruit should be ready for picking about 60 days from sowing – check seed packet details for ideal fruit size.

LATE SUMMER
Keep picking and feeding. Keep a watch for pests and diseases. When watering, avoid getting the leaves wet and remove any damaged or diseased-looking leaves.

EARLY AUTUMN
Picking should start to slow down. When it finally stops, put all the old plants on the compost heap.

> **TIP**
> Seed is expensive – you can raise just a couple of plants, keeping the rest of the seed you bought for next year. Alternatively, visit your garden centre in early summer for ready-grown young plants.

VARIETY SELECTOR

Large greenhouse cucumber
• 'Flamingo', 'Galileo'.

Small-fruiting outdoor cucumbers
• 'Passandra', 'Ilas'.

Small-fruiting outdoor cucumbers
• 'Gracius'.

Very small-fruiting outdoor cucumbers
• 'Rocky', 'Green Fingers'.

Outdoor gherkin
• 'Venlo'.

Majestic sweetcorn
Sweetcorn needs plenty of space and is not the most productive crop, but once you've tasted the sweetest corn fresh from your garden, you'll be sure to find a gap for a few plants each year.

Sweetcorn

With new super-sweet varieties, sweetcorn has got to be one of the most child-friendly vegetables.

✪✪✪✪✪	VALUE FOR MONEY
✪✪✪✪✪	MAINTENANCE
✪✪✪✪✪	FREEZE/STORE
CROPPING SEASON: LATE SUMMER–EARLY AUTUMN	

Sweetcorn looks fantastic in the garden. It is ornamental in its own right, with tall grass-like stems producing large, arching tassels in midsummer. Each plant will provide you with a single cob – two if you're lucky. As each plant needs around 30 cm (12 in) square they're not the most economical of plants in terms of space. However, because they grow almost vertically, it is possible to plant in between. A crop of lettuce, spring onions or turnips is a possibility, as is planting with your winter brassicas or winter squashes, which will continue to grow well after your sweetcorn has been harvested and eaten.

Where to grow Sweetcorn is a wind-pollinated plant and needs to be fertilised from the pollen produced on its tassels. To ensure this happens, it is best to plant sweetcorn in blocks (3 x 3 or 5 x 5) rather than in rows, or hills (clumps) of three to four plants, with the clumps 60 cm (2 ft) apart.

VARIETY SELECTOR
- 'Swift': super-sweet variety.
- 'Mirai Bicolour': bi-coloured super-sweet – a combination of white and yellow kernels.
- 'Red Strawberry': an unusual variety – the kernels can be made into popcorn.

Sweetcorn plants like plenty of sunshine so you'll need to select a sunny spot, and as they grow tall, nowhere too windy either. And because they become large plants, they'll need plenty of organic matter worked into the soil before you plant.

As they are tender plants, they are usually started late in the garden. You can get the crop growing, and therefore harvesting earlier, by starting plants off in pots, or growing under fleece. However, for a simple life, you can sow direct from the last frost until early summer.

One word of warning: sweetcorn can be pollinated by different varieties of sweetcorn – if your neighbour is growing an unusual variety, watch out for some rogue-coloured kernels!

Types and varieties Intense breeding has now produced many varieties with a super-sweet taste – so sweet that the cobs can be eaten fresh off the plant! There is also a range of unusual-coloured varieties – often heritage or old varieties that, while they aren't as sweet as the super-sweets, make an interesting display on the plate and have a rich flavour.

Pests and diseases Mice can eat the seeds if sown direct – if this is a problem, start your seeds off in pots indoors. Slugs can also attack young plants – use appropriate defence measures, at least while the plants are very small.

Harvesting and storage When the tassels on the cob start to shrivel and go brown, the sweetcorn inside should be almost ripe. Check by peeling away one of the leaves around the cob and push your thumbnail into a kernel. If the liquid is creamy, the sweetcorn is ready; if it's watery leave for a few more days. New varieties of sweetcorn keep their sweetness for longer after they've been picked, but they're still best eaten fresh off the plant.

In the kitchen Throw onto a late-summer barbecue, seasoned with olive oil, salt and pepper. Alternatively, they can be boiled, or the kernels cut off the cob and used to make pancakes or soup. Kernels of certain varieties such as 'Red Strawberry' can be dried and used to make popcorn.

CALENDAR

MID-SPRING

Plant individually in small pots. Use long, narrow pots if possible. Sweetcorn needs a temperature of at least 15°C (59°F) to germinate and does not like very cold conditions.

LATE SPRING/EARLY SUMMER

In warmer areas, you can consider sowing sweetcorn direct into the ground. Plant seeds 1 cm (½ in) deep and cover with fleece to help keep the warmth in.

Once any threat of frost has passed, plant out your sweetcorn grown in pots or remove the fleece. Space plants about 35 cm (14 in) apart.

MIDSUMMER

Tap the tassels gently, which helps the pollen to drop down, pollinate the flowers and form the cobs.

LATE SUMMER

Check cobs for maturity and harvest as and when ready.

INTERCROPPING SWEETCORN

1 Once you've raised your sweetcorn plants, plant them direct in the soil 50 cm (20 in) apart each way in early summer.

2 Sow a row of dwarf beans or lettuce in between each row of sweetcorn, or plant out a couple of young winter squash plants.

Aubergine

With their large purple flowers and brightly coloured fruit, aubergines look just as good on the patio as they do on the plate.

✪✪✪✪✪	VALUE FOR MONEY
✪✪✪✪✪	MAINTENANCE
✪✪✪✪✪	FREEZE/STORE
CROPPING SEASON: LATE SUMMER–MID-AUTUMN	

In the past, growing aubergines was reserved to those gardeners who had long, hot summers, with little chance of frost. These egg-shaped fruits, which are related to tomatoes, hail from the warmer climes of India and China, and are a staple vegetable in those cuisines. Aubergines are now part of our weekly supermarket shop but with a little care and attention it's possible to grow aubergines almost anywhere.

Traditionally, in cooler climates, aubergines were grown in greenhouses, with constant warm temperatures ensuring that the large, purple fruits swell to maturity before the weather turns cool. With the breeding of aubergines creating more and more varieties, most are now perfectly happy sitting on a patio in a pot

Regal vegetable
Aubergines are one of the most ornate vegetable plants, with downy silver foliage, delicate purple flowers and impressive white or purple fruits.

AUBERGINES MADE EASY

1 Grow in a frost-free area until any threat of frost has passed. A windowsill or greenhouse will do fine.

2 Plant out – one plant per container at least 30 cm (12 in) in diameter or three to a growing bag. Plant deeply to help prevent the plant from toppling over once covered in fruit.

3 Pinch out the growing tip, feed and water regularly.

4 Once the plant starts to flower, feed it with a tomato fertiliser. Your first aubergines should start to form in a matter of a few days.

VARIETY SELECTOR

In the greenhouse

- **'Moneymaker'**: good greenhouse variety with large purple fruit.
- **'Mohican'**: produces decent-sized white fruit.

On the patio

- **'Ophelia'**: produces a small but plentiful supply of dark purple fruit.
- **'Bonica'**: great-tasting large purple fruits.

Small and sweet
The flesh of small aubergines varieties is usually sweeter than the larger fruiting kinds.

CALENDAR

EARLY SPRING
For the best choice of varieties, raise from seed. Start seeds off in small pots. Sow in multi-purpose compost and keep plants somewhere warm (a propagator if you have one, see page 201) – they need a constant temperature of 20°C (68°F).

MID-SPRING
Keep plants somewhere warm and in good light. If you don't want to raise plants from seed, garden centres will be selling young plants at this time, but the choice of varieties won't be as good as with seed.

LATE SPRING
Pot on into larger pots if you're keeping in the greenhouse. Plant out either in the garden or into large 5-L (1½-gallon) pots containing compost and slow-release fertiliser.

EARLY SUMMER
If your plants are destined for the patio and you haven't done so already, plant into large containers now. Leave on the patio once all threat of frost has passed. Pinch out the growing tip when the plant reaches around 20 cm (8 in) to encourage the plant to bush out.

MIDSUMMER
Keep watering well and start including a tomato feed. Watch out for pests.

LATE SUMMER
Pick over the plants every week. They should keep producing fruit for up to six weeks until early autumn.

---

or growing in a bed. Grown well, a single pot can produce around 50 fruit of the smaller-fruiting types. Choose a large-fruiting variety, and you'll get between five and 10.

Where to grow
Aubergines are one of the most attractive vegetable plants to grow. They produce large, velvety leaves and large, exotic-looking purple flowers. The plants are usually fairly compact, reaching no more than 50 cm (20 in). This means they need little in the way of support too.

Because they're fussy about the temperature, aubergines are often grown in a greenhouse in cooler climates. If you have some greenhouse shelves available, it's definitely worth adding a pot or two of aubergines. If you don't have a greenhouse, a large pot on the patio is the best option. Choose a pot that holds around 5 L (1½ gallons) of compost. Use general multi-purpose compost and add a handful of slow-release fertiliser. This will give it a good start, but when the plant starts to flower, begin feeding with a tomato fertiliser to encourage flower and fruit production.

Types and varieties
Any variety will succeed in a greenhouse. Outdoors, your choice is more limited, but it's better to go for the smaller-fruiting types. As well as dark purple, you can also find white-fruiting aubergines, as well as many with pretty speckles and flecks of colour. If you really want to try something unusual, then there are

orange, yellow and green varieties, such as 'N'Goya', 'Toga' and 'Kermit'.

Pests and diseases
Outside aubergines are usually fairly trouble-free, although flee beetles are sometimes a problem. To avoid an attack, protect your plants with fine mesh. In the greenhouse, however, where temperatures and humidity are much higher, they can be a magnet to pests. Like other greenhouse crops, they can suffer from spider mite, whitefly and aphids. You can use an organic pesticide to try to control these pests, or use biological controls (see page 217). These are natural enemies of the pests that can be introduced to devour the pests.

Harvesting and storage
Aubergines should start to ripen in late summer. You'll need to harvest the fruits regularly rather than in one go. Refer to the packet instructions to find out how big the fruits are meant to be, and pick once they've reached this size. Don't leave too long as seeds will start to grow inside, making them inedible.

In the kitchen
In the past, aubergines were salted before cooking to remove bitterness. With better breeding, new varieties don't have this problem. Simply chop, slice and fry. Aubergines can be used in Mediterranean and Asian cuisines. They are fantastic grilled on the barbecue, or roasted whole, with the inside scooped out and made into a dip.

Pepper

Sweet, juicy and colourful, these Mediterranean vegetables look fantastic growing on the patio.

✿✿✿✿✿ VALUE FOR MONEY
✿✿✿✿✿ MAINTENANCE
✿✿✿✿✿ FREEZE/STORE
CROPPING SEASON: MIDSUMMER–MID-AUTUMN

If you're growing tomatoes, it's definitely worth having a go with peppers too. They can be tricky to grow in cooler climates, only in that they need a long, hot summer to fruit well. If you have a greenhouse you can easily cheat, but many varieties also do well on the patio in large containers. They look stunning too, with large red, yellow and orange fruits.

Where to grow It is possible to grow peppers outdoors in the ground, but there is nothing more disheartening than nurturing a plant from seed only to find that you've run out of summer and the small green fruits are never going to ripen. If you're keen on success, it's definitely worth growing in a greenhouse if you have one. Even if you don't, peppers grown in a container on a hot, sunny patio will also do well. They're beautiful plants too, so even if you're growing in a greenhouse, make sure they are easily visible to enjoy when you are walking by.

Like aubergines, peppers don't grow particularly large – up to around 50 cm (20 in). Some varieties naturally bush out, creating attractive-shaped plants. Others have a tendency to grow straight up. If your plant is more like the latter, pinch out the growing tips when the plant is around 20 cm (8 in) high. This will encourage the plant to bush out. Peppers are generally self-supporting, but when laden with large fruits they can sometimes struggle to keep upright. It is a good idea therefore to insert a short cane and tie the main stem in, ensuring the plant doesn't flop.

They can also be grown in a large container – choose one that holds around 5 L (1½ gallons) of compost. Alternatively, they can be grown in a growing bag – three per bag – or outside in the garden.

Types and varieties Peppers come in a variety of shapes, and not just the typical bell shape, but there are now much longer, more chilli-like varieties too. Then of course there are the colours. Red is most common, but orange and yellow varieties are available to gardeners, as well as dark purple and brown too.

GETTING THE MOST OUT OF YOUR PEPPERS

1 When plants are about 20 cm (8 in) tall, pinch out the growing tip using your thumb and finger. Be careful not to damage the rest of the plant.

2 Remove the first fruits that form in early summer to encourage plants to bush out and fruit more heavily.

Vibrant peppers
Peppers come in all shapes, colours and sizes and can bring some brightness to your patio.

VARIETY SELECTOR

In the greenhouse

- 'New Ace': decent, red greenhouse variety.
- 'Gypsy': another red variety – better indoors than out.
- 'Sweet Chocolate': a dark purple large-fruiting variety.

All varieties prefer long, hot summers with plenty of sun, preferably in a greenhouse. However, some do alright on the patio too, but you'll need to choose your variety carefully.

Pests and diseases Peppers are likely to suffer from the same pests as tomatoes, cucumbers and aubergines when growing in the greenhouse – namely whitefly, red spider mite and aphids. If you're growing in a greenhouse keep a close eye on your plants, and if necessary, reach for an organic spray.

Harvesting and storage Make sure you know the colour of your peppers and pick them when ripe – usually in late summer and early autumn. Green, unripe peppers can be picked off the plant at the end of the season. Leave on a sunny windowsill and they may ripen up, otherwise use them green. Once ripe, the fruits will be much sweeter.

Keep picking fruits as they ripen as this will encourage more fruit to develop. You can store them in the fridge until you need them but once picked they'll last only a couple of weeks.

In the kitchen Peppers can be used in Asian and Mediterranean cooking. They can be enjoyed raw in salads or roasted. You can blacken the skins on the barbecue or under the grill. They will peel off easily, leaving sweet, succulent flesh underneath.

CALENDAR

EARLY SPRING
Sow a couple of seeds in a small pot of multi-purpose compost. You'll need a propagator or warm windowsill to maintain the required temperature of 20°C (68°F). Once germinated, remove the weaker seedlings.

MID-SPRING
Once the seeds have germinated, the pots can be moved to a cooler place – between 12 and 18°C (53 and 64°F).

LATE SPRING
Pot on to a larger 5-L (1½-gallon) pot or plant in a growing bag, or plant outside in a bed. They'll still need to be kept under cover or indoors if there is a threat of cold weather. If you didn't get around to growing from seed, buy from your local garden centre now.

EARLY SUMMER
Place in the sunniest spot available. If plants are becoming leggy, pinch out the growing tips to encourage them to bush out.

It's hard to do, but removing some of the earlier fruit that develop now will encourage the plant to develop a lot more.

MIDSUMMER
Start watering more frequently as the weather warms up, keeping the compost just moist. Also, start feeding with a tomato feed to encourage more flowers and fruit.

LATE SUMMER
Pick off your fruit as they ripen.

EARLY AUTUMN
Fruiting should be plentiful at this time, so keep picking and watering.

MID-AUTUMN
If the weather is starting to turn cooler, bring any outdoor plants indoors if you can to encourage ripening.

LATE AUTUMN
Pick off any existing fruit and use in the kitchen.

Chilli

Cousins of the peppers, chillies add fire to your food and colour to your kitchen garden.

✿✿✿✿✿ VALUE FOR MONEY
✿✿✿✿✿ MAINTENANCE
✿✿✿✿✿ FREEZE/STORE
CROPPING SEASON: MIDSUMMER–MID-AUTUMN

Originating from Central and South America, chillies were first spread to the rest of the Americas then on to Asia. Popular in Mexican and Asian cuisines, chillies are similar to peppers in looks and growing requirements, the only difference being the heat of the fruit! The small bushy plants produce green, variegated and even black glossy leaves that look attractive in any garden, greenhouse or even on a windowsill. But it's the colour of the small chillies themselves that provide a real show. Even if you don't use chillies much in your cooking, a chilli plant can be as ornamental as any flowering plant.

Chillies have become extremely popular with gardeners in recent years. Intense breeding has created hotter and hotter chillies and gardeners like to outdo each other with the varieties they grow – and eat. The hotness is due to the chemical capsaicin held in the flesh and seeds. The more capsaicin, the hotter the chilli. This heat can be measured and is reported in Scoville heat units. One of the hottest so far is the 'Dorset Naga', which has a heat-rating of over 900,000 Scoville units! Chilli festivals have become really popular in recent years. Usually taking place in late summer, they offer a chance to look at the huge range of chilli plants available to gardeners and to taste how hot they really get.

Where to grow In the garden the growing requirements of chillies are exactly the same as peppers – hot and sunny conditions over a long season. But again, while some varieties only do well in a greenhouse, others will be happy on a sunny patio. They're tender plants, so you can only grow them outside during the seasons that are free from frost. For most gardeners it won't be worth growing in the ground and in any case, these small, highly attractive plants suit being grown in a pot, to

Fiery characters
Brightly coloured chillies look fabulous in the garden, greenhouse and on the windowsill. Dry the fruits and they'll provide heat to your food for the whole year.

allow you to appreciate their attractive fruit close-up. If you select one of the smaller varieties, then you can even grow on a windowsill in the kitchen or conservatory.

Types and varieties Ranging in height between 25 and 50 cm (10 and 20 in), chillies are rather compact. They come from the capsicum family and are actually short-lived perennials – meaning they would, if the weather permitted, last more than a year. In the garden it's more usual to treat them like an annual – growing from seed and fruiting all in a single year. There are thousands of varieties of chilli to choose from, varying in colour from

green, yellow and orange, to red and purple. All also vary in their hotness too, but this depends on the exact growing conditions – it's not uncommon to find two chillies on the same plant with different levels of heat.

Harvesting and storage Chillies should be harvested when ripe. You can store fresh chillies in the fridge or freeze whole and use individually when required. Chillies often ripen together. You can cut off the whole plant, and leave it hanging upside down to dry. Alternatively, pick off chillies individually and leave in the sun or in a very low oven to dry off. These can be crushed and sprinkled into the cooking pot when required. Be careful when handling chillies – their hotness can easily transfer to your fingers, so make sure you wash your hands after touching them.

In the kitchen Famous in Mexican and other Central American dishes, chillies are a common ingredient. Chillies are also used regularly in Asian and Mediterranean cooking to add heat to dishes when they are usually fried at the beginning of cooking, along with onions and garlic. The seeds of chillies are usually hotter than the flesh – if you prefer a milder taste, then leave the seeds out. Otherwise chop finely and add the whole chilli, including the seeds.

VARIETY SELECTOR

Hot chillies

- 'Habanero'.

Milder chillies

- 'Hungarian Wax': starting sweet, the heat intensifies.

Best for a patio

- 'Filius Blue', 'Mirasol', 'Purple Tiger', 'Numex Twilight'.

Best for a windowsill or greenhouse

- 'Explosive Blast', 'Paper Lantern'.

CALENDAR

EARLY SPRING

Sow seeds individually in small pots to a depth of around 1 cm (½ in). You'll need somewhere with a constant temperature of 20°C (68°F) – use a heated propagator if you have one.

MID-SPRING

Seeds should germinate in a fortnight. Once germinated, the temperature can be cooler, with a minimum of 12°C (54°F). Pot on into slightly larger pots and keep well watered and in a sunny, warm spot.

LATE SPRING

Plant out into the final pots of up to 5-L (1½-gallon) capacity if the varieties are quite large. Smaller varieties should cope with a 2-L (½-gallon) pot, but they will require more attention to keep them well watered. Pinch out the growing tips if the plants are looking leggy.

EARLY SUMMER

If you are growing them outside, place the plants on the hottest part of your patio. Make sure the plants are protected or taken back indoors if there is any chance of frost at night.

MIDSUMMER

If plants are becoming top-heavy, stake using a short cane, and tie in with string. If the flowers don't seem to be setting fruit, give the plants a little tap to distribute the pollen, or even try using a small paintbrush.

LATE SUMMER

Start to harvest your chillies as they ripen.

CHILLI VARIETIES

'Explosive Blast' is an ornamental chilli with clusters of different coloured fruits.

'Filius Blue' carries purple-blue, egg-shaped fruits that ripen to red, losing their pungency in the process.

'Numex Twilight', an attractive, drought-resistant plant, yielding medium-hot fruits.

'Mirasol', the name means 'looking at the sun' and the plant carries an abundance of upwards-pointing chillies.

Tomato

Whether you have a windowsill, patio or greenhouse, there are varieties of sweet, succulent tomatoes suitable for all situations.

✪✪✪✪✪ VALUE FOR MONEY
✪✪✪✪✪ MAINTENANCE
✪✪✪✪✪ FREEZE/STORE
CROPPING SEASON: MIDSUMMER–MID-AUTUMN

Tomatoes have got to be the most well-loved and popular salad fruit. And home-grown tomatoes taste so much better than shop-bought, so this is definitely one crop that's worth growing year after year.

It's no wonder they're so popular: inch for inch, tomato plants are one of the most bountiful and space-worthy crops to grow – just one growing bag with three plants can provide around 15 kg (33 lb) of tomatoes. If the weather isn't suitable outdoors for this tender South American plant, then greenhouses can be filled up with tomatoes throughout the warmer months. Rich in vitamins and antioxidants, they are best enjoyed fresh from the garden through the summer and early autumn, and in salads and Mediterranean-style dishes. The excess at the end of the season can be dried, frozen, puréed or turned into chutney.

Where to grow There are tomatoes for almost all situations of the garden (and house!). New breeds mean that small-fruiting varieties can be grown in pots small enough to fit on a windowsill. Although they won't give you a huge supply of tomatoes, there may be enough to throw into a salad every week or so.

For larger harvests, opt for growing in the garden. On the patio or in the greenhouse, tomatoes can be grown in growing bags or containers. Some trailing or bush varieties also look decorative and are perfect for a hanging basket. Whichever container you choose, compost from a growing bag is ideal, preferably peat-free.

Tomatoes also do well planted straight into the border – whether in the greenhouse or outdoors. If growing in a rotation, they can be planted out either with, or to follow on from, early potatoes.

Types and varieties Intense breeding has produced a huge range of tomato varieties. *Colour* Red is still the favourite. Nowadays there is a range of oranges, yellows and even striped varieties.
Size Ranges from fruits measuring less than 1 cm (½ in) in diameter to larger 'beefsteaks'.
Flavour Think about what you want the tomatoes for before you choose the variety to grow – cherry tomatoes are great for salads, plum varieties are ideal for cooking and beefsteak tomatoes are good for slicing in sandwiches. For the biggest croppers, go for a salad variety.

Container tomatoes
Recent breeding means that tomatoes can now be grown in small containers and baskets, producing a plentiful supply of small and extremely sweet fruit.

Ripe for picking
Tomatoes come in all shapes and colours. It's worth trying a few types such as cherry, plum and salad types, to provide contrasting tastes and colours in your dishes.

TOMATOES IN FOUR EASY STEPS

1 In late spring, buy three young tomato plants, or raise three plants from seed – a good place to start is with the cherry tomato cordon varieties, such as 'Sungold'. Also, get a growing bag and a bottle of tomato feed – that's all you need.

2 Once all threat of frost has passed, cut three evenly spaced holes in the growing bag, push the compost out of the way and carefully plant the tomatoes into the bag. Gently press down the soil around the base of each plant, and water.

3 Insert and secure three 2-m (6 ft 5-in) high canes next to each plant, being careful not to damage the plants. After four weeks, start to feed as instructed with the liquid tomato food. As the plants grow, tie them to the canes. As side shoots develop, remove them from the plant, as shown here.

4 Leave the fruits on the plant until they are really ripe – they taste even better when they're allowed to ripen on the plant. Take into the kitchen and enjoy!

Ripen on the vine
Leaving the fruit on the plants until they're really ripe will produce the best flavour.

Climate Tomatoes are tender plants, but can be grown outdoors if the temperature stays above 21°C (70°F) for more than 10 weeks. Areas that suffer from diseases like blight make outdoor growing tricky – so if possible they're safest grown in a greenhouse.

In the garden

Planting and training When planting out tomatoes, plant deep. Roots will grow out from the stem and provide greater support for the plant above. For bush varieties, these can be left to sprawl on the ground – you can always use a plastic or permeable fabric to keep the fruits clean, or alternatively use a loose wire cage made of chicken wire wrapped around the plant as a means of support. Cordon varieties need more maintenance. You'll need to train the leading shoot up a cane or string. Nip out side shoots as they grow. Later in the season you'll need to nip off the leading shoot either as it reaches the top of the greenhouse or towards the end of summer. That way all the energy will go into ripening the fruit already on the plant.

Feeding If you are growing your tomatoes in a pot or growing bag, feeding is essential. You'll need to start feeding your plants around four to six weeks after planting out. You can use a regular plant food until the fruits start to form, then switch to a liquid tomato food. High in phosphate, this feed will ensure a bumper crop.

Mulching If you are growing in the ground, add a good, deep layer of garden compost or other bulky organic matter (see pages 218–223) in the spring. Start to feed with a liquid tomato feed in summer.

Watering Tomatoes hate to dry out, and doing so can lead to blossom end rot (see below). Watering during dry spells is therefore essential in the ground. In a container, watering up to twice a day may be necessary at the height of summer. Think about setting up an automatic irrigation system (see page 215).

Pests and diseases Blossom end rot is a problem caused by fluctuating temperatures, insufficient water, excessive heat or calcium deficiency. Ventilating the greenhouse,

GROWING TOMATOES FROM SEED

1 Sow seeds individually in seed modules in mid-spring.

2 Prick out the seedlings into small pots and keep indoors until after the last frost date.

3 When the seedlings are around 15 cm (6 in) high, it is time to transfer them to growing bags in the greenhouse or plant outside.

SEEDS OR PLANTS?

Tomatoes have got to be one of the easiest plants to grow. Throw a tomato onto a compost heap and seedlings will soon emerge. However, if you want to grow a range of varieties, it may be cheaper (and easier) to buy a few young plants from your local garden centre than several packets of seed, although the range of varieties bought this way may be limited. Stored properly, tomato seed can last many years, but if you've missed the sowing time (see Calendar), then head for the garden centre to see what you can pick up.

dampening down the greenhouse floor and watering regularly can all help.

Aphids, spider mite and whitefly can all cause a gardener some concern when growing tomatoes. Pesticides and biological controls are available or you could try companion planting (see pages 226–227).

One major problem that affects tomatoes is blight – a fungal disease that spreads on the wind. You can use a preventive fungicide spray, but you'll need to use this through the whole season. If blight is a problem in your area, consider growing only in a greenhouse. This way, the blight spores are less likely to come into contact with the plant. Once infected, the plant and all fruit are quickly ruined.

Harvesting and storage Tomatoes should be picked when they're as juicy and ripe as possible. If you're only making weekly trips down to your plot, picking tomatoes that are just turning pink is still fine. Just leave them on a sunny windowsill to ripen up. Tomatoes in the greenhouse may need to be picked a couple of times a week. Expect tomatoes right into late autumn if the weather stays mild. However, once the weather turns, you'll need to collect everything. Try ripening in a paper bag with a banana. Alternatively just use green tomatoes, either fried or in a pickle.

VARIETY SELECTOR

- 'Gardener's Delight', 'Cherrola': best cherry varieties.
- 'Shirley': best salad variety.
- 'Incas': best plum variety.
- 'Black Russian', 'Brandywine': best beefsteak varieties.
- 'Hundreds and Thousands', 'Tumbler': best basket varieties.
- 'Red Robin': best for a windowsill.

In the kitchen Tomatoes are delicious in salads, soups or puréed. If there's a glut, you can make salsas, chutneys, jams and pickles, or dry them in the sun (in hot areas) or in the oven (see pages 240–241). Excess tomatoes can be frozen whole or puréed for winter use.

CALENDAR

LATE WINTER

If you have a heated greenhouse, you'll be able to start seed off now in a propagator – they'll need 18°C (64°F) to germinate.

MID-SPRING

For growing in an unheated greenhouse or outside, sow indoors in small pots.

Prick out individually into small pots once plants have germinated, and keep indoors until after the last frost date.

LATE SPRING

Plant out tomatoes in their final positions – in pots, baskets or in the ground. Plant no more than three plants per growing bag, aim for a pot size of 15 L (3.5 gallons) for pot-grown, and as big a basket as you can manage to cut down on watering.

In the ground, set a plant every 45–60 cm (17–23 in).

EARLY SUMMER

Start feeding with a specialist tomato feed once the first fruits have formed.

Nip off all side shoots from cordon varieties.

Start to water every day.

MIDSUMMER

Keep nipping out side shoots and feeding plants. Start to harvest tomatoes as the first fruits ripen. Watch out for pests such as spider mite and whitefly.

LATE SUMMER–EARLY AUTUMN

Nip out the leading shoot on cordon varieties.

Pinch out side shoots and remove any yellowing leaves.

LATE AUTUMN

Pick the last of the ripe fruit and any unripe fruit before the first frosts hit.

STEM AND FLOWER CROPS

These stem and flower crops include some of those that are more tricky to grow. However, if you just love broccoli and have a real addiction to fennel, they're worthy of space in any vegetable garden. For those of you who have less time, why not try some of the perennial vegetables such as asparagus and globe artichokes?

Broccoli and Calabrese

If you decide to grow only one member of the cabbage family, make it broccoli. The tender, sweet flower buds and stems are well used in the kitchen.

◐◐◐◐◯ VALUE FOR MONEY
◐◐◐◐◐ MAINTENANCE
◐◐◐◐◐ FREEZE/STORE
CROPPING SEASON: LATE SUMMER–MID-SPRING

Ready for harvest
The calabrese broccoli is similar to other broccoli but it produces a single head.

Broccoli stems
When the main head has been harvested, the plant will produce side stems for later harvest.

A real superfood, broccoli is one of the most popular brassicas to grow. It's meant to help prevent cancer as well as heart disease, and it's also rich in vitamins and folic acid. You can grow broccoli almost all year round.

Where to grow Broccoli and calabrese need plenty of space. They can become large plants, needing around 40–60 cm (16–24 in) between plants, depending on the variety. Grow with the rest of your brassicas, or intercrop overwintering purple-sprouting broccoli, which really does grow quite large, with sweetcorn (see page 86). Here you may need to stake as with Brussels sprouts, pushing in a cane and tying in (see page 56). Like other brassicas, broccoli is a greedy crop so sprinkle over a general-purpose fertiliser before you plant.

Types and varieties Traditional broccoli produces lots of side shoots with small heads of flowers. Stems and flowers are picked when the buds are still tight, in early spring. Often these flowers are purple or white.

Calabrese, originating from Calabria in Italy, is similar, but instead produces a single large stem with a large flowerhead. Picked before the flowers open, this gives a single large head of broccoli. Unlike broccoli, calabrese doesn't need a cold spell, and so will be ready for picking in midsummer from a spring sowing. While sprouting broccoli is also grown in spring, most varieties need a cold spell, and will be ready for picking in late winter. Recently, new varieties of broccoli have become available, which allow you to pick broccoli in the autumn from a spring sowing.

Pests and diseases Broccoli suffers from all the same pests and diseases as cabbages (see page 55). Grow and protect with the other members of the cabbage family. For crops left over winter, birds, especially pigeons, can be a real problem. You'll need to use netting to keep them at bay.

Harvesting and storage Calabrese can be picked in midsummer from a spring sowing. If you space the plants fairly wide apart, once you've cut the main

VARIETY SELECTOR

Calabrese

- 'Green Magic', 'Decathalon', 'Tiara'.

Sprouting broccoli

- 'Bordeaux', 'Spike', 'Wok Brocc'.

Purple sprouting broccoli

- 'Claret', 'Red Arrow'.

White sprouting broccoli

- 'Early White Sprouting', 'White Eye'.

stem, leave the plants to grow. Further side shoots will keep growing, and these can be picked right into winter. Broccoli is worth picking over every week to ensure you pick before the flowers open, and it should be eaten straight away. Alternatively, you can blanch for a minute or two, drain, then freeze.

In the kitchen Young broccoli and calabrese can be tender enough to eat raw. Otherwise, steam, stir-fry or add to soups.

TIP

Space calabrese wide apart for large main heads, or close together for smaller main heads and lots of side shoots.

HOW TO MAXIMISE YOUR BROCCOLI CROP

1 Plant out the seedlings at least 45 cm (18 in) apart.

2 Cut off the main head when the tight flower buds have formed.

3 Leave the plant to produce side shoots and keep picking these as they grow.

CALENDAR

EARLY SPRING

This is a good time to start off calabrese. Sow seeds individually in small pots, about 1 cm (½ in) deep.

MID-SPRING

You can still sow calabrese now. Start to sow winter-sprouting broccoli in the same way. Prepare your vegetable bed by digging over and adding some fertiliser.

LATE SPRING

Now's the time to sow summer-sprouting broccoli. Once the plants have grown on, plant out in the garden. Spacing will depend on the variety. Cover the crop with fine mesh to protect it from birds and other pests.

EARLY SUMMER

Make sure all your plants are planted out. Firm in well and provide a cane for support for tall varieties.

MIDSUMMER

Water plants well during dry spells and while they're becoming established. Add another sprinkling of fertiliser over the surface. Start to pick heads of calabrese when the heads are formed.

LATE SUMMER

Keep picking calabrese side shoots.

EARLY AUTUMN

Start to pick summer-sprouting broccoli.

MID AUTUMN

Pick over the plants.

LATE AUTUMN

Calabrese and summer-sprouting broccoli will finish around now.

EARLY TO MID-WINTER

Keep your winter-sprouting broccoli protected from birds by covering it with netting.

LATE WINTER

Start to pick winter-sprouting broccoli, and continue picking into mid-spring.

Cauliflower

This is a difficult vegetable to grow, but new growing techniques make it just a little easier.

○○○○○ VALUE FOR MONEY
○○○○○ MAINTENANCE
○○○○○ FREEZE/STORE
CROPPING SEASON: ALL YEAR ROUND

Cauliflowers are one of the trickiest vegetables to grow. Not only do they suffer from every brassica-family pest and disease imaginable, but they're also liable to bolt. They also need harvesting as soon as they're ready – if left outside their curds can spoil. In spite of that, cauliflowers are a rewarding crop to grow – in addition to the traditional white types, there are purple and green, as well as the pointy romanesco types. Best of all, cauliflowers are usually ready for picking when little else is available. If you get your timing right you can have cauliflower from autumn into spring.

Where to grow Grow cauliflowers with your other cabbage-family crops, preferably under a fine mesh to try to keep many of their pests at bay. Enrich the soil with compost, and add a general-purpose fertiliser just before you plant out. Traditionally cauliflowers should be planted about 45 cm (18 in) apart each way, giving the plants plenty of space to grow and produce large curds. However, grow them much closer together and you'll be rewarded with smaller, but a larger overall weight of curds from the same space.

Cauliflowers are often split into summer, autumn and winter varieties. Winter varieties are generally very hardy and will survive through a long period of cold. The summer and autumn varieties are generally harvested the year they are planted – from late summer right through to early winter.

For a bit of interest, it's worth trying a coloured variety, and especially some of the new romanesco types.

Pests and diseases As troublesome as any other cabbage-family crop (see page 55). Flea beetle, slugs, snails, caterpillars, aphids and cabbage root fly can all be a problem. (See pages 226–227 for controls.)

Creamy curd
A popular winter vegetable, cauliflowers are now available in a variety of colours.

Harvesting and storage The outer leaves protect the cauliflower curds, but you'll need to pull them back to check their progress. When ready, curds should be coloured as expected, and the individual flower buds should not be distinguishable. Cut below the curd using a sharp knife. They can be kept in a cool, dark place for a week or so, or alternatively, broken up into pieces and frozen.

In the kitchen Use in soups, stews or even turn into a pickle, such as piccalilli.

VARIETY SELECTOR

Summer and autumn cauliflowers
- 'Aviso', 'Moby Dick': white.
- 'Graffiti': purple.
- 'Panther', 'Emeraude': green.
- 'Cheddar': yellow.

Winter cauliflowers
- 'Winter Aalsmeer', 'Walcheren', 'Winter Pilgrim'.

Romanesco cauliflowers
- 'Amphora', 'Veronica'.

CALENDAR

EARLY SPRING
Start sowing now for an early summer crop. Sow seeds individually in small pots in a cool greenhouse or cold frame.

MID-SPRING
Keep sowing a few seeds now, which will spread out the harvest later.

LATE SPRING
Plant out your first sowing. For mini cauliflowers, space out 25 cm (10 in) each way between plants. For regular-sized cauliflowers, go for around 45 cm (18 in) each way. Water well at planting, but not after.

EARLY SUMMER
Plant out your later sowing now, as above.

MIDSUMMER
Start to harvest your early sowing. Make another sowing now for a late-autumn harvest.

LATE SUMMER
If the soil becomes dry, give your plants a really good soaking once or twice a week to prevent bolting.

EARLY AUTUMN ONWARDS
Keep a lookout for pests and harvest when ready.

Kohlrabi

An unusual vegetable, where the swollen stem makes for an interesting crop.

✪✪✪✪○ VALUE FOR MONEY
✪✪✪✪○ MAINTENANCE
✪✪✪✪○ FREEZE/STORE
CROPPING SEASON: LATE SPRING–EARLY WINTER

Kohlrabi is part of the brassica family, but this is the only member where the stem is the edible part. Plants grow to around 30 cm (12 in) high, but around halfway up the stem, it starts to swell into a ball. This swollen part of the stem is the edible part, making a tasty, tender (if picked at the right time) and sweet treat.

Exotic vegetable
The swollen stems of kohlrabi are delicious both raw and lightly cooked.

Where to grow Kohlrabi can be quick-growing, reaching an edible size within eight weeks. To avoid problems with pests, it is best grown with your other brassicas, under a fine mesh. However, it can also be grown as a quick-growing crop among some other slower-growing plants such as sweetcorn, or grown quickly once another crop has been taken out, say, after broad beans.

Because it's quick-growing, you can also make several sowings through the spring and summer, which spreads out the harvest well.

Red kohlrabi
Red forms of kohlrabi look almost alien-like, but they taste just as good as the other colours.

Types and varieties There is not much in the way of breeding of new kohlrabi varieties, but there are still some interesting forms available in purple, green or white. All have creamy white flesh with a turnip-like flavour.

Pests and diseases As with other brassicas, kohlrabi can suffer from a variety of pests (see page 55). However, they are said to be a bit tougher than other brassicas, and so may be worth a go even if you've failed with others. They are also supposedly more heat- and drought-tolerant than other types too.

Harvesting and storage Harvest on a regular basis when the stems reach golf ball size. Left to grow to the size of a tennis ball, the flesh turns woody. They are also fairly tough and will survive some of the cold weather if not harvested in time.

They're not worth storing for very long, so eat when they're fresh.

In the kitchen Picked young and tender, they can be peeled and chopped into salads. They can also be steamed.

CALENDAR

EARLY SPRING
Sow individually in small pots or modules in a cool greenhouse or cold frame.

MID-SPRING
You can start to sow direct into the soil – make a shallow drill and go for a couple of seeds every 10 cm (4 in) or so in rows 30 cm (12 in) apart. Take out the weakest seedling if two come up at each place.

LATE SPRING
Plant out your early harvest 10 cm (4 in) apart. Keep sowing direct into the soil, as above.

EARLY SUMMER
Your first crop should be ready for harvesting. Keep sowing right up to late summer if you want a plentiful supply of kohlrabi.

Fennel

The aniseed-flavoured fleshy stem of this plant is perfect in salads and fish dishes.

⬤⬤⬤◯◯ VALUE FOR MONEY
⬤⬤⬤◯◯ MAINTENANCE
⬤⬤◯◯◯ FREEZE/STORE
CROPPING SEASON: LATE SPRING–EARLY AUTUMN

Fennel is a rather unusual vegetable in the garden, but is becoming more popular in the supermarket. Despite it being a bit tricky to grow, there's little reason not to give this plant a try. Fennel produces fine, feathery foliage, much like the herb, however, this plant is grown to produce a swollen fleshy base to its stem. It has juicy, crunchy stems, a bit like celery, and a fine aniseed flavour.

Where to grow
Fennel prefers deep, rich soil. It will grow on sandy and heavy clay soil, provided that the soil is kept constantly moist. It also doesn't like the cold. Because of this it's best not to sow fennel too early in the season because it is liable to bolt. Fennel sometimes bolts when it has been disturbed when being grown. It's a good idea to start fennel off in small pots, then plant out individually. This way the roots are not disturbed.

Types and varieties There aren't many varieties of fennel; however, some do claim to resist the urge to bolt.

Pests and diseases Slugs can be a problem, particularly early on in the plant's growth. Other than this, fennel has few problems.

Harvesting and storage Plants can mature in as little as 10 weeks after sowing. Cut off the bulbous stem 2.5 cm (1 in) above the soil level. Leaving the root in the ground encourages the plant to reshoot. Don't leave the plants standing for too long as, again, they may bolt.

In the kitchen The fine aniseed flavour of fennel goes well with fish of all types and works well braised in the oven.

VARIETY SELECTOR

- **'Tauro'**: an early maturing variety with some resistance to bolting.
- **'Amigo'**: produces slightly flattened bulbs, with good bolting resistance.
- **'Finale'**: very flat bulbs, but good bolting resistance.

CALENDAR

MID-SPRING
Sow a couple of seeds in small individual pots or modules.

LATE SPRING
Keep the strongest seedling going (thin out the weakest) and plant out in the garden after a few weeks of growing. Give plants plenty of space – around 30 cm (12 in) each way.

EARLY SUMMER
You could still sow a row or two directly in the soil now – around 1.5 cm (⅝ in) deep. Sow a few seeds every 30 cm (12 in) and thin out if more than one comes up at each point.

MIDSUMMER
Water your plants well through any dry spells. Start to harvest early crops.

LATE SUMMER
Keep watering and harvesting.

TIP
Use the feathery foliage in the kitchen as well as the bulbous stems. Cut off the foliage with scissors as required.

Feathery fennel
Fennel is tricky to grow, but if you succeed, you'll be rewarded with crunchy, sweet and tender stems perfect for salads.

Leek

Leeks are one of the few vegetables you can continue to harvest right through winter.

✪✪✪✪✪	VALUE FOR MONEY
✪✪✪✪✪	MAINTENANCE
✪✪✪✪✪	FREEZE/STORE
	CROPPING SEASON: LATE SUMMER–EARLY SPRING

Just like their cousin, the onion, leeks are an incredibly versatile crop. They are well known for standing through the cold of winter, allowing you to pull a stem or two any time you need. They're also a good summer crop. Grown close together, 'baby leeks' can be picked when they resemble salad onions, or left to become larger. Baby leeks are expensive in the supermarket, but very easy to grow at home.

Hardy crop
When there is little else to harvest in mid-winter, you'll be pleased that you planted a couple of rows of leeks.

GROWING BABY LEEKS

1 Sow several seeds in small pots in spring.

2 Once they've germinated, plant these clumps out in the garden, spaced 30 cm (12 in) apart.

3 The young plants will push each other apart and produce a fine crop of young baby leeks.

Where to grow Leeks should be grown alongside your other onion-family members and moved around the garden every year (see pages 22–23). If you don't have much space in your garden, they can be grown in a pot on the patio. Here, sow seeds 2.5 cm (1 in) apart and cover with compost. Water well and you'll be able to pull leeks when they reach pencil thickness. Leave a few to grow even bigger.

Types and varieties There is little difference in colour and flavour between varieties. It's best to go with an F₁ variety, since they are generally higher yielding and hardier than some of the open-pollinated varieties – but be careful, because if you're growing them as baby leeks you'll need plenty of seed, and some varieties can be expensive.

Pests and diseases Relatively trouble-free compared to onions, but leek rust can be a problem. Small, orange spots appear on the leaves but there is little you can do. Just make sure plants don't suffer from lack of water in the summer. Remove all affected leaves and discard them.

Harvesting and storage Harvesting of leeks can span from midsummer right into the following spring. If you've planted them close together, you can start pulling very small leeks in the summer and use them like salad onions. Left a little longer, more can be harvested when the stems are around 2–3 cm (¾–1¼ in) in diameter. By this time there should be a plant every 20–30 cm (8–12 in). These can be left in the ground and pulled whenever they're needed in the kitchen. Because they're happy left standing outside, there is no need to harvest and store.

How to get leeks all year In mid-spring, sow leeks direct into the ground. Sow seeds thickly, aiming for a seed every 1–2 cm (½–¾ in). Once the seeds have come up, thin out to every 2.5 cm (1 in). Leeks can start to be pulled after around 10 weeks. Be careful not to disturb the neighbouring plants, which will continue to grow. Keep pulling until you have a plant every 20–30 cm (8–12 in). These can be left to mature to full size and pulled through the winter right up to next spring.

In the kitchen Leeks have a mild oniony flavour and can be used as an onion replacement. Their tender stems are popular steamed or used in soups and stir-fries.

Grow your own seed
Leave one or two plants in the garden and they'll run to seed. The white flowers become so tall they may need some support, but they should produce a good crop of small, black seeds that can be used to grow more leeks.

TIP

CALENDAR

EARLY SPRING
Sow in small pots or modular trays. Plant one seed in each and cover with compost. Leave in a cool greenhouse or cold frame.

MID-SPRING
Water seedlings and feed if necessary with a liquid fertiliser.

LATE SPRING
Transplant into the ground. Make a hole with a dibber around 10 cm (4 in) deep and drop the young leek into the hole. Water. Keep around 30 cm (12 in) between rows and space 15 cm (6 in) apart.

EARLY SUMMER
Water well and keep weeds down.

MIDSUMMER
Keep watering if it's dry.

LATE SUMMER
You can start to harvest baby leeks now, or leave to grow on in the ground right up to next spring.

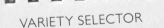

VARIETY SELECTOR

- **'Bandit'**: a hardy winter leek, producing a large crop and a good choice for growing as baby leeks as the seed is cheap.

- **'Carlton'**: a more expensive variety, but a strong grower with excellent flavour.

- **'Oarsman'**: another expensive variety, but probably the best you can find with good resistance to rust.

High-return crop
Leeks are a valuable winter crop, which are perfect for adding to hearty winter casseroles or soups.

Salad onion

This onion crop is a good
vegetable for those eager
for a quick crop.

| ✪✪✪✪✪ VALUE FOR MONEY
| ✪✪✪✪✪ MAINTENANCE
| ✪✪✪✪✪ FREEZE/STORE
| CROPPING SEASON: LATE SPRING–LATE AUTUMN

Salad onions, or spring onions, are a fast-
growing crop, perfect for using in salads or
stir-fries. If you're new to gardening and new
to onion-growing, this is a good place to start,
since it's both a quick crop to mature and one
that can be sown any time between early
spring and early autumn.

Where to grow It's a good idea to keep
salad onions with any other onions you have,
rotating them around the garden each year (see
pages 22–23). However, as salad onions take
up such a small amount of space and can be
sown right through the growing season, they're
a good choice for any patch of spare ground
you have. For example, a short row can be
sown between larger brassicas early in the
season, or sown in place of a crop of broad
beans or peas, which finish in summer.

GROWING SALAD ONIONS IN A CONTAINER

1 Select a container 30 cm (12 in) in diameter
or 5 L (1½ gallons) in volume and fill with
multi-purpose compost.

2 Scatter seed individually every 2.5 cm
(1 in) across the surface of the pot.

3 Cover with a layer of compost and water
with a fine rose.

Quick croppers
A quick-growing crop, you can start harvesting salad onions in just six to eight weeks.

If you are short of space, salad onions are brilliant in containers. You can sow fairly thickly and you'll have plenty of onions for pulling.

Whether you're growing in containers or in the ground, they can be sown outside from early spring onwards. Sowing every few weeks through the growing season will provide you with fresh salad onions right through winter.

Types and varieties
Most traditional salad onions tend to produce a small bulb at the end. Japanese bunching onions are similar, except for the fact that they're much straighter, without a bulb. Some varieties are crosses of the two types. For a bit of interest, there are now even red salad onions, which look good both in the garden and on the plate.

Pests and diseases
These quick-growing onions are relatively trouble-free, but can still suffer from white rot and downy mildew, which affect all members of the onion family. If your crops are affected by this problem, it's best to destroy the harvest and don't grow onions in that part of the garden again.

Harvesting and storage
Salad onions can grow in as little as 10 weeks. As soon as they're pencil thickness, start to harvest, gently pulling the stems. If the soil is firm, loosen with a garden fork.

Salad onions taste best fresh from the garden. It's therefore not worth storing them in the fridge for more than a week. They'll stand well enough in the ground – just pull a few at a time as you need them in the kitchen.

In the kitchen
Salad onions are traditionally used as a garnish, but their milder flavour means they're good in salads too. They are often used in Asian stir-fries, or to replace onions in cooked dishes, particularly when you want a milder flavour.

CALENDAR

LATE WINTER
Prepare your soil by digging over well and removing any perennial weeds.

EARLY SPRING
Start to make your first sowings. Make a shallow trench, about 1–2 cm (½–¾ in) deep and around 10 cm (4 in) wide, and sprinkle seeds along it, aiming for a seed every 2.5 cm (1 in). Cover with soil.

MID-SPRING
You can still sow now, as above.

LATE SPRING
It's worth making another sowing, even if you made one last month, to spread out the season.

EARLY SUMMER
Continue to sow now, as above, or think about sowing into small gaps as they open up in the rest of the vegetable garden.

MIDSUMMER
Start to water if your soil is dry. Your early sowings can start to be harvested.

LATE SUMMER
You can keep sowing, and watering as necessary to keep the plants growing.

EARLY AUTUMN
Keep harvesting your earlier crops through the autumn.

4 Young onions will start to swell at the base after just a few weeks.

5 Start to pull salad onions when they're pencil thickness. Leave others to grow a little more.

VARIETY SELECTOR
- 'Elody': bulbous white salad onions.
- 'Guardsman', 'Ishikura': straight white salad onions.
- 'Deep Purple', 'Rossa Lunga di Firenze': red salad onions.

Celery

An extremely popular salad vegetable in the kitchen, but one that is tricky to grow in the garden.

✪✪✪○○	VALUE FOR MONEY
✪✪✪✪✪	MAINTENANCE
✪✪✪○○	FREEZE/STORE

CROPPING SEASON: EARLY SUMMER–LATE AUTUMN

Celery, like fennel, prefers warm but moist conditions. These can be difficult to sustain in a vegetable patch when crops often dry out in the summer. So, celery is really only worth a go if you've got time to devote to this crop. Given the right conditions, you'll be rewarded with long, distinctively flavoured crunchy stems that are fantastic eaten raw as well as used in soups and stews.

Where to grow Celery seed can be tricky to germinate. Seeds need light to grow, so sow on the surface of a small pot or tray of compost. Cover either with a thin layer of vermiculite, which allows light through, or place some clingfilm or a piece of glass over the top to keep the surface of the compost moist. The

GERMINATING CELERY SEED

1 Fill a small pot with compost and sow a few seeds on the surface.

2 Cover with a thin layer of vermiculite, and mist with a fine spray. Alternatively, after watering, you could cover the pots with clingfilm.

3 Mist regularly with water and keep at a constant temperature of 15°C (59°F). Keep the pots in a propagator to ensure the humidity is kept high, and the temperature constant.

Crunchy celery
New varieties of self-blanching celery mean that they're much easier to grow in the garden – as long as you keep them well watered.

seeds also need a temperature of around 15°C (59°F).

It's worth growing celery in the vegetable garden only if you can devote some time and effort to these plants, making sure they're well watered. They prefer rich, moisture-retentive soil, with a pH of around 7 (see page 219).

Types and varieties
Celery used to need trenching up, where soil was pushed against the stems as they grew to preserve their pale colour and tender stems. Now there are new varieties called 'self-blanching' – meaning that you don't need to keep pushing soil against the stems every couple of weeks. Self-blanching celery produces long-stemmed plants that reach up to 45 cm (18 in) high. They don't like the weather too cold, so are best grown in the summer. You can find celery in a range of colours, not just green: there are varieties with creamy-yellow stems as well as ones with pinkish-red stems.

Pests and diseases Celery fly and carrot root fly can both be pests. The easiest way to prevent damage is to cover your crop with fleece or fine mesh. Slugs can be a problem because the soil is kept constantly wet. Use appropriate controls to keep them at bay.

Harvesting and storage Once the celery looks ready for harvesting, use a garden fork to ease the plant out of the ground and cut off the root. Once cut, it will only remain fresh for a week or so. Plants may bolt or be damaged by frost if left in the ground as the weather turns cool, so it's worth harvesting all plants before the weather turns too cold.

In the kitchen The unusual flavour of celery works well with onion and carrot as a base for all sorts of stews. It also works well in soups. French crunchy celery is popular with children and is great eaten as a crudité.

CALENDAR

MID-SPRING
With a minimum temperature of 15°C (59°F) (use a propagator), sow seed on the surface of a tray of multi-purpose compost. Keep moist and at a constant temperature.

LATE SPRING
Once germinated and grown on, start acclimatising the plants to cooler conditions.

EARLY SUMMER
Plant the seedlings out in the garden around the last frost date when they have several true leaves. Plant in rich, moisture-retentive soil, with around 25 cm (10 in) of space each way. Water the plants well and cover with fine mesh.

MIDSUMMER
Keep watering the plants at least twice a week.

LATE SUMMER
Keep watering. Plants should be ready to start harvesting now.

EARLY AUTUMN
Keep watering and harvesting.

VARIETY SELECTOR
- 'Giant Red': red stems.
- 'Golden Self-Blanching': yellow stems.
- 'Ventura': easier to grow, tasty.

Tasty crop
If you get the watering right, celery can be a productive and rewarding crop to grow.

Asparagus

One of the most expensive vegetables to buy in the supermarket but probably one of the easiest to grow — however, you will have to wait a year or two for a crop.

✪✪✪✪✪ VALUE FOR MONEY
✪✪✪✪✪ MAINTENANCE
✪✪✪✪✪ FREEZE/STORE
CROPPING SEASON: MID-SPRING–LATE SPRING

Asparagus is a perennial vegetable, which means that you need to plant it only once and it keeps coming back year after year. The first two years you should not harvest as the plant settles in and bulks up. However, after this period you'll be able to pick spears of asparagus from mid-spring to early summer. Plants are either male or female. Males produce larger spears; females produce seed and smaller spears. You don't need to grow males and females together to produce a crop.

Minimum temperature range
-34°C (-30°F) to -2°C (29°F).

Succulent stems
Once the plants are established, you'll be able to pick fresh asparagus from the garden for at least six weeks.

Where to grow Unlike many other vegetables that move around the garden each year, you'll have to find a spot to keep your asparagus permanently. Find an open site with well-cultivated ground, which is free from any weeds. Enrich the soil with some homemade compost. You'll have to order plants (known as crowns) in the winter, and these will be

PLANTING NEW CROWNS

1 Dig a trench around 40 cm (16 in) wide.

2 Lay the crowns on a mound in the centre of the trench, spreading the roots on either side. The top of the crown should be around 10 cm (4 in) below the surface of the soil.

3 Aim for a plant every 45 cm (18 in) along the trench, and leave 90 cm (3 ft) between trenches if you're planting a block.

4 Cover with soil and a layer of homemade compost.

VARIETY SELECTOR
• 'Backlim', 'Mondeo' and 'Purple Pacific' are all good choices.

CALENDAR

MID-SPRING
Create your new asparagus bed. Established plants should start producing spears for cutting now.

LATE SPRING
Keep cutting established plants, but stop cutting now if your plants are only two years old.

MIDSUMMER
Stop cutting established plants now. Apply a fertiliser and add a thick layer of homemade compost.

LATE AUTUMN
Cut the dead foliage down to the ground.

delivered in mid-spring. After planting out, keep the plants well watered and the plots weed-free. Don't consider picking any spears in the first year, and in the second, just pick for three to four weeks in late spring, to encourage the plants to develop even further. After the second year, you should be rewarded with well-established plants that produce fern-like foliage through the summer.

Types and varieties Modern hybrids produce only male plants, which means they yield more spears than female plants. You'll need to order crowns (one-year-old plants) in the winter for delivery in the spring.

Pests and diseases Asparagus succumbs to only one main pest, which is the asparagus beetle. This serious pest is easy to identify – the yellow and black beetles cover the spears in early spring. The easiest solution is to try to pick off the beetles as you see them

– otherwise they will damage the spears. Also, after your second-year harvest, harvest all stalks during the harvest period.

Harvesting and storage After the second year, you can start to harvest from mid-spring for around six to seven weeks. Wait until the spears reach around 10 cm (4 in) in height with a tight bud. Using a sharp knife, cut the spear around 2.5–5 cm (1–2 in) below the surface of the soil. You'll need to check the plants at least twice a week as they can grow very quickly. Asparagus doesn't store well, so should be used as you harvest it. Alternatively, it can be frozen – blanch for a couple of minutes before doing so.

In the kitchen Asparagus is best eaten lightly steamed or stir-fried to appreciate its subtle flavour. Tender asparagus is also good raw in salads, grilled or barbecued, or cooked in risottos.

Globe artichoke and Cardoon

Globe artichokes are statuesque plants. They are worth growing if you have plenty of space and enjoy the unique flavour of this perennial vegetable.

Cardoon bud
Artichokes and cardoons may not be the most productive crop for the space they take up, but they do make for interesting looking plants.

✪✪✪✪✪ VALUE FOR MONEY
✪✪✪✪✪ MAINTENANCE
✪✪✪✪✪ FREEZE/STORE
CROPPING SEASON: LATE SPRING–EARLY SUMMER

Globe artichokes are elegant, silver-leafed plants with beautiful thistle-like flowers that can look good in an ornamental border as well as the kitchen garden. They require a lot of space, reaching 1.2 m (3 ft 9 in) high and around 1 m (3 ft 2 in) wide, and since they are perennial, you'll need to devote part of your garden to them for at least two or three years.

You can buy young plants from the garden centre, but they're also fairly straightforward to raise from seed. You won't get a huge crop in your first year, but look after them well and they'll return the favour by producing a good crop of fleshy edible buds year after year.

Minimum temperature range
-18°C (0°F) or above.

Where to grow Artichokes prefer rich, moisture-retentive soil and a fairly sunny spot. They don't like strong winds or cold conditions, so avoid areas that suffer badly from frost.

Types and varieties There are few named varieties of artichoke, and often plants from the same packet vary in vigour and performance. It's a good idea to discard the weaker plants and concentrate your efforts on the stronger performers. There is some choice when it comes to colour. As well as green, there are also artichokes with a purple tinge.

In the garden As they are perennial plants they'll slowly grow larger each year, producing more edible buds. Keep the plot weed-free and mulch in spring with a good dose of homemade compost or equivalent. After four years or so the yield may reduce, and it is probably a good time to either take cuttings from original plants or start again from seed.

Globe artichokes
There are not many varieties to choose from, but it's worth trying both green and purple versions, if you have the space.

CALENDAR

LATE WINTER
Sow seeds in a seed tray, cover with a dusting of compost and germinate in a brightly lit place indoors.

EARLY SPRING
Select the strongest seedlings and plant into larger pots. Grow in the greenhouse or cold frame.

MID-SPRING
Feed plants with a general fertiliser if necessary.

LATE SPRING
Plant out into the garden, leaving around 90 cm (3 ft) between plants. Mulch well.

EARLY SUMMER
Water plants and as buds form, harvest for the kitchen.

LATE AUTUMN
Cut dead stems back to the ground and keep the plot weed-free. Mulch each spring.

Pests and diseases Globe artichokes and cardoons are generally trouble-free.

Harvesting and storage The edible part of the globe artichoke is the immature bud and the stem just below. The whole bud can be eaten when very young and the bud is very tight. However, artichokes are most commonly picked when the bud is larger, just before it starts to open into flower. In the first year you'll get only a single bud. But in further years, side shoots will produce many more, often up to 12 per plant. These are produced over the summer. Cut with around 10 cm (4 in) of stalk.

In the kitchen Young buds can be eaten whole. Larger buds will need to be prepared. This usually means boiling for 20 minutes or so, then cutting out the fleshy bottom of the bud, leaving the bristly developing flower or 'choke'. You can also eat the fleshy base of each scale – a favourite way is dipping in melted butter or French dressing and running it against your teeth to remove the flesh.

Flowering artichoke
Once flowered, it's not worth trying to harvest. Just enjoy the plant for its architectural beauty.

VARIETY SELECTOR
• **'Green Globe'**: this variety produces elegant plants, good enough to plant in the flower border.

• **'Purple Globe'** or **'Romanesco'**: good for cooler regions and makes attractive purple-coloured artichokes.

• **'Violet Globe'**: produces abundant purple artichokes. Good flavour.

Sprouting seeds

Grown on the kitchen windowsill, this is definitely one crop you can succeed with right through the year.

⬢⬢⬢⬢⬡	VALUE FOR MONEY
⬢⬢⬡⬡⬡	MAINTENANCE
⬢⬢⬡⬡⬡	FREEZE/STORE
CROPPING SEASON: ALL YEAR ROUND	

Tasty morsels
Sprouting seeds are quick and easy to grow and are a great way to keep you eating healthily right through the year.

Sprouting seeds have been popular for some years, and are a mainstay in vegetarian and vegan diets. However, even if you're not a vegetarian, these healthy and nutritious sprouts are simple to grow and tasty to eat. They're a good choice for growing in the winter when very little else is available in the garden and can provide you and your family with some fresh salad right through the year.

Seed companies have caught on to their popularity and have been extending the range of the seeds available for sprouting. You'll need to buy seed especially for sprouting – not because the seed is any different to those you grow in your garden, but just that you need lots more. Also, you need to make sure that the seed has not been treated with pesticides.

Where to grow To grow sprouting seeds all you need is a jar; however, there are plenty of specialist sprouting kits that you can buy. The best of these are tiered, allowing you to sprout several different seed types on separate tiers of the sprouter. These are ideal and take up little space in the kitchen. Alternatively, if you're trying sprouting seeds for the first time and want to see whether they're for you, just use an old jam jar, and cover the lid with plastic wrap or a piece of cheesecloth.

Next get hold of the seed. You can buy it from your regular seed supplier, or alternatively, health food shops often stock seed for sprouting.

Each seed will require slightly different growing requirements, so consult the seed packet, but the basics are essentially the same. First, soak your seed for the specified length of time – usually overnight – in fresh water.

Then rinse the seed and transfer into the sprouter or jar. The seed will need to be rinsed through, preferably twice a day. Using a sprouter with holes to allow for rinsing is best and easier than using a jar. Leave on a windowsill, covered and out of direct sunlight. After anything between three and 10 days the seed will have sprouted and be ready for eating.

You can store the sprouted seed in the fridge for a few days, but it will need to be rinsed each day.

Types and varieties There are lots of seeds that are sold for sprouting – some are quicker to sprout than others, while some are tastier. Here's a quick guide to what's around.
Alfalfa Five days to harvest.
Crunchy stalks with a nutty flavour.
Fenugreek Five days to harvest.
Crispy stalks, with a mild curry taste.
Mung bean Three days to harvest.
Large beans that produce chewy, fat sprouts.
Radish Four days to harvest.
A strong radish flavour, with a hot aftertaste.
Sunflower Five days to harvest.
Crunchy sprouts with a slight pea flavour.

In the kitchen Sprouted seeds are great in stir-fries, and the bigger-seeded types, such as mung bean and fenugreek, are perfect for this. The smaller seeds, such as alfalfa and radish, are great in salads and sandwiches.

Sprout variety
There are lots of different sprouting seeds to choose from. All have a different texture and taste so it's worth trying a few before you decide on your favourite.

Microgreens

A cross between sprouting seeds and baby-leaf salads, microgreens make a pretty garnish and add zing.

⊙⊙⊙⊙⊙ VALUE FOR MONEY
⊙⊙⊙⊙⊙ MAINTENANCE
⊙⊙⊙⊙⊙ FREEZE/STORE
CROPPING SEASON: ALL YEAR ROUND

Microgreens are essentially very young leafy plants. Unlike sprouting seeds which get eaten before the leaves have grown and developed (see opposite), microgreens are picked and eaten when the first young leaves start to grow. While mustard and cress are favourites among children, microgreens are becoming fashionable in restaurants too. Adding a sprinkling of young seedlings to salads can really pack a punch. There are all sorts of seeds you can use for growing microgreens – basil, celery, coriander, fennel, radish, sorrel and watercress are all popular, as are those mentioned below. While very little of the plant is actually used, you'll still be able to taste its intense flavour.

Where to grow Microgreens can be grown almost all through the year, but you'll need either a bright windowsill, or ideally a greenhouse or polytunnel. Because you're picking the plants when they're very young you do end up harvesting very little. For this reason, it is quite labour-intensive and requires a fair amount of space to get decent amounts. It's worth growing just a tray or two to begin with, to see whether this crop works for you.

You'll need some large seed trays to grow microgreens, filled with multi-purpose compost. Seeds are sown thickly onto the compost, and kept moist and somewhere light and warm. In a matter of a week or so, the seeds should have germinated. Microgreens are harvested by just snipping off at the base when the seed leaves have opened out.

Types and varieties You'll need to buy seed especially for growing as microgreens because you'll need a lot more seed than if you were growing full-size plants. Seed suppliers are tapping into this new area of gardening and are quickly increasing their ranges.

Miniature salads
Microgreens are essentially baby leaves that are harvested early on in their lives.

Broccoli Six days to harvest. Crunchy stalks with a mild, but slightly spicy broccoli flavour.
Chervil Ten days to harvest. Usually grown as a herb, these microgreens have a slight aniseed flavour.
Red mustard Six days to harvest. A popular choice with schools, but worth growing at home too for their spicy crunchy stems.

Harvesting and storage Microgreens won't store, so you'll need to time your growing to perfection. Once harvested, use immediately.

In the kitchen Add a sprinkling onto meals at dinner parties to give that restaurant-style presentation, or add a handful to salads.

Chervil
Use chervil as a microgreen to add a hint of aniseed to your dishes.

Red mustard
Attractive mottled red leaves will bring a dash of colour to a salad bowl.

Edible flowers

For gardeners who want to show off
their skills, adding a few edible flowers
to a dish can really brighten up a meal.

⬢⬢⬢⬡⬡	VALUE FOR MONEY
⬢⬢⬢⬢⬡	MAINTENANCE
⬢⬢⬢⬢⬡	FREEZE/STORE
CROPPING SEASON: ALL YEAR ROUND	

There are hundreds of plants that produce
edible flowers, but some are more tasty than
others. Most are used fresh, added to salads
or drinks. Some are used in hot food to
provide colour, while others are used in
preserves. Many edible flowers also make
attractive garden plants. It's certainly worth
growing a few in your kitchen garden or patio
to brighten up the area, while providing a bit of
colour to your food. Saffron and elderflower
are common flowers used in supermarket
products, but to really show off, why not try
growing violets, nasturtiums or borage?

Where to grow Edible flowers come
in all shapes, sizes and colours. You'll need to
think about the final size of your plant and
decide where it can fit in before you grow it.
Many people grow their edible flowers at the
entrance to their vegetable plot, along a
pathway or in between herbs. This makes an
attractive and colourful entrance to your

Sweet violets
Edible flowers, such as sweet violets, can look
stunning in the garden as well as being a useful
addition in the kitchen.

garden, while also ensuring that you can eat
everything that you grow. Because the flowers
vary widely in their cultivation it's not possible
to list every site, situation and growing method
for each one. Try selecting a few, follow the
seed packet instructions, and see how you get
on. Don't expect hundreds of flowers, but
appreciate the few you do get, and enjoy their
colour in the garden and flavour in the kitchen.

Harvesting and storage Pick flowers
early in the day. Handle them gently as they can
quickly bruise. If flowers have insects nestling
inside, gently tap to remove or just leave to
one side until they leave. It's best not to wash
the flowers if you can help it, but you can dip
the flowers in ice-cold water to refresh them

just before serving in a salad. Some flowers,
such as courgette and nasturtiums, can be used
whole, while others, such as pot marigolds and
daisies, will need their petals tearing off.

In the kitchen Sprinkle petals of
daisy-like flowers over salads just before
serving, or add larger flowers, such as
nasturtiums, in with baby leaves. Deep-fry
lightly battered courgette flowers, and try
violet and sweet bergamot in tea. Stronger
flavours of lavender and sweet William are
reserved for using in small amounts in baking.
Use basil and oregano flowers just as you
would their leaves. Borage, with its bright blue
flowers, looks great added to summer drinks.

Daylily
In some Asian cuisines, all parts of the daylily
are eaten: flowers, buds and leaf shoots.

VARIETY SELECTOR

The list of edible flowers is lengthy. Some of them you may have growing in your garden already, and you can pick a few flowers as you need them, leaving the rest to enjoy in the garden. Others you'll need to grow specially, particularly those raised from seed.

PERENNIALS

You should be able to buy these from garden centres as plants.

Pinks *(Dianthus)*
The flower of this popular garden plant, which you may have growing in your garden already, can have a heady scent of cloves with a sweet flavour. Add petals to ice cream and fruit salads.

Chives *(Allium schoenoprasum)*
This common garden plant produces pretty pink flower heads. Sprinkle these onto salads or use as a garnish in soups and stews.

Rose *(Rosa)*
Rose petals can be added to salads. Some have an unpalatable taste so try before you harvest.

Lavender *(Lavandula)*
These strongly flavoured flowers can be added in small quantities to cakes. You can even add some to ice cream.

Daylily *(Hemerocallis)*
Flavours of this common garden herbaceous perennial vary. It is thought that the lighter the colour of flower, the sweeter the flavour. Try before you eat and add to salads.

Sweet violet *(Viola odorata)*
These can provide colour in salads, but their taste is nothing special, with just a hint of perfume. Violets can be dried and used in tea.

Daisy *(Bellis perennis)*
A common plant found in the lawn or growing as a weed. The flowers are perfectly edible. There are cultivated forms too, with larger, sometimes more colourful, flowers. All are edible – just pick off the petals and add to salads.

Daisy
As well as looking great in the garden, with their tangy flavour, daisies make an interesting and unusual addition to salads.

Borage
Borage is a pretty plant and a useful nectar-rich species to encourage bees into your garden.

Nasturtium
Nasturtiums are easy to grow from seed and, given a sunny, dry spot, will grow and flower well all summer long.

FLOWERS TO GROW FROM SEED

These flowers won't last more than a year, but are easy to raise from seed and can be great for filling space in your garden or patio.

Pot marigold *(Calendula officinalis)*
These easy-to-grow annuals can be sown direct to produce their bright orange flowers throughout the summer. They have a faint peppery taste and are a good choice for adding colour to cakes and salads.

Sweet rocket *(Hesperis matronalis)*
This pretty plant produces spires of pale purple flowers. They have a slight perfumed flavour. Add them to salads.

Nasturtium
Probably the most well-used edible flower because the plant flowers so prolifically. This plant is easy to grow from seed each year, and there is a wide selection of colours and varieties to choose from. The flowers are often used in salads.

Borage *(Borago officinalis)*
This large plant is easy to grow and will reach up to 1 m (3 ft 2 in) in height. It produces lots of pretty blue flowers during the summer. The flowers are sweet and can be added to puddings and ice creams, and also look great added to a summer punch.

Courgette
If you've got too many courgettes, pick the flowers before they set fruit. These buttery yellow flowers are delicious battered then deep-fried, or alternatively they can be eaten in salads.

Basil
If your basil plants start flowering, don't fear, just pick the flowers and add them to your Mediterranean dishes instead.

HERBS

If you're passionate about cooking as well as gardening, herbs will have a real presence in your garden. Some perennial herbs, such as bay and rosemary, are easy to grow and will add structure and style to your garden. Others, such as basil, parsley and coriander, are worth growing in larger quantities, allowing you to grab handfuls for the cooking pot throughout the season.

Bay

Bay leaves bring flavour and depth to sauces and stews.

○○○○○ VALUE FOR MONEY
○○○○○ MAINTENANCE
○○○○○ FREEZE/STORE
CROPPING SEASON: ALL YEAR ROUND

Bay trees are often grown for their elegant appearance and are a good choice for any garden – not one used just for growing food. They can be grown as standard trees and survive well in containers, and for that reason are often found on patios or terraces all over the world. However, it's their aromatic leaves that are also used in cooking that really make this plant worth keeping on the patio. Step outside at any time of year and your plant will yield fragrant leaves that can be used in Italian sauces, soups and even desserts.

Minimum temperature range

-18°C (0°F) or above.

Where to grow
Bay trees are often grown in the ground, and while they can be damaged by extreme cold or wet conditions, they'll come through most winters unscathed.

If you are planting in the garden, select a spot that gets some sun and is sheltered from strong winds and out of any frost pockets.

You'll most often see bay grown in a container. Bay trees trained into tall standards with a ball-shaped head have become popular in garden centres. They survive well in containers and require little attention – except for regular watering.

Types and varieties
You'll mostly just see the species *Laurus nobilis* with its bright, shiny green leaves.

Pests and diseases
Bay can suffer from scale insects. They attach themselves to the leaves and bark and encourage the growth of sooty mould. The best way to get rid of these insects is by scrubbing the leaves and stems with soapy water. Then rinse.

Harvesting and storage
Pick leaves as required. When pruning in midsummer,

Year-round seasoning
Bay trees look stunning in the garden and their leaves, either fresh or dried, can be used in the kitchen all year round.

leave prunings to dry and store dried leaves for use later in the year.

In the kitchen
Tear leaves in two to release the flavour and add to soups, sauces and stews.

CALENDAR

MID-SPRING
If you have a container-grown tree, add a sprinkling of slow-release fertiliser in the spring. If necessary, re-pot into a larger container – this is a good time to do this.

LATE SPRING
Keep watering the plant through the rest of spring and summer.

EARLY SUMMER
The plant should have put on some new growth. Now is the time to clip the plant back into its original shape – or consider trying some topiary shapes.

MIDSUMMER
Keep watering and pick leaves as required for the kitchen.

LATE AUTUMN
Move the container-grown plant to a more sheltered spot out of any direct wind.

BAY PRUNING AND MAINTENANCE

1 By early summer you can cut back your bay tree. If it is already pruned into a ball or other shape, keep stepping back to take a look as you work slowly around the shrub.

2 Scale insects often attack bay trees – use a bowl of warm soapy water and a sponge scourer to gently remove the scale and mould by rubbing the leaves and stems.

Basil

While not the easiest of herbs to grow, basil is probably one of the most rewarding and the most useful in the kitchen.

●●●●○ VALUE FOR MONEY
●●●●○ MAINTENANCE
●●●●○ FREEZE/STORE
CROPPING SEASON: EARLY SUMMER–MID-AUTUMN

Genovese basil
The leaves of Genovese basil are perfect for growing in bulk – collect all in one go to make pesto, then freeze for later use.

Basil is used in lots of cuisines, but most famous is its use in Italian and Asian cooking. Each style of cooking uses one of the two distinct types of basil. Sweet basil is used in Italian cooking to make pesto and add flavour to pasta sauces. 'Thai' basils, with their stronger, spicier flavour and thicker, hairy leaves, are used in Asian cooking.

Whichever types you go for, their growing requirements remain the same – they prefer hot conditions, and if not continually picked, will quickly run to seed.

Where to grow Basil can be sown direct and grown in the garden anytime in the summer months. Sometimes it's grown in pots on the patio or even on the windowsill. Watered and fed often enough, a single pot will give a continual supply. If you want to make pesto, it's worth growing a much larger amount in the garden, then freezing the fresh leaves for making pesto at a later date.

Supermarkets often sell basil, and other herbs, growing in a small pot. You can use these as young plants and encourage them to carry on growing through the season.

Pests and diseases Basil is generally trouble-free.

Harvesting and storage Basil can be frozen then used in cooking or for making pesto. Otherwise just add leaves straight from the garden to the pan.

In the kitchen Used widely in both Asian and Italian cooking, the chopped leaves are often added to dishes in small amounts just before they're served to add flavour.

MAKING THE MOST OF SHOP-GROWN BASIL

1 Buy a pot of supermarket basil. Remove the plastic and soak the pot in water.

2 Plant in a larger pot, with multi-purpose compost and a sprinkling of slow-release fertiliser.

3 Keep the basil on a sunny windowsill and pick as required.

CALENDAR

MID-SPRING

Start sowing now in small pots indoors. Sprinkle a few seeds on the surface of a small pot filled with compost and cover with a dusting of compost. Keep moist. The seed may take a couple of weeks to germinate.

LATE SPRING

Once the seedlings have grown to around 15 cm (6 in), pinch out the tip to encourage them to bush out. Pot them into larger containers, filled with multi-purpose compost and a slow-release fertiliser.

EARLY SUMMER

Sow seeds in larger pots on the patio or direct in the soil. Move young plants sown in the spring outside.

MIDSUMMER

Start to harvest the leaves and pick off any developing flowers.

LATE SUMMER

You can keep sowing seed until late summer for a harvest into autumn.

EARLY AUTUMN

If you have space, move your containers to the greenhouse to keep the plants growing.

VARIETY SELECTOR

Italian or sweet basil
- 'Greek': a small-leafed version.

Genovese basil
- 'Sweet Green', 'Neapolitan'.
- 'Red': a red leafed basil.

Thai basil
- 'Siam Queen': pretty purple flowers.
- 'Lime Mrs Burns': lime scented.
- 'Holy': purple stems, pink flowers.

BASIL VARIETIES

'Greek' basil
Used in Greek cuisine, this is a compact form with tiny leaves less than 1 cm (½ in) long.

'Siam Queen' basil
An attractive form of Thai basil, 'Siam Queen' has an excellent aroma and flavour.

Holy basil
Native to India, holy basil is used in Ayurvedic medicine as well as the kitchen. It is a great container plant.

'Lime Mrs Burns' basil
Lime-scented leaves that can be used in cooking, chopped in salads or used to make fresh herbal tea.

Chervil

With its parsley-like flavour, chervil is a favourite winter herb.

✪✪✪✪✪ VALUE FOR MONEY
✪✪✪✪✪ MAINTENANCE
✪✪✪✪✪ FREEZE/STORE
CROPPING SEASON: MID-SPRING–LATE AUTUMN

This hardy annual is often used in French cooking. It has a parsley flavour, but with a hint of aniseed. The leaves are rich in vitamin C and iron and can be used to make a refreshing tea. In the garden, it's an easy herb to grow, but should be sown regularly for a constant supply of fresh leaves.

Types and varieties Stick to the species *Anthriscus cerefolium*.

Where to grow Plants reach around 60 cm (2 ft) in height and around 30 cm (12 in) across. It can be a scruffy-looking plant, so it's best kept in the vegetable garden. It grows quickly and can soon set seed, after which it will die. Therefore, sowing seed every two to four weeks will provide you with a regular supply. Chervil grows best in semi-shade as full sun will encourage it to bloom and die. You could try growing it in between other taller and longer-growing crops such as sweetcorn or some brassicas.

Pests and diseases Generally, trouble-free, but watch out for greenfly.

Harvesting and storage To keep its fresh, aniseed flavour, chervil is best picked and used immediately. If you have too many leaves all ready for picking, they can be chopped and frozen immediately.

In the kitchen Chervil leaves can be chopped and used in soups and sauces, and go particularly well with vegetable, fish and chicken dishes. Adding the herb towards the end of cooking will help to retain its flavour.

Attractive foliage
The delicate leaves of chervil can look attractive in their own right.

CALENDAR

EARLY SPRING
Start to sow chervil direct in the ground. Draw out a drill about 1.5 cm (⅝ in) deep and add a few seeds every 20 cm (8 in). Cover with soil.

MID-SPRING
Thin out seedlings if more than one comes up at each station. Sow another row of seeds now.

LATE SPRING
Start to pick leaves as they become ready.

SUMMER
Continue to sow chervil for another harvest in eight weeks or so.

EARLY AUTUMN
Make a final sowing now for herbs through the winter. Although chervil is hardy, you may want to protect it with a cloche or fleece to keep the leaves in good shape.

GROWING CHERVIL IN CONTAINERS

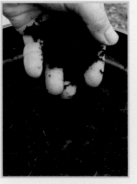

1 Fill a pot with multi-purpose compost.

2 Sow a seed every 5 cm (2 in) and cover with a dusting of compost. Water.

3 Cut chervil 5 cm (2 in) from the base – young leaves should start to grow again from the base.

Chives

A relative of the onion, this perennial herb is both pretty and productive in kitchen gardens.

✿✿✿✿✿	VALUE FOR MONEY
✿✿✿✿✿	MAINTENANCE
✿✿✿✿✿	FREEZE/STORE
CROPPING SEASON: EARLY SPRING–LATE AUTUMN	

The pinky flowers of chives make this one of the most attractive herbs to grow. It can be grown in a pot on the patio or even in an ornamental border. It is often used as edging too, down the side of a path or along the front of fruit trees, for example. The leaves can be picked all through the summer and well into autumn.

Minimum temperature range
-40°C (-40°F) to -2°C (29°F).

Where to grow Chives can be grown from seed, or bought as young plants from the garden centre. They're pretty simple to grow from seed, and once established will last for many years. In fact, after a couple of years' growth, an established clump can be dug up, split and re-planted around the garden. It's a worthwhile herb to grow as it's so productive.

Chives can be grown in a pot, and as long as they are kept watered, will keep producing new stems for picking all through the summer. Alternatively, just grow them around your garden either in rows or in small clumps and enjoy the pretty flowers that will be covered with bees in early summer.

Types and varieties There's little to choose from, but as well as the common pink flowering type, you may also come across white-flowering chives. All grow to around 25 cm (10 in) in height.

Pests and diseases In theory, chives will suffer from the same diseases as onions, garlic and leeks (see page 46), but in reality they are usually trouble-free.

Harvesting and storage Snip off leaves at the base as required.

Tasty seasoning
Chives can be used as a border plant. What's more, they're extremely productive.

In the kitchen Chives can be used to add a delicate onion flavour to almost anything, but are often chopped finely and added as a garnish on soups and stews.

CALENDAR

MID-SPRING
Seed can be sown now either direct in the ground or in pots. Sow around 1–2 cm (½–¾ in) deep.

LATE SPRING
Young leaves will be starting to emerge. If you sowed into pots, make sure plants are kept well watered.

EARLY SUMMER
Start cutting leaves as you need them in the kitchen. Cutting off at the base of the plant will encourage more stems to be produced.

LATE AUTUMN
Tidy up plants now by removing any dead or dying foliage.

DIVIDING CHIVE PLANTS

1 Dig up a whole plant using a spade.

2 Gently pull it apart with your fingers into smaller clumps with roots.

3 Re-plant these small clumps around the garden.

Coriander

Another favourite in the kitchen, coriander is a must for anyone who likes cooking Indian or Middle Eastern dishes.

○○○○○ VALUE FOR MONEY
○○○○○ MAINTENANCE
○○○○○ FREEZE/STORE
CROPPING SEASON: EARLY SUMMER–MID-AUTUMN

Productive herb
Regular sowing of coriander through the spring and summer will provide a plentiful supply.

Coriander is a well-loved herb, but its reputation is one of a tricky-to-grow plant. However, sow at the right times and there's a good chance you can harvest year-round.

Where to grow Coriander grows well in a pot, as well as in the ground. A large container is ideal on the patio where you can keep an eye on it and you can pick leaves as often as you like. Traditionally, coriander was sown in the spring; however, it does just as well when sown in the autumn. Considering it originates in southern Europe and Asia, it's actually a pretty hardy plant and will survive most winters outside unscathed. For best results and a lengthy supply of leaves, it's probably best to make a couple of sowings: one in spring and one in autumn. When the finer, feathery leaves start to grow you know that the plant is about to set seed. There's not much you can do at this stage. Either leave the plant to flower, and collect what seeds are produced, or start again.

Types and varieties Varieties are now being bred that are less likely to bolt and produce more leaves.

Pests and diseases Generally trouble-free, but slugs and snails can be a problem.

Harvesting and storage Wait until the plants are around 15 cm (6 in) high, then snip the leaves with a pair of scissors around 5 cm (2 in) from the base of the plant as required. Leaves should . Use immediately in the kitchen. Seeds can be collected and dried in a paper bag. Store in the kitchen in an airtight container. They can be crushed with a pestle and mortar when needed.

In the kitchen Fresh coriander leaves are often added to Indian dishes just before serving. They're also added to South American, Caribbean and Middle Eastern dishes. Small amounts can be added to salads.

CALENDAR

LATE SPRING–EARLY SUMMER
Fill a large container with multi-purpose compost and add some slow-release fertiliser. Sprinkle a seed every 5 cm (2 in) on the surface. Cover with a dusting of compost and water. Alternatively, sow a row of seed 0.5 cm (¼ in) deep, and thin plants to around 10 cm (4 in).

MIDSUMMER
Keep watering, and don't let the plant dry out, both in the ground and in a pot. Pick leaves as required. Picking leaves can help to prevent the plant from running to seed.

LATE SUMMER–EARLY AUTUMN
Make another sowing. Using a large container will be more successful for growing over winter. Plant in the same way as above. Your spring sowing is probably finished; wait to collect the edible seeds.

AUTUMN–WINTER
You can keep your summer/autumn-sown container outside, but place it in a sheltered spot.

SPRING
Start to harvest the leaves from the pot you sowed last year.

GROWING CORIANDER IN CONTAINERS IN WINTER

1 Choose a small pot, and in early autumn, fill with multi-purpose compost.

2 Add a sprinkling of seed, water, and cover with clingfilm.

3 Remove the clingfilm when the seeds have germinated and place on the windowsill.

VARIETY SELECTOR
- 'Cilantro': good for both leaves and seed.
- 'Confetti': produces ferny leaves with a sweet flavour.
- 'Leisure': a good choice for the production of leaves.

Dill and Fennel

These pretty herbs produce a fine feathery foliage with large saucer-shaped flowers.

✪✪✪✪✪	VALUE FOR MONEY
✪✪✪✪✪	MAINTENANCE
✪✪✪✪✪	FREEZE/STORE

CROPPING SEASON: LATE SPRING–MID-AUTUMN

The leaves of dill and fennel are often used in fish and potato dishes. Dill has a subtle aniseed flavour, whereas the flavour of fennel is slightly stronger. While dill is an annual, its larger cousin, fennel, will survive in the garden for some years. If you're going to grow just one of these, go for fennel. The plant is much more attractive – especially the bronze-leafed version – and it's much easier to grow.

Minimum temperature range
Fennel: -29°C (-20°F) to 5°C (40°F).

Where to grow Dill is a fairly small herb and it's worth growing a few plants from seed for your herb garden. Fennel is a much larger plant, often reaching 2 m (6 ft 5 in) high. It's an attractive plant too, and often found in ornamental borders as well as in kitchen gardens. Because it grows so big, it's not worth trying it in a pot.

If plants dry out, they can quickly run to seed, so plant in an area that won't go short of water.

Types and varieties There are a few varieties of dill. 'Hera' is often grown for its leaves, whereas 'Mammoth' is usually grown for seed, which can be collected and dried.

There are just two choices of fennel – either green- or bronze-leafed. Both reach up to 2 m (6 ft 5 in) in height.

Pests and diseases Dill and fennel are generally trouble-free.

Alluring blooms
The ethereal flowers and foliage of dill and fennel are a common sight in kitchen gardens.

Harvesting and storage Cut leaves as required. For dill seed production, use a variety such as 'Mammoth' with its huge seed heads. These can be cut and dried in a large paper bag to collect the seed.

In the kitchen Leaves can be added to yogurt and cucumber, and eaten with fish, often smoked salmon. Seeds can be added to soups, pickles and potato salads.

CALENDAR

EARLY SPRING
You can start to make sowings now, but germination may be sporadic. Create a 1.5-cm (⅝-in) drill and sprinkle seeds thinly along it. Aim for a seed every 2.5 cm (1 in). Cover the drill with soil.

MID-SPRING
Sow the seed of dill direct in the ground in short rows, about 2 cm (¾ in) deep.

LATE SPRING
Thin out seedlings so there's a plant every 15 cm (6 in) or so. If you're growing fennel, buy just one or two plants from the garden centre and plant out immediately into rich, fertile and moisture-retentive soil.

EARLY SUMMER
Keep plants well watered and start to cut as a herb.

MID–LATE SUMMER
Cut off flower heads and save the seed if required either for cooking or regrowing next year.

Feathery fronds
The feathery, green fronds of dill can be used in a wide variety of dishes in the kitchen.

Lovage

This giant of a herb gives a hearty, meaty flavour to soups and stews.

- ✪✪✪✪✪ VALUE FOR MONEY
- ✪✪✪✪✪ MAINTENANCE
- ✪✪✪✪✪ FREEZE/STORE
- CROPPING SEASON: MID-SPRING–LATE AUTUMN

As a perennial, lovage will last for a long time in the garden but as it can reach up to 1.5 m (5 ft) in height when in flower, it needs plenty of space. You'll need only a single plant as each one grows into a large clump. It's an attractive plant, with shiny, green leaves and long, tall stems. It was originally used by the ancient Greeks who believed chewing the stems would aid digestion. The leaves are also believed to have an antiseptic effect on the skin.

Minimum temperature range
-40°C (-40°F) or above.

Where to grow Lovage prefers deep, rich, moist soil. It is happy in semi-shade or full sun, but does need a plentiful supply of water to keep it going in the summer. It's a good idea to add plenty of well-rotted organic matter to the site before planting, and more each spring around the plant. As it's a perennial, it will look after itself, coming back each year. To stop the plant getting too big, consider dividing it every few years. Spring is a good time to do this.

Types and varieties *Levisticum officinale* is the species that is normally grown; it produces tiny yellow flower clusters in summer.

Pests and diseases Relatively trouble-free, but leaf-miners can often spoil the leaves. If this becomes a big problem, cut down and put the leaves in a bin bag. Water well and the plant should return. Slugs and snails can also be troublesome.

Harvesting and storage Leaves are worth picking fresh, which are available all through the growing season. If you do want to store some leaves, they can be frozen whole, then crushed before use.

Giant of the herb garden
Reminiscent of celery in looks and taste, this sturdy but attractive herb is easy to grow.

CALENDAR

LATE SPRING
Sow in the greenhouse or on the windowsill. Add one or two seeds to each small pot and cover with a dusting of compost.

EARLY SUMMER
Once the seedling is big enough, plant it out into the garden. Mulch the plant with compost and water well.

MIDSUMMER
If you didn't get around to sowing seed, just buy a single plant from the garden centre – much easier when you need only one plant.

LATE SUMMER
All through the summer and autumn, leaves can be picked. If you cut the leaves right back, make sure you water the plant to encourage new growth.

In the kitchen Lovage has a particular flavour, somewhat similar to celery. The leaves can be used to add robust flavours to soups and stews, and it's also a good choice to add when making stock. The root and stem can also be used in cooking as a vegetable, but it can be somewhat bitter.

DIVIDING AN ESTABLISHED LOVAGE CLUMP

1 Use a garden fork to dig out a large clump of lovage.

2 Using a spade, cut the clump into smaller, more manageable pieces and replant.

Oregano

Also known as marjoram, this herb picked fresh is so much tastier than the stuff you get dried in the supermarket.

⊙⊙⊙⊙⊙ VALUE FOR MONEY
⊙⊙⊙⊙⊙ MAINTENANCE
⊙⊙⊙⊙⊙ FREEZE/STORE
CROPPING SEASON: ALL YEAR ROUND

Used in Mediterranean dishes, oregano adds flavour to sauces. It's fantastic used fresh, but it can also be dried and stored for winter use.

Minimum temperature range
-29°C (-20°F) to 5°C (40°F).

Where to grow This plant is very well behaved in the garden. It reaches around 30 cm (12 in) high, and in midsummer produces pretty pink flowers. These can be cut down at the end of summer and the plant will regrow the following year. It's also a great-smelling plant, and for that reason is a good one to plant around the edges of permanent beds and borders, particularly in sunny, dry spots where the aromatic foliage can be enjoyed as you brush past.

Types and varieties The wild type of oregano, *Origanum vulgare*, is the one often found in garden centres, but there are other versions too. There's a yellow form, *Aureum*, which produces a brightly coloured carpet of leaves in the spring. Whereas most species will keep coming back year after year, there are some varieties which aren't hardy, such as 'Sweet Marjoram', and these will have to be grown from seed each year.

Pests and diseases Trouble-free.

Harvesting and storage Leaves can be picked throughout the growing season. For drying, pick in the summer and dry by hanging upside down in the greenhouse. Dried leaves can be stored in airtight containers.

In the kitchen Use fresh leaves in marinades for meat and fish or add to pasta sauces. Dried leaves can be used through the winter in tomato sauces or sprinkled onto pizzas.

Mediterranean gem
This aromatic herb is a must for any lover of Mediterranean food.

CALENDAR

MID-SPRING
Buy one or two young plants from the garden centre.

LATE SPRING
Plant out in the garden. Choose a dry, sunny spot. Oregano prefers dry, sandy soils so if necessary, add some coarse sand to heavy soil.

EARLY SUMMER–EARLY AUTUMN
Keep picking fresh leaves.

EARLY AUTUMN
Cut back flowering stems to the base.

HOW TO DRY OREGANO

1 Cut long stems of oregano in early to midsummer.

2 Tie stems together at the base and hang upside down to dry in a greenhouse or bright kitchen.

Mint

STAR PLANT
CHEF'S FAVE, FRESH OR DRIED

This refreshing herb is simple to grow – just make sure it doesn't take over your garden!

✪✪✪✪✪	VALUE FOR MONEY
✪✪✪✪✪	MAINTENANCE
✪✪✪✪✪	FREEZE/STORE

CROPPING SEASON: EARLY SPRING–MID-AUTUMN

Mint is a shade-loving, moisture-requiring plant. It grows in rich, moist soil and, with the aid of its roots, can be rampant in the garden.

In the kitchen and elsewhere, mint is widely used. Food, cosmetics and aromatherapy all make use of this herb. It's used in medicines too, to aid digestion, and as an antiseptic and a decongestant.

MINT VARIETIES

Black peppermint
Dark green-purple leaves and stems, with blue flowers in summer. This variety is also great for the pot.

Ginger mint
A pretty, spicy-scented, variegated-leaved variety. This variety has pink flowers through summer.

Versatile herb
Fresh mint can be used both in cooking and in tea to provide a refreshing drink.

There are hundreds of varieties of mint. All differ slightly in their growth habit but markedly in their scent and taste. From peppermint, with its strong, minty flavour, to lemon mint, spicy Moroccan mint, pineapple mint and even chocolate mint – all give an extra dimension to the minty flavour.

Minimum temperature range
-34°C (-30°F) to -2°C (29°F).

Where to grow
All mints are easy to grow in the garden, but need to be restrained. If left on their own, they'll quickly spread through the soil, taking over large swaths of garden.

Often mint is planted into a sunken large pot or container, with the lip of the container 1 cm (½ in) or so above the soil level. This helps to keep the mint in check. Alternatively, just grow in a raised pot.

If you are going to plant mint directly into the soil, then at least every couple of years you'll need to dig it out and replant it where it came from!

Types and varieties
Mint is a perennial, and if cut down at the end of autumn, it will come back again in the spring with fresh leaves. There are around 30 species of mint, and many, many named varieties, often with unusual tastes. It's a good idea to have a variety growing in your garden with a good, plain minty flavour, which is great for making tea and using in food. It's also a nice idea to select a couple of more unusual-smelling and -tasting varieties (see below). It's easiest to buy mint as plants from garden centres or specialist herb suppliers – this way you'll be sure of getting the variety you want.

Pests and diseases
Trouble-free but can suffer from rust. Just cut down any affected foliage. Water well and feed with a fertiliser to encourage new shoots.

Harvesting and storage
Cut fresh stems of mint when required. Mint can be dried, or chopped finely then frozen for use throughout winter when there is little available in the garden.

In the kitchen
Drop whole stems into boiling water for refreshing mint tea. Use to make traditional mint sauce to go with lamb, or try in Greek, Moroccan and Middle Eastern dishes.

Chocolate mint
Incredible chocolate flavours are released when this variety is crushed. Also a stunning plant in the garden.

Lemon mint
A useful aromatic plant. When crushed the leaves release a wonderful lemon scent.

Peppermint
Another good culinary choice, the fresh taste of peppermint is also wonderful used fresh in tea.

Spearmint
Has the strongest minty flavour. Spearmint extract is used in all sorts of products from toothpaste to drinks.

CALENDAR

EARLY SPRING
Order young plants from a specialist nursery, or buy plants from a garden centre.

MID-SPRING
Plant out in the garden, giving each plant plenty of room– at least 30 cm (12 in) square. Alternatively, plant in a large container and sink into the ground. Use multi-purpose compost with a slow-release fertiliser added.

LATE SPRING ONWARDS
However you've planted your mint, it prefers rich soil and plenty of moisture. If the weather turns dry, give your plant a good watering. Start to pick stems as they grow. Keep watering and feeding to encourage new growth.

AUTUMN
If your plant is overcrowded, consider digging up, splitting and replanting smaller, thriving sections.

Parsley

This well-used herb is a must
for any gardener and cook.

○○○○○ VALUE FOR MONEY
○○○○○ MAINTENANCE
○○○○○ FREEZE/STORE
CROPPING SEASON: ALL YEAR ROUND

Parsley is probably the most well-used herb
in the kitchen – certainly in quantity. It can be
used in abundance in all sorts of food, adding
flavour and a certain freshness. Parsley is also
very easy to grow. It's available in garden
centres as young plants, but as you'll probably
need a few plants to keep you going for most
of the year, it's worth growing this herb from
seed. It doesn't grow well in the winter, but it
will produce leaves throughout the spring,
summer and autumn months. If you do want
parsley in the winter too, then either growing
in the greenhouse, or growing under cloches
or fleeces is the way to go.

Minimum temperature range
-40°C (-40°F) to -2°C (29°F).

Where to grow If you're short of space,
parsley will grow happily in a container. It also
looks extremely attractive too, and many
people grow parsley for its ornamental value
– its fresh, green leaves can look attractive in
containers mixed with flowers or on the edge
of a path or border. But if your aim is to
produce a really good supply of leaves for the
kitchen, it's best to devote a bit of the herb or
vegetable plot to this plant.

Parsley will happily grow in full sun or
partial shade. It prefers a good, rich soil
and, given the right conditions, can produce
large plants. You can keep the plants small,
however, by picking leaves regularly through
the season. While some advocate chopping the
plant right down in one go, parsley will keep
growing if you just pick one or two stems
at a time.

Types and varieties Parsley can be
split into two main groups, based on the leaf
shape. Curly-leafed varieties were once the

Perfect with fish
Parsley is easy to grow from seed, and it is
worth making regular sowings to provide
for your kitchen all through the year.

most commonly grown and are thought to stand up well to cold, unfavourable weather. Nowadays though, the flat-leafed parsleys are becoming more popular. Their taste is thought to be a bit stronger, but their texture is less coarse. Flat-leafed parsley is a common ingredient in many Mediterranean dishes, but it is in fact just as hardy as the curly types.

Within these two groups there are a few varieties – selected for their vigour and resistance to bolting (see Variety selector).

Pests and diseases Parsley is trouble-free.

Harvesting and storage Cut down whole plants about 2 cm (¾ in) from their base and the plants should regrow.

Alternatively, just pick leaves when required. Parsley is biennial so once flower shoots start to form, either leave to enjoy the flowers or dig up and start again.

If you have lots of parsley it can be picked, chopped and frozen in a resealable plastic bag.

In the kitchen Use whole leaves in salads or as a garnish. Chop leaves finely and add to sauces, salads, soups and stews.

PARSLEY VARIETIES

Curly-leaved parsley
Tends to have slightly tougher leaves, and is often used in a kitchen garden as an ornamental edging plant.

Flat-leaved parsley
Flat-leaved varieties tend to have softer leaves and can be just as productive as the curly types.

CALENDAR

MID-SPRING
Sow seeds in small pots or modular trays. Sow just one or two seeds per pot and cover with a dusting of compost.

LATE SPRING
Seeds can be slow to germinate, but once grown, plant out in the garden about 15 cm (6 in) apart. Alternatively, plant individually in mixed containers.

EARLY SUMMER
Start harvesting leaves.

MIDSUMMER
It's worth making another sowing now, either in pots or direct in the ground, for leaves throughout autumn and into spring next year.

LATE SUMMER
Plant out young plants sown last month. Keep all plants, particularly young seedlings, well watered. Keep picking leaves.

AUTUMN
Pick leaves throughout the season.

EARLY WINTER
Cover plants with cloches or fleece to keep leaves looking good for picking over winter. Don't pick too much during this time to allow the plant to survive into spring.

VARIETY SELECTOR
Curly-leafed parsley
• 'Champion Moss Curled', 'Rosette'.
Flat-leafed parsley
• 'Plain Leaved 2'.

Rosemary

This useful culinary herb makes an elegant, attractive and aromatic plant to grow in any garden.

✪✪✪✪✪ VALUE FOR MONEY
✪✪✪✪✪ MAINTENANCE
✪✪✪○○ FREEZE/STORE
CROPPING SEASON: ALL YEAR ROUND

Pretty flowers
Rosemary is a beautiful plant in its own right, and worthy of a spot or pot in every garden.

The scent of rosemary is enough to make you think of Mediterranean holidays. This shrubby plant is now cultivated almost everywhere and is a useful herb both in the garden and in the kitchen. It's an evergreen, so looks good almost all year with its pine needle-like leaves and pretty blue, white or pink flowers. Despite heralding from the Med, it's pretty tough too. It will survive in most gardens, but can be damaged by long periods of cold weather. It has a habit of flowering not just in the summer, but in winter too, making it a useful plant for pollinating insects such as bees towards the end of autumn.

Minimum temperature range
-18°C (0°F) or above.

Where to grow
Because it's a shrubby perennial, once planted it will happily stay there for many years. Choose a sunny, sheltered spot with well-drained soil. You could plant a single specimen, or grow them into a hedge, by planting several plants together, 60 cm (2 ft) apart. Others have a prostrate growing habit – perfect for growing over walls or on a gravel path. Usually the plant will reach around 1 m (3 ft 2 in) or so in height, but it can be pruned to keep it much smaller.

Types and varieties
There are a number of varieties and types of rosemary. All essentially taste similar but their growth habit and flower colours vary.

Pests and diseases
Rosemary is trouble-free.

Harvesting and storage
Rosemary can be picked whenever it's required. The main growing season is spring and summer, and a mass of foliage will be available for harvesting as required during these seasons. A little can be harvested outside this time.

In the kitchen
Rosemary combines well with lamb. Whole sprigs can be pushed into roasts and the flavour infused. It also works well with chicken, roast potatoes and sauces. Sprigs can also be added to salad dressings.

CALENDAR

MID-SPRING
Buy individual plants from the garden centre.

LATE SPRING
Dig over the soil well, add some coarse sand if the soil is heavy, and plant.

EARLY SUMMER
Once the plant has flowered, it can be pruned back into shape. Take cuttings from early to midsummer to propagate new plants.

VARIETY SELECTOR
Ground-hugging rosemary
• The Prostratus Group grows 30 cm (12 in) high and spreads along the ground. Usually light blue flowers in summer.
White-flowering rosemary
• *Rosmarinus officinalis var. albiflorus*.
Pink-flowering rosemary
• 'Roseus'.
Blue-flowering rosemary
• *Rosmarinus officinalis*.
Good for hedging
• 'Miss Jessopp's Upright' reaches 2 m (6 ft 5 in) in height.

PROPAGATING ROSEMARY

1 In midsummer, select side shoots that are about 10 cm (4 in) long. Pull down on these individually, tearing them off the parent stem. These are known as heel cuttings. Remove all the lower leaves and pinch out the tip.

2 Push individual cuttings into small pots filled with gritty compost. Water and cover pots with a clear plastic bag and leave somewhere cool and out of direct sun.

Sage

This pretty Mediterranean herb is popular in the herb garden. Easy to grow, it will look good all year round.

⭘⭘⭘⭘⭘ VALUE FOR MONEY
⭘⭘⭘⭘⭘ MAINTENANCE
⭘⭘⭘⭘⭘ FREEZE/STORE
CROPPING SEASON: EARLY SPRING–EARLY WINTER

This shrubby plant is often used in Mediterranean cooking. It produces thick, downy leaves that provide a rich flavour when cooked with meat. You don't need much to impart their flavour, so you'll only need a single plant in the garden. Because it's an evergreen perennial, it's easiest to buy plants from the gadren centre rather than growing from seed.

In the garden, sage is a pretty plant, and grown next to other Mediterranean herbs, such as rosemary and thyme, it will continue to look good throughout the year. Because it's perennial, you'll be able to keep picking leaves all year round too.

Minimum temperature range
-29°C (-20°F) to -2°C (29°F).

Where to grow
This plant likes fairly well-drained soil and a sunny spot. It prefers alkaline soil, but would grow in most soils. If your soil is heavy, consider digging in some gravel or coarse sand to improve the drainage. Plants don't reach more than 60 cm (2 ft) in height and spread. Place just one or two plants in your perennial herb garden and it will provide you with leaves for years to come.

If the plant becomes straggly, consider taking some cuttings in the summer and propagate your plant to produce new ones for the following year.

Types and varieties
The most common sage used in cooking is plain garden sage (*Salvia officinalis*). There are others, particularly with purple or variegated leaves. Try 'Purpurescens' for colourful purple foliage, or 'Tricolor' with leaves in pink, cream and green. One to try in containers is pineapple sage (*Salvia elegans* 'Scarlet Pineapple'). It's not hardy like the other sages, so you'll either have to move it somewhere frost-free during the winter months or start again the following year. It has striking red flowers and pineapple-

Aromatic leaves
The slightly furry evergreen leaves of sage make this herb an essential for the winter kitchen garden.

scented leaves, but is not necessarily the best for cooking.

Pests and diseases
Sage is trouble-free.

Harvesting and storage
Pick leaves as you need them. Leaves can be dried but as you should be able to pick leaves for most of the year, it isn't usually necessary. In the winter, you can continue to pick leaves, but covering the plant with a cloche or fleece will help to protect the plant and keep the leaves looking good.

In the kitchen
Add to meat such as pork or lamb when roasting. It's often used in stuffings or you can add it to oil to impart its flavour. Wonderful with squash.

PROPAGATING SAGE

1 Remove some stems from this year's growth and remove the lower leaves.

2 Insert individual stems into small pots filled with multi-purpose compost.

3 Water well and cover with a plastic bag. Keep somewhere in good light but out of direct sun.

CALENDAR

EARLY–MID-SPRING
Buy plants from the garden centre. You'll need only one, but try some different forms to add colour to your garden.

LATE SPRING
Grow on in a pot in a sheltered spot until all threat of frost has passed, then plant in a well-drained, sunny spot in your garden. Sage can also be grown in a container.

EARLY SPRING YEAR 2 ONWARDS
Each year in early spring, cut back plants to around 15 cm (6 in) above the ground to prevent the plant going leggy.

Tarragon

This somewhat leggy perennial herb is an attractive, productive plant for the herb garden.

✪✪✪✪✪	VALUE FOR MONEY
✪✪✪✪✪	MAINTENANCE
✪✪✪✪✪	FREEZE/STORE

CROPPING SEASON: LATE SPRING–EARLY AUTUMN

Tarragon is a pretty plant and a good choice along a path or entrance. It grows fairly tall for a culinary herb, to around 90 cm (3 ft), but its feathery leaves do look attractive. Tarragon is often used to complement fish and chicken, particularly cold dishes. With its faintly aniseed flavour, it works well with delicately flavoured foods, and is the main herb used in béarnaise sauce.

Minimum temperature range

-40°C (-40°F) to -8°C (19°F).

Where to grow
Grow tarragon in a warm, dry spot. Go for direct sun if you have it and make sure the soil is well drained. It can be a fussy herb and will die off if the soil remains cold and wet for a long period. It's a slow grower, but does get quite big, so give it plenty of space and this perennial will keep coming back year after year.

Types and varieties
There are just a couple of types to choose from. Russian tarragon is sharp in flavour but disliked by many. French tarragon (*Artemisia dracunculus*) is considered to be far superior with a much more subtle aniseed flavour.

Pests and diseases
Generally trouble-free, but can suffer from rust – reddish spots appearing on the leaves. If this poses a problem, just cut the plants right down to the ground and remove any infected foliage. Water and feed, and the plant should return.

Temperamental tarragon
A tall plant, tarragon can be fussy and won't do well in every garden.

Harvesting and storage
Harvest stems around halfway up the plant throughout the growing season as you need them. Tarragon can be chopped and frozen to be used in winter months.

In the kitchen
Look out for tarragon in recipes using chicken and fish.

DIVIDING TARRAGON PLANTS

1 Once the weather and soil start to warm up, dig up the clump of tarragon with a garden fork.

2 Using another fork, insert both into the middle of the root clump and pull the forks apart. This splits the plant without damaging too much root.

3 Replant the smaller clumps immediately and water in well.

CALENDAR

SPRING
Buy plants from the garden centre. Make sure you look for French tarragon and avoid Russian tarragon. Plant in a sunny, well-drained spot. You'll only need one or two plants, but leave plenty of space around them.

SUMMER
Cut leaves as required in the kitchen. If you have plenty, consider freezing some in a resealable plastic bag.

AUTUMN
If the plant gets too big after a year or two, consider lifting the plant and splitting it. Sections can be planted up around the garden.

Thyme

This small, shrubby plant is a must for any herb garden. It grows well in a container or window box too.

✪✪✪✪✪	VALUE FOR MONEY
✪✪✪✪✪	MAINTENANCE
✪✪✪✪✪	FREEZE/STORE

CROPPING SEASON: ALL YEAR ROUND

Thyme plants rarely reach higher than 30 cm (12 in). Many are ground-hugging plants that produce an aromatic carpet of leaves; others are taller and produce short spires of pink or purple flowers. Whichever variety you go for, thyme is useful in the kitchen too.

Minimum temperature range
-34°C (-30°F) to -2°C (29°F).

Where to grow
Like the other Mediterranean herbs, thyme prefers a dry, sunny spot. If the soil isn't well drained, consider digging in some coarse sand, and where the soil is acid, think about adding some garden lime in the spring before planting. Because the plants remain small, thyme grows well in containers too, as well as in small crevices in walls or in cracks in paving. A bit like lavender, thyme plants don't last too long, becoming straggly and leafless after a few years:

A variety of varieties
There are lots of varieties of thyme to choose from, and it may be worth selecting a few to grow.

replace plants when they get to this stage. Plants are best bought at the garden centre or by mail order. They're tricky to grow from seed but it is possible if you want a lot of plants. To make more of your plants, you can propagate thyme from cuttings in early summer.

Types and varieties
There are hundreds of varieties of thyme. The most common culinary herb is common thyme (*Thymus vulgaris*). This is the one you're likely to find if you want to grow thyme from seed. There are plenty of other thymes as well, often varying in habit, flower colour and flavour.

Pests and diseases
Trouble-free.

CALENDAR

SPRING
Prepare the soil in spring by digging over and adding coarse sand to improve drainage. Buy plants from the garden centre, and plant out in the garden. Varieties vary in height and spread, so consider this when planting.

SUMMER
Leaves can be picked throughout the season. Once the plant has finished flowering, trim it back to neaten. Cuttings can be taken in late summer to propagate plants for next year.

Harvesting and storage
In theory, this evergreen plant can be picked all year, but during winter the plant becomes very straggly. Cut whole stems and either pull off leaves to use, or throw in whole stems.

In the kitchen
Whole stems can be used in stocks and when roasting meat and potatoes. Remove the leaves from the stems and chop finely to add directly to sauces or stuffings.

GROWING COMMON THYME FROM SEED

1 Sow seed in mid-spring in multi-purpose compost in small pots.

2 Place the pots in a propagator and ensure the temperature remains fairly constant and above 15°C (59°F).

VARIETY SELECTOR
- *Thymus vulgaris*: a good choice if you're growing from seed and want plenty of plants.
- **'Archers Gold'**: a ground-hugging variety, which produces golden leaves and has a mild flavour.
- **Lemon thyme**: reaching up to 30 cm (12 in) in height, this lemon-scented thyme produces pink flowers in the summer.
- **Caraway thyme**: reaches just a few inches in height. Produces dark green leaves with a smell of caraway. Good with meat.

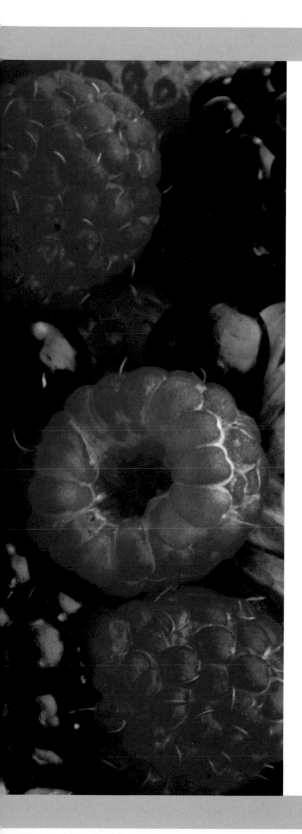

FRUIT CROPS

Fruit can be even easier to grow than vegetables. Just an annual prune and a mulch of compost and your fruit crops will reward you for years to come. Soft fruits require little space and can be grown in a pot if necessary, while some tree fruit reach much loftier proportions suitable only for larger gardens. Select your varieties carefully for both suitability to your garden and your palate – once they're planted, you'll have to keep harvesting, year after year.

TREE FRUIT

The first fruits worth considering for a place in your garden are tree fruits. While some varieties and rootstocks need to be planted in open ground and are liable to cast shade, others can be grown alongside paths or even in containers.

Apples, pears, plums and other tree fruit are incredibly rewarding to have in your garden and are a simple way of growing food.

Apple

Whatever size garden you have, there'll be an apple tree that looks good and produces delicious fruit.

✪✪✪✪✪   VALUE FOR MONEY
✪✪✪✪✪   MAINTENANCE
✪✪✪✪✪   FREEZE/STORE
CROPPING SEASON: LATE SUMMER–MID-AUTUMN

When you think about an apple tree from your childhood it's probably a big one, with a swing hanging off it or branches low enough to climb. Although a tree of this size will certainly be productive, there are smaller apple trees that can bear just as many fruit.

If your garden is big enough, an orchard is the traditional place to grow apples. Set among a wildflower meadow, orchards are havens for wildlife. The blossom provides nectar for bees and other pollinating insects, while the trees themselves provide food and shelter for all manner of invertebrates. And in the winter, the windfall of apples provides food for garden birds.

But even in a small garden, an apple tree can be a useful plant, not just for wildlife but for your garden too. Apples can be trained into all sorts of shapes and, if you get the right rootstock, sizes too. They can be placed along paths, in front gardens, at the back of an ornamental border, against walls and fences, as well as in the productive part of the garden.

Minimum temperature range
-40°C (-40°F) to -2°C (29°F).

Where to grow Apples do best in sunny spots, out of any harsh winds. They prefer rich, fertile soil that doesn't easily dry out. Saying this, apples (particularly the culinary types) also do well in semi-shade, and if you improve your soil with plenty of organic matter will survive in most soil types. If the ground is really unsuitable then you can even grow apples in containers.

The position you have in mind will determine the variety you finally go for when buying a new tree. While some varieties are more vigorous than others, it's the rootstock that will determine the final size of the tree.

Productive apple trees
Low-maintenance apple trees will supply you with plenty of fruit in the autumn, which can be stored through the winter too.

Rootstocks All apple trees are grafted. This means the stem of the selected variety has been grown onto the root of another variety. These rootstocks, as they are known, have specific characteristics that will ultimately determine the vigour and final size of your selected apple variety. Your choice of rootstock can also be decided by the ➤

PLANTING A BARE-ROOT APPLE TREE

1 Clear the area around where you are going to plant the tree, removing any perennial weeds. Dig a good-sized plant hole (much larger than the roots), and ensure the tree goes in at the same depth as it has been originally grown.

2 Drive a stake vertically into the ground. This will support the tree as it grows.

3 Spread the roots of the bare-rooted tree out well over a low mound and push back the original soil.

4 Use a tree tie to ensure the tree remains secured to the stake, and if rabbits are a problem, consider adding a trunk protector, which wraps around the base of the stem, preventing rabbits, squirrels and other pests from nibbling at the bark.

5 Fill the planting hole in with the original soil and add a sprinkling of a general-purpose fertiliser on top of the soil. If you are planting by a wall, ensure the tree isn't too close to it. Aim to plant it about 25–35 cm (10–14 in) away from the foot of the wall.

6 The tree will need regular watering in its first year. Give it a watering can-full every week during the spring and summer. If it's really hot, a couple of times a week will be necessary. In subsequent springs, ensure the base of the tree is well mulched. Add a sprinkling of fertiliser and loosen the tree tie as the trunk widens.

quality of the site you have in mind. More vigorous rootstocks will do better on poor soils than a dwarfing rootstock, for example.

There are around six main rootstocks you can choose from. Sometimes you won't get a choice of rootstock, but if you go to a specialist fruit nursery, the selection of combinations of rootstock and varieties will be much greater. Here are a few listed:

M27 This is an extremely dwarfing rootstock with plants reaching from 1.5–1.8 m (5–5 ft 9 in). Needs good soil and can also be grown in a container.

M9 This is known as very dwarfing, with a mature height of 2.4–3 m (7 ft 8 in–9 ft 8 in). Needs good soil and is useful for training into small cordons and espaliers.

M26 This dwarfing rootstock will create a tree from 3–3.5 m (9 ft 8 in–11 ft 4 in). Needs good soil. You should use this rootstock for small trees, as well as cordons and espaliers.

MM106 This semi-dwarfing rootstock produces a tree from 4–5.5 m (13–18 ft). A good choice for a medium-sized garden, and can be used on poorer soils for cordons and espaliers.

MM25 Known as a vigorous rootstock, the mature height will reach from 4–5.5 m (13–16 ft 4 in). A good choice if you want a larger tree or if you want to train it into more elaborate shapes. A good choice for poor soil.

M2, MM111 These very vigorous rootstocks can produce trees up to 9 m (29 ft 5 in) in height and should be used only for orchards.

Types and varieties

Once you've worked out the ultimate size of the tree you want, you'll need to decide what sort of apples you'd like in your garden.

Apple trees need at least one other apple tree nearby to pollinate the fruit. This can be a crab apple or other edible apple. If your garden is small, your neighbours' apple trees may also help.

Apples can be separated into dessert apples (for eating fresh) and culinary/cooking apples (for cooking). While dessert apples are often crunchy, sweet and juicy, culinary apples have a much sharper taste and turn readily into a purée. Additionally, apples start to ripen in midsummer, with early varieties being ready to be picked first. Later-ripening varieties will be ready as late as mid-autumn and often these store much better over the winter months too.

Tree forms and growing methods

Bush and standard The most common shape of apple tree grown in gardens is a bush type or standard. This basically means having a stem or trunk of anything from 60 cm–2 m (2–6 ft 5 in). The top part of the tree is pruned in the winter to produce a compact round or goblet shape.

The other tree shapes are used where space is short. There are a number of shapes you can attempt.

Cordon The most common shape is the cordon. It is usually grown at an angle of around 45 degrees, against a wall or fence. Growing at an angle allows you to get a longer trunk for a given height, and so maximises your crop. Because the side branches are kept very short, you can plant trees close together – up to 60 cm (2 ft) apart.

Espalier Another common shape is the espalier. This is also commonly grown against a wall or fence, where the longer side branches are trained in a two-dimensional form, often horizontally along the wall.

Step-over The other type of espalier is a step-over, where a single stem is trained horizontally as low as 15 cm (6 in) to allow you to step over it – perfect for edging a path.

Pests and diseases and other problems

When apples grow well, they grow in abundance. However, they do suffer from their fair share of ➡

TREE FORMS AND GROWING METHODS
(FOR PRUNING AND TRAINING FRUIT TREES SEE PAGES 206–209)

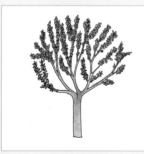

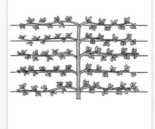

Bush or standard
The most common apple-tree shape with the highest yield, this form should be pruned in winter to maintain its round shape.

Cordon
A compact form useful for small spaces. Cordons are grown at an angle of 45 degrees. Regular pruning is essential.

Espalier
An attractive compact form, the high-yielding espalier works well grown against boundary walls or fences.

Step-over
A step-over is a single-armed espalier, and is useful for when space is limited. They are pruned in the same way as espaliers.

problems. This shouldn't put you off growing apples though, but there are some things to watch out for.

Sometimes trees underperform, simply because they're short of food. This is especially true if they're growing in the lawn or meadow. Adding around 100 g per sq m (3½ oz per sq yd) of general-purpose fertiliser each spring, applying a mulch, and removing a circle of grass 1 m (3 ft 2 in) around the base of the tree will all help. If fruit are small or you are only getting fruit every other year, you need to remove some fruit in the spring. This thinning out of fruit will help the fruit that are left to grow on and ripen. The tree should also have enough energy to repeat fruiting the following year.

Caterpillars can damage the leaves of apple trees but most are not a problem. Codling moths, however, are.

Apple orchard
It's unlikely you'll be growing trees on a commercial scale – just one or two trees, well spaced in your garden, should be plenty.

REJUVENATING A NEGLECTED APPLE TREE

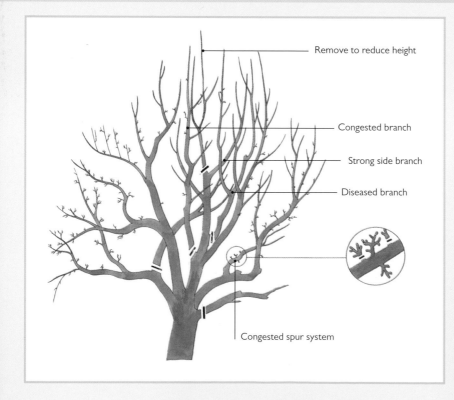

Remove to reduce height

Congested branch

Strong side branch

Diseased branch

Congested spur system

You can encourage a neglected apple tree to crop well again and improve the fruit quality by pruning. Renovation work should be carried out during the dormant season.

1 Cut out any diseased, split or otherwise damaged branches. Cut well back into healthy wood, or remove the branch completely if badly affected.

2 If the tree is very congested, cut out some branches to let in more light, especially in the centre of the tree. Remove crossing or badly placed branches, cutting them right back to the point of origin.

3 If the tree is too tall, cut back the tallest branches to strong side branches.

4 Thin out the spurs drastically (see page 207). It may be necessary to remove some entirely, cutting them flush with the stem. Avoid leaving clusters of spurs closer than 23 cm (9 in) apart.

5 Clean up any major pruning wounds and seal with a specialist wound paint, available from garden centres.

Powdery mildew can also be a problem. Make sure the tree has been pruned appropriately, and ensure that it isn't suffering from a lack of water. Scab – where the fruits are damaged – is caused by a fungus. Again, the best advice is to try to keep the tree healthy through regular pruning, mulching and watering where necessary, and clear away fallen leaves and fruit in the autumn.

Harvesting and storage As apples can ripen any time between midsummer and late autumn, it's a good idea to know what variety you have. However, once apples start dropping, you know it's time to start picking. It's a good idea to pick over a number of weeks, harvesting the most ripe fruit first. The fruit should be stored somewhere cool, dark, and if possible, slightly damp. A cellar, cool shed or garage would be fine. Store on trays and check over fruit regularly, removing any that start to rot. Those harvested later in the season generally store for longer.

In the kitchen Ripe fruit can be eaten straight off the tree – at least those varieties that are sufficiently sweet. Culinary varieties tend to be sharper in flavour, and whether you're making an apple sauce to go with your Sunday roast pork, or creating an apple pie or crumble, adding sugar is a necessity.

VARIETY SELECTOR

Dessert apples

- 'Beauty of Bath', 'Discovery': midsummer ripening.
- 'Red Devil', 'Scrumptious': late summer/early autumn ripening.
- 'Falstaff', 'Rosemary Russet': mid-autumn ripening.

Culinary (cooking) apples

- 'Grenadier': midsummer ripening.
- 'Bountiful': early autumn ripening.
- 'Bramley's Seedling': mid-autumn ripening.

Storing apples
Apples can be stored in boxes in a cool dark place, but preferably not piled up, since one rotten apple will spoil the whole box.

CALENDAR

EARLY SPRING
A good time to plant your apple trees. Plant at least two trees to ensure good pollination.

MID-SPRING
Make sure your trees are well mulched and fed with fertiliser.

LATE SPRING
Hang up your codling moth traps.

EARLY SUMMER
Ensure all perennial weeds have been removed and are not growing back. Thin out the number of fruit.

MIDSUMMER
Ensure your tree doesn't go short of water.

LATE SUMMER
Trees grown in a restricted form, such as cordons and espaliers, need to be pruned back now.

EARLY AUTUMN
Start to pick fruit as they ripen.

MID-AUTUMN
Clear up fallen fruit and diseased leaves.

LATE AUTUMN
Finish harvesting the fruit.

WINTER
Prune all your trees now. Go for an open goblet shape for trees, or cut back to keep the original shape of espaliers and cordons, ensuring you don't cut off the larger buds likely to turn into flowers.

Pear

Delicious pears taste good both
cooked and ripened off the tree.

○○○○○	VALUE FOR MONEY
○○○○○	MAINTENANCE
○○○○○	FREEZE/STORE
CROPPING SEASON: LATE SUMMER–MID-AUTUMN	

Ripe pears
The heavy cropping and juicy, sweet
texture of pears means it's worth
making space in any fruit garden.

Pear trees are renowned for being slow to fruit.
And it's true that a newly planted tree will take
a couple of years to really start to bear fruit.
However, if you've ever been rewarded with
moving into a new house and finding a pear
tree in the garden, you'll know that every
garden should have one.

Pears can be grown like apples, either
as standard trees, often shaped into an
open goblet shape, or trained as cordons
or espaliers.

Because pears are a bit more fussy about
the weather and prefer warmer conditions,
particularly early in the season, training them
against a sunny wall or fence is ideal. That way,
they take up little room. Just an annual prune
and a little care and attention through the
season, and you'll have a productive tree
for many years to come.

Minimum temperature range
-34°C (-30°F) to -2°C (29°F).

VARIETY SELECTOR

- **'Conference'**: the most reliable
pear of all, good cropper and
good tasting.

- **'Merton Pride'**: red blushed.

- **'Concorde'**: a modern variety
which starts cropping when it's
fairly young.

- **'Beth'**: small, sweet fruits. Starts
cropping when young.

- **'Catillac'**: produces large flowers
and fruit. A hard pear that keeps
well and is good for cooking.

Where to grow
Pears need a long
growing season, and are therefore slightly more
difficult to grow than apples. Their blossom
comes out in early spring, which needs
pollinating and protecting from frosts, and their
fruit tend to ripen later than apples. In cooler
areas, it's safest to grow pears against a wall
or fence. This way, the flowers and fruit are
provided with some protection against
potential harsh weather. In warmer areas,
growing in an open garden will allow you to
grow a large tree.

Pears are fairly unfussy when it comes to
soil, as long as it's not very chalky or overly
wet. It's worth mulching your soil with
well-rotted compost each year, but apart
from that, and annual pruning, they need little
other care.

Pears, like apples, are grafted onto
rootstocks. This ensures they grow to a
specified size and helps them be vigorous
enough to produce plenty of fruit. Once you've
selected a spot for your pear tree, selecting
your rootstock is crucial to making sure it fits
into its allotted space.

Rootstocks
Most pears are sold on
rootstocks from quince trees. They're named
either Quince A or Quince C. Quince C
produces a smaller tree of around 3 m
(9 ft 8 in) and should be used where you want
to keep a tree small. Quince A can produce a
tree of 4 m (13 ft) or more – ideal if you want
a large tree, or if your soil is very poor. When
it comes to espaliers, cordons and step-overs,
you won't have a choice: the supplier will use
the most appropriate rootstock. They are also
sold on one of a series of OX×F rootstocks of
various sizes.

Types and varieties
There are not as
many pear varieties as you would think. They
can be broadly separated into dessert (for

eating) or culinary (for cooking). They can also
be separated into groups, depending on when
they flower. Most pears need another tree in
the vicinity to cross-pollinate with, and these
should flower at the same time. 'Conference'
and 'Williams' Bon Chrétien' are two that
don't need to be cross-pollinated, so are
perfect if you just want one tree. Earlier
flowering trees that should be planted together
include 'Durondeau' and 'Merton Pride'. Later
ones include 'Concorde', 'Beth' and 'Comice'.

Growing methods and pruning
The size of tree you wish to grow and the
shape you train it into will all depend on your
garden and the space you have within it. Pears,
on the whole, can be trained exactly the same
way as apples, as either standalone trees or as
cordons or espaliers, usually trained against a
fence or wall (see page 141).

Once grown into the desired shape, the
pear tree will need regular pruning (see pages
206–209). Overgrown trees can be cut down
to size too. Here, the best time to prune is in
mid-winter.

Pests, diseases and other
problems
One problem with pear trees
can be a lack of fruit. This is often caused by a
cold spring affecting the blossom. If frosts are
predicted when in bloom, try covering with a
fleece during the night, making sure you
remove it in the morning.

Fruit can often be affected by scab (where

black spots appear on the fruit). The only treatment is to rake up affected leaves and fruit and burn them, as well as ensuring your tree is well pruned, with any cracked or damaged shoots cut out. Fireblight is a disease that affects whole branches, where they can turn black and appear to be burnt. The best option is to cut out diseased branches well below where they have been affected.

Birds and wasps can also damage fruit, but there isn't much you can do about it, apart from drape a fine mesh over the tree.

Harvesting and storage The best time to pick pears is just before they ripen – that way they'll store for longer. It can be tricky to know exactly when to pick them, and often the best way is to start picking individual pears and try them. Another way is to twist the stem – if the pear comes off easily, it's ready.

Pears are best stored at around 5°C (41°F) in a tray, laid out separately. Try a cold cellar or garage during winter. Most pears don't keep too well, so eat them within two months.

In the kitchen Fresh pears picked from the garden often don't even make it into the kitchen, but if they do, there are plenty of recipes that use pears. Poaching pears in wine is a classic way of cooking them. Otherwise, use fresh in salads. They also work particularly well with strong cheese.

REJUVENATING AN OLD PEAR TREE

A very old pear tree is often best replaced with a new one, but a tree that has simply been neglected can often be rejuvenated. Do this during the dormant season.

1 If the tree is large, it is a good idea to mark the branches to be removed with chalk or string, then stand back to check that you've picked the right ones. If the tree is large or complex, remove dead or diseased wood before continuing, so that you can assess the remaining branches more clearly.

2 Next remove crossing and badly placed branches. Where there is a choice, retain the branch with the most or the fattest buds.

3 Start to shape the tree, aiming for a wine-glass outline, removing branches less than 60 cm (24 in) apart if this will not spoil the shape. Again, where there is a choice retain the one with the most or fattest buds.

4 If height is a problem, cut the central branch back to an outwards-pointing side branch. If the tree is large you must remove big branches with care. A tree more than 4.5 m (15 ft) high should be tackled by a qualified tree surgeon.

5 Thin the fruit spurs as described for rejuvenating neglected apples (see page 142).

Reduce height to improve shape

Badly crossing branch

Excessive growth

Dead or diseased wood

Overcrowded spurs

CALENDAR

EARLY SPRING
Plant your pear tree now. Use a stake and tree tie to keep it in place. You may need to plant more than one for good pollination. Make sure your trees are given an annual sprinkling of fertiliser and are well mulched with homemade compost.

MID-SPRING
If blossom comes early and frosts are forecast, be ready with some fleece to protect the flower buds. If you are growing it against a wall, ensure the system of wires is in place for training.

LATE SPRING
Make sure your young tree doesn't go short of water.

EARLY SUMMER
Thin out the numbers of fruit if the tree is heavily laden to one to two per cluster, as shown at right.

MIDSUMMER
Keep watering in the first couple of years.

LATE SUMMER
Trees grown in a restricted form, such as cordons and espaliers, need to be pruned back now.

EARLY AUTUMN
Start to pick fruit as they ripen.

MID-AUTUMN
Clear up fallen fruit and diseased leaves.

LATE AUTUMN
Finish harvesting your fruit.

WINTER
Prune your pear tree. Remove crossing, diseased and damaged branches. Cut back long shoots but keep the short fruiting spurs that produce the flowering buds.

Plum, Gage and Damson

For a cooler climate, plums are one of the most reliable fruit, and their taste can rival even the sweetest peaches and cherries.

○○○○○ VALUE FOR MONEY
○○○○○ MAINTENANCE
○○○○○ FREEZE/STORE
CROPPING SEASON: MIDSUMMER–MID-AUTUMN

If you want to eat tasty plums, gages and damsons, you have little choice but to grow your own. Supermarket plums are usually restricted to tough-skinned varieties with an insipid watery flavour. But the juicy, sweet flavours of Victoria plums and greengages are something worth coveting. They're not the easiest tree fruit to grow, however. While they do well in cool climates, late frosts can seriously affect their crop. Pests and diseases can be a problem too, and while they don't take very much pruning, it takes only a couple of years for a tree to get out of hand. Prune conservatively each year, mulch and feed well, and a tree should reward you with fruits through the midsummer and autumn.

Minimum temperature range
-34°C (-30°F) to 5°C (40°F).

Where to grow Plums don't like to be grown through grass, so it's worth growing at the back of a border or against a sunny fence or wall. As plums come into flower early, you'll need to make sure they're sited where they can be protected from late frosts. If your garden does suffer from late frosts, consider growing a plum tree against a west- or south-facing wall, so that you can throw a fleece over the tree to protect the flowers.

They like good, rich soil that's well drained, but will do fine on heavier or lighter soils, which are worth improving with homemade compost each spring. At this time, also sprinkle a handful of general-purpose fertiliser around the base of the tree.

Planting and pruning Buy a tree in winter; plums are best planted during the dormant season. There's a better choice of varieties and sizes from a specialist nursery.

Juicy fruit
Often untidy and unattractive trees for much of the year, plum trees are worthy of a space for their juicy fruit alone.

It's not possible to grow plums as cordons, but they can be trained against a wall as a fan (see page 141). Alternatively, site in a sunny open position in the garden for a larger tree.

Once grown into the desired shape, the plum tree will need regular pruning (see pages 206–209).

Rootstocks
Plum trees, like other tree fruit, come grafted onto rootstocks to determine the size of tree.
Pixy The smallest rootstock, creating a tree up to 3 m (9 ft 8 in) in height. Starts cropping after three to four years.
St Julien A A slightly larger tree of up to 5 m (16 ft) will be produced with this rootstock. A good choice for poor soils, or for a large fan against a wall.

Types and varieties The wild plum (*Prunus spinosa*) produces fruit that are only worthy for flavouring alcohol. While sloe gin is popular, there is so much more you can do with a harvest of sweet, juicy plums. The wild plum was crossed with another species, the cherry plum (*Prunus cerasifera*), and together this created the garden plum. You can find varieties that are plump, sweet and juicy, ideal for eating straight off the tree. There are also those that are good for cooking with.

PLANTING A CONTAINER-GROWN PLUM TREE

1 Dig a planting hole that is larger than the rootball of the tree.

2 Plant the tree, and using a tree stake, tie in the tree to prevent it swaying in the wind. Mulch with homemade compost.

Gages are similar to dessert plums, but their fruit are smaller and usually green or yellow. Gages are slightly trickier to succeed with.

If your climate is inclement, then think about choosing a damson. These fruit are perfect for making jam and are generally tougher than plums, surviving cold weather and resisting diseases.

For a really tough plum, consider a bullace. The fruit matures later than plums, but is good for cooking and the tree is very hardy.

Pests, diseases and other problems

Plums have a lot going for them taste-wise, but they do suffer from plenty of problems too.

Silverleaf is one of the worst diseases; here, leaves take on a silvery sheen and whole branches can die back. The only solution is to cut whole branches off. To prevent this disease, only prune the tree in the summer months as pruning in winter gives the disease a place to enter the tree. The same is true for another disease – canker. Here, small 'shots' appear in the leaves and areas of bark become sunken and a sticky liquid oozes out.

Plum leaf-curling aphids can also seriously affect leaves, but shouldn't affect the tree too badly. However, plum maggots can get into the fruit and spoil them. If this is a problem, you can buy special traps to hang in the tree.

One common problem with plums is a total lack of fruit. This is usually caused by late frosts damaging the flowers, causing them to drop off. If frosts are forecast when the tree is in flower

you'll need to try to cover as much of the tree with garden fleece as you can to offer some protection.

Branches can sometimes become heavily laden with fruit, which causes them to snap. Try supporting heavy branches with a stake or other support. Alternatively, thin out the fruits to one every 2 cm (¾ in).

Harvesting and storage Plums, gages and damsons will crop, depending on the variety, any time between late summer and late autumn. Give the fruits a squeeze and, when soft to the touch, they'll be ripe. Taste one or two before picking any more.

Some fruits, such as bullaces and damsons, will crop later, and while they may still have an acidic flavour, will be fine for making jams or chutneys.

In the kitchen Plums are the ideal late summer fruit. Picked straight off the tree, they're tasty and sweet. They can be used in puddings and pies too.

Damsons make excellent jam and along with bullaces are a great choice when making chutney. Here the rich, sweet flavours develop over time with the chutney tasting great after storing for at least six months.

VARIETY SELECTOR

Plum

• **'Victoria'**: heavy cropping, large pale-red fruit.

• **'Czar'**: good for cooking, sharp flavour.

• **'Kirke's'**: really good-flavoured plum, likes good growing conditions.

Gage

• **'Cambridge Gage'**: best gage you can buy, small yellow-green fruit.

Damson

• **'Prune'**: good flavour, small fruit.

CALENDAR

EARLY SPRING

YEAR 1
Dig over the soil well and plant your tree. Use a tree stake and tie in the tree to prevent it swaying in the wind. Mulch with homemade compost.

YEAR 2 ONWARDS
Protect early blossom with fleece if frost is forecast.

MID-SPRING

YEAR 1
Prune the tree in the first year in early spring. Cut back the leading shoot and all side shoots.

YEAR 2 ONWARDS
Add a couple of handfuls of balanced fertiliser and a few bucket loads of homemade compost.

LATE SPRING

Hang up your codling moth traps. Carry out pruning of young trees now to create the desired shape.

EARLY SUMMER

Thin out the numbers of fruit if the tree is heavily laden.

MIDSUMMER

Ensure your tree doesn't go short of water. This is the time to prune older trees. Don't prune any later than this.

LATE SUMMER

You may have to support the very heavily laden branches with a wooden stake to prevent them breaking off.

EARLY AUTUMN

Leave plums to ripen on the tree and start to pick fruit as they are ready.

MID-AUTUMN

Clear up fallen fruit and diseased leaves.

Sweet cherry

If you love the taste of cherries, there is nothing better than being able to grow and pick your own.

✪✪✪✪✪	VALUE FOR MONEY
✪✪✪✪✪	MAINTENANCE
✪✪✪✪✪	FREEZE/STORE
CROPPING SEASON: MIDSUMMER–EARLY AUTUMN	

Sweet cherries deserve to be more widely grown. Their sensational flavour is second to none when picked fresh from the garden. However, they're renowned for being tricky. They tend to grow into large, unwieldy trees and they're fussy about growing conditions, requiring a warm spot and good weather conditions from early spring. However, there are now smaller-growing varieties available, and these allow you to protect the trees from late frosts as well as from birds, which have a habit of pinching all the best fruit.

Minimum temperature range
-29°C (-20°F) to -2°C (29°F).

Juicy cherries
Sweet cherries can turn into huge trees, but if you're not careful birds will steal the lot.

PRUNING AN ESTABLISHED SWEET CHERRY FAN

Weak side branch

Main branch that has grown too tall

1 Prune established fan-trained sweet cherries in summer to restrict the amount of leafy growth and encourage the formation of fruit buds for the next year. Remove the growing tips of new shoots when they have made five or six leaves (cut out completely any shoots growing directly towards the wall).

2 Shorten these same shoots to three buds in early autumn. Remove any dead wood, and thin very congested spurs (remains of old shoots) at the same time.

3 Very tall shoots at the top of the fan can be cut back to a weaker side branch to reduce the size. Other strong upright shoots can be reduced in vigour by tying them down towards the horizontal.

Where to grow Sweet cherries require a sunny spot. They also need to be sheltered from strong winds and in a place where frost is least likely. Try growing against a sunny south- or southwest facing wall.

The most widely available cherries are grafted onto the Colt rootstock. This can produce a free-standing tree of over 5 m (16 ft) tall. Too big for many gardens, there are now a couple of alternative rootstocks, which claim to produce much smaller trees. These are called 'Tabel' and 'Gisela', and produce trees around 2–3 m (6 ft 5 in–9 ft 8 in) high.

All cherries are best planted during the dormant season. Choose a fairly well-drained spot, and if necessary improve with some homemade compost or similar organic matter. Sweet cherries are prolific croppers, so each spring you should mulch the tree with a 5-cm (2-in) layer of organic matter as well as a good handful of general-purpose fertiliser.

Types and varieties Unlike acid cherries, many sweet cherry varieties need pollinating by another cherry. To make things more complicated, some cherries are incompatible with others. For an easy life, it's safest to choose one of the few self-pollinating varieties. This way, you'll only need a single tree.

Pruning and training Trees can be pruned into a fan (see opposite and page 209) or allowed to grow into a tree. Sweet cherries fruit on old wood, so unlike acid cherries, it's a good idea to do as little pruning as possible once you've created the shape you want. Take off any crossing branches and any that look diseased or weak in the summer.

Pests and diseases The worst problem to affect cherries is birds eating them. This is frustrating, as you see the fruits ripening, only for them to disappear overnight! By keeping the tree small you will be able to drape a fine mesh over it during this time.

Fruit can also crack and sometimes fall off the tree before it is ripe. These problems are related to the weather, and there is little you can do. Some varieties are more affected than others. 'Lapins' is a good choice for cracking resistance.

Another disease that affects cherries is silver leaf. Carrying out any pruning in the summer is the best way to avoid this problem.

Harvesting and storage Sweet cherry trees can be more prolific than acid cherries, mainly because of their larger size. In a good year you can get as much as 45 kg (100 lb) from a tree. You can freeze cherries after they've been cleaned, but the best option is to eat them fresh.

In the kitchen Eating as a fresh fruit is the best way to appreciate this delicious crop.

CALENDAR

EARLY SPRING

Dig over the soil well and plant your tree. Use a tree stake and tie in the tree to prevent it swaying in the wind. Mulch with plenty of homemade compost. You may need to plant more than one tree, depending on the variety, to ensure good pollination. Mulch an established tree well and add a good few handfuls of general-purpose fertiliser.

MID-SPRING

If frost is still forecast, you may need to protect flowers from frost with a fleece. Now is a good time to prune your young tree.

LATE SPRING

Water the tree regularly in the first couple of years, and if the weather is dry thereafter.

EARLY SUMMER

Protect developing fruit from birds. Pick over the tree for ripe fruits when they're ready.

MIDSUMMER

Ensure your tree doesn't go short of water.

LATE SUMMER

A good time to prune an older tree is when it has just finished fruiting. Trees fruit on one- or two-year old wood, as well as the spurs of older wood. Now is a good time to reduce the size of your tree.

PRUNING A SWEET CHERRY BUSH

If bush cherries are not pruned they quickly become tall with few branches near the ground.

Once a bush form starts to fruit, reduce the number of main branches to seven or eight, to maintain an open tree that is easy to pick. Established trees may need only the top shoots thinned or cut back to reduce height, but prune back hard, old or neglected shoots to stimulate new growth.

VARIETY SELECTOR

- **'Lapins' (Cherokee):** large, dark red, almost black, fruits that crop in midsummer.

- **'Celeste':** makes a more compact tree with dark red fruits.

- **'Stella':** the most widely grown sweet cherry with dark red fruits.

Sour succulence
Acid cherries are perfect for cooler climates, since they will tolerate lower temperatures than sweet cherries (see pages 148–149).

Acid cherry

Hardier cousins to the sweet, dessert cherries, acid cherries are great for desserts, pies and jams.

✪✪✪✪✪	VALUE FOR MONEY
✪✪✪✪✪	MAINTENANCE
✪✪✪✪✪	FREEZE/STORE
CROPPING SEASON: LATE SUMMER–EARLY AUTUMN	

If your climate is chilly and unlikely to support sweet cherries, you may have more success with acid cherries. These cherries originate in southwest Asia and have been bred to produce varieties such as 'Morello' and 'Nabella'. The fruits from these trees are more acid, or sour, in flavour than the sweet cherries (see pages 148–149) and are perfect for cooking with, or even for making drinks such as cherry brandy.

Minimum temperature range
-34°C (-30°F) to -8°C (19°F).

Where to grow
Acid cherries are actually a more suitable garden tree than sweet cherries. They grow to a diminutive 3-m (9 ft 8-in) tall tree. They can be trained as a fan, as well as being left to grow as a standard tree, and they also thrive on all aspects – even growing on a north-facing wall, where little other fruit does well. Nevertheless, they will still thrive in a warm, sheltered spot, and as they flower in mid- to late spring, you may need to protect the blossom from frost.

Types and varieties
Unlike many sweet cherries, all acid cherries are self-fertile. This means they don't need another tree growing nearby to aid pollination.

As with other fruit trees, acid cherries are grafted onto a rootstock of another type. Here, it's easy. Colt is the most well-used rootstock, and will produce a tree of around 3 m (9 ft 8 in), and is suitable for all forms, including fans grown against a wall.

As far as varieties go, there isn't much choice here either. 'Morello' is an old variety, but produces really good-flavoured fruit. 'Nabella' is a more recent introduction with similar dark red fruits, which is meant to crop even more heavily than 'Morello'.

Pruning and training Acid cherries bear on new wood, so need to be pruned fairly hard each year to encourage new growth. Once you pick the fruit, cut back branches to vigorous new growth. Once you have the shape of tree you want, just try cutting back about a third of the branches each year.

Pests and diseases See Sweet cherry on pages 148–149.

Harvesting and storage A decent-sized tree can produce around 13.5–18 kg (30–40 lb) of fruit; a fan tree somewhat less. Fruit should be picked when they've coloured to a dark red and are fully ripe. Try to cut the fruit off with the stalk, rather than pulling it off the stalk. All the fruit won't necessarily be ripe at the same time, so you may need to pick over the tree a few times. Fruit can be frozen or used fresh.

In the kitchen Acid cherries are good only for cooking as they need a decent amount of sugar to sweeten them up. However, they do have an excellent flavour and are worthy additions to summer pies and desserts. For a real bumper crop, consider turning the excess into jam for eating in the winter months.

CALENDAR

EARLY SPRING
Dig over the soil well and plant your tree. Use a tree stake and tie in the tree to prevent it swaying in the wind. Mulch with plenty of homemade compost. Mulch an established tree well and add a good few handfuls of general-purpose fertiliser.

MID-SPRING
Now is a good time to prune your young tree.

EARLY SUMMER
Protect developing fruit from birds. Pick over your tree for ripe fruits when they're ready.

MIDSUMMER
Ensure your tree doesn't go short of water.

LATE SUMMER
A good time to prune an older tree is when it has just finished fruiting. Remove some of the old fruited wood to promote new growth which is likely to flower next year.

PRUNING AN ESTABLISHED ACID CHERRY FAN

Surplus new shoot

New shoots that will replace it

Old shoot that has fruited

1 In late spring or early summer, thin the new shoots to 7.5–10 cm (3–4 in) apart along the main branches, and tie them in to retain a good fan shape. Where possible, allow a shoot to develop at the base of each sideshoot that is bearing fruit.

2 When the crop has been gathered, cut the shoots that have fruited back to the replacement that was tied in during early summer pruning. If the fan starts to crop mainly around the edges, cut back some of the three- or four-year-old branches in early spring to stimulate new growth.

Correct cherry pruning
A good cut angles down away from the main stem of the tree.

Peach, Nectarine and Apricot

More suited to warmer climes, peaches, nectarines and apricots can also be grown in containers on a sunny patio.

⬤⬤⬤◯◯ VALUE FOR MONEY
⬤⬤⬤⬤◯ MAINTENANCE
⬤⬤◯◯◯ FREEZE/STORE
CROPPING SEASON: LATE SUMMER–EARLY AUTUMN

To enjoy peaches, nectarines and apricots at their best it's worth trying to grow your own. They prefer a warm climate with a long growing season. However, they are fully hardy and actually need a cold period to encourage winter dormancy. But, because they flower very early – as early as late winter – the flowers do need to be protected from frost, and where pollinating insects aren't around, you'll need to pollinate the flowers yourself.

They are often grown as large specimens, trained as a fan against a sunny wall. However, there are now varieties available that are specially bred for growing in a pot. This means that they can be moved to somewhere frost-free very easily, and returned outside when the weather warms up.

Minimum temperature range
-29°C (-20°F) to -2°C (29°F).

Where to grow If you have a sunny, south- or west-facing fence or wall, then you could try growing a peach, nectarine or apricot tree against it. A tree grown on St Julien A rootstock is best for this, and it will reach around 1.8 m (5 ft 9 in) high and 4 m (13 feet) wide. You'll need to improve the soil with some well-rotted compost, and make sure the soil isn't alkaline. Plant the tree about 25 cm (10 in) away from the wall, leaning towards it. Add general-purpose fertiliser in the spring, and a mulch of homemade compost.

Peaches, nectarines and apricots all flower very early in the season. If you're growing outside, then you may need to cover the emerging flowers.

If growing in a container, plant in multi-purpose or soil-based container compost. Mix in a slow-release fertiliser and top this up each spring. Keep the plants well watered and feed with a tomato fertiliser through summer.

Ripe apricots
Succulent apricots, peaches and nectarines are now a reality for most gardeners with many smaller forms suitable for growing in a container.

POLLINATING FLOWERS

1 If pollinating insects are few and far between in early spring, consider hand-pollinating your crop. Use a paintbrush to dab pollen onto the stigma of each flower.

2 When the fruit has set, thin the fruit in early summer to around one every 10–15 cm (4–6 in).

Types and varieties

The best choice outside is to grow trees as a fan which will help protect them from the worst of the weather and the disease peach leaf curl.

The best rootstock to choose is St Julien A, then combine with one of the varieties below:

Peaches 'Duke of York' crops by mid summer. 'Peregrine', with crimson skin and white-coloured flesh, crops later, by late summer. 'Rochester' is a good, reliable cropper but also ripens in late summer. The fruits have a lovely yellow flesh.

Nectarine 'Early Rivers' is the earliest ripening, by midsummer, and has juicy, pale yellow flesh. 'Lord Napier' ripens later and has crimson-skinned fruit.

Apricots 'Moorpark' is the best of the varieties available. It ripens by late summer and has orange and red-flushed fruit.

Growing in a container

You'll need trees specially grown for this purpose. Make sure they're on the dwarf Pixy rootstock. These varieties should require very little pruning, except for removing dead, diseased or misplaced stems.

Peaches 'Bonanza', 'Garden Anny' and 'Garden Lady' all fruit in mid summer.

Nectarine 'Nectarella' is a good choice for patio nectarines.

Apricot 'Golden Aprigold' and 'Golden Glow' are the best on offer.

Pests and diseases

If you're growing in a greenhouse or conservatory, peaches, nectarines, and apricots can suffer from spider mite. Here, the biological control *Phytoseiulus* mite introduced onto the tree will help to control them.

Outside, there can be worse problems. Peach leaf curl is a fungal disease that affects both peaches and nectarines, and to some extent apricots. It causes blistering on the leaves which become distorted and die. You can spray with a copper-based fungicide, but the best control is to try to keep the tree dry between mid-winter and mid-spring.

Pruning and training

The best time for pruning is in summer. If the tree is growing up against a wall or fence, follow the advice for cherries on formative pruning to get the shape you want. Trees fruit on year-old wood. Each year, prune most of the side shoots out, but keep a couple and tie these in through the summer. In late summer, cut out the shoots that have fruited and the ones you tied in will replace these the following year.

Harvesting and storage

The best time to harvest peaches, nectarines and apricots is when they're ripe, or almost ripe. If the flesh is soft and the fruit easily comes away from the tree, it's ready. While ripe fruit can be eaten straight away, any unripe fruit can be laid out carefully to ripen indoors.

In the kitchen

Best used as fresh fruit.

CALENDAR

EARLY SPRING

YEAR 1

Dig over the soil well and plant your tree. If you are growing against a wall, attach horizontal wires set at no less than 60-cm (2-ft) intervals. Cut back to start to train as a fan.

YEAR 2 ONWARDS

Keep the protection against frost and peach leaf curl that you erected in late autumn or winter in place. Mulch the tree well every year and add a good few handfuls of general-purpose fertiliser.

MID-SPRING

Hand-pollinate if necessary. Remove any polythene protection you had in place.

LATE SPRING

Start to tie in growth against the horizontal wires. Thin fruits when they reach the size of a walnut.

EARLY SUMMER

Water the tree in the first couple of years, and if the weather is dry thereafter.

MIDSUMMER

Start to pick fruits as they ripen.

LATE SUMMER

Keep picking fruits. If you need to prune in later years, now is a good time to do it. Trees fruit on stems produced the previous year, so old stems, including ones that have fruited, need to be slowly replaced with new ones to boost your harvest.

WINTER

Erect a rain and frost protection cover for your tree.

VARIETY SELECTOR
Container
Peaches
• 'Bonanza', 'Garden Anny', 'Garden Lady': all fruit in midsummer.
Nectarines
• 'Nectarella': good choice for the patio.
Apricot
• 'Golden Aprigold', 'Golden Glow': the best.

VARIETY SELECTOR
Outdoors
Peaches
• 'Duke of York', 'Peregrine', 'Rochester'.
Nectarines
• 'Early Rivers', 'Lord Napier'.
Apricots
• 'Moorpark'.

Plump figs
Figs can be more productive than you think, and kept under control, can make extremely handsome garden plants.

Fig

Keep a fig tree contained and it will reward you with sweet, sticky fruit in late summer.

✿✿✿✿✿	VALUE FOR MONEY
✿✿✿✿✿	MAINTENANCE
✿✿✿✿✿	FREEZE/STORE
CROPPING SEASON: LATE SUMMER–EARLY AUTUMN	

The fruits of the fig tree are somehow rather exotic. Despite being grown in the UK since the 16th century, it wasn't until the 18th century that they became popular in walled gardens. Here, the warmth and shelter of the wall encouraged fruit-ripening. They are widely grown with little attention all over the Mediterranean where the low rainfall, absence of frosts and long, hot summers encourage two crops of figs a year. In other areas, just one late summer crop is as good as you can hope for.

CREATING A PLANTING PIT

1 Dig out a pit and line it with four vertically placed paving slabs to create a square-shaped planting hole. Aim for a hole around 45 cm (18 in) deep and 60 cm (2 ft) square. The tops of the slabs should stand above the soil surface so roots can't grow over. Fill the bottom 10–15cm (4–6 in) with broken pots or rubble.

2 Fill the pit with soil and plant the tree in the centre, but lean it towards the wall.

3 Cut back the main stem by a third and after attaching wires or canes to the wall, start to encourage the tree into a fan shape.

Minimum temperature range

-12°C (10°F) and above.

Where to grow

Fig trees are extremely vigorous, and will happily produce a plentiful supply of leaves, at the expense of fruit. For that reason, to be successful, it's best to try to contain the roots. Either grow in a container or line the planting pit with impermeable materials (see below left).

Against a south- or west-facing wall is a good place to site a fig. The foundations of the wall will help to curtail its growth, and the drier conditions suits the plant well. However, during spring and summer the plant may require some additional watering if it is very dry. It's also a good idea to add a handful of general-purpose fertiliser to the base of the tree.

Figs are generally fairly unfussy about the soil they grow in, but they do need it to be well drained. If your soil is heavy, try adding some grit or well-rotted compost.

Types and varieties

Unlike other fruit trees, figs haven't been grafted onto more well-behaved rootstocks – hence the need to curtail their growth. However, this makes choosing a variety to grow much easier.

Once you've chosen the variety, you'll need to decide on the shape of tree to buy. Trees are often sold as 'bushes' in small pots. These are young trees that will take some time to settle in. Alternatively, you can buy larger forms, in the shape of a fan, for example – perfect for growing against a wall. If you're thinking of growing in a container, select either a young tree, or a larger, multi-stemmed bush.

Pruning and training

To create a fan against a wall, you'll need to do most of your pruning in spring after the worst of the frosts are over. By summer, you'll need to start tying in the developing shoots, so the fruit can start to ripen. It's a good idea to pinch out the growing tips in summer too to encourage fruit ripening.

In a container, consider aiming for a multi-stemmed bush. This encourages more fruit to set. A couple of years after planting, prune the tree to ground level. This will encourage lots of shoots to emerge from underground. Removing around a third of them each year will keep encouraging more to be produced and keep the plant small.

Pests and diseases

Figs are generally trouble-free. Birds will probably be your worst pest – they have a habit of picking the fruit just before they're ripe. Here, netting the tree is your only option.

Harvesting and storage

Figs develop on the axils of the leaves in young side shoots. They develop in autumn and over winter as small pea-sized fruit. They grow on the following year and start to ripen from mid- to late summer. You'll need to pick figs when they're ripe. You can tell they're ripe as they look heavy, hang downwards and often start to split. If the fruit is a little under-ripe, it can be ripenened on a sunny windowsill. To appreciate their flavour, eat soon after picking.

In the kitchen

Figs are often eaten as fresh fruit, straight from the garden. The skin can be easily peeled off and the sweet, sticky flesh eaten. Alternatively, consider using in salads with mozzarella and Parma ham. If you really have too many, they can be dried – cut in half, sprinkle with a little sugar and place in a warm oven direct on the rack for a few hours. The dried fruits can be eaten as a snack. You can also turn them into jam.

VARIETY SELECTOR

• **'Brown Turkey'**: considered to be the most reliable variety. Produces a good crop of purple fruits with sweet, red flesh.

• **'Violetta'**: a really tough fig – thought to be the hardiest, and produces exceptionally flavoured fruit.

CALENDAR

LATE SPRING

YEAR 1

Usually bought in a container, fig trees are best bought in late spring when the worst of the winter weather is over. Restrict root growth by creating a planting pit to encourage heavier fruiting.

YEAR 2 ONWARDS

Cut back as hard as you like, creating a shape that suits your garden. Cut out crossing, damaged or diseased branches too. Some figs may be set now, but if the season is short they will not ripen.

EARLY SUMMER

Water your tree, especially in the first few years. If you have restricted the roots, they may struggle to find enough water during dry spells, so water when necessary.

MID- TO LATE SUMMER

Pinch out the growing tips, which encourages more fruit to be set. These 'embryo' fruit should overwinter and ripen by next summer. Check fruit regularly and pick when ripe. You may need to protect developing fruits from birds.

AUTUMN

If you're likely to have a cold winter you can protect the developing fruit with fleece; however, in reality this is difficult to achieve.

EARLY SPRING

YEAR 2 ONWARDS

Apply a couple of handfuls of general-purpose fertiliser, plus a good layer of homemade compost.

SOFT FRUITS

Strawberries, raspberries and currants are the taste of summer. New varieties are now extremely high-yielding as well as bursting with flavour. While they're both healthy and nutritious, most soft fruits are also easy to grow and despite being expensive in the supermarket, at home this is one glut you won't mind having to deal with.

Strawberry

The sweet, succulent fruit of the strawberry is synonymous with summer.

○○○○○	VALUE FOR MONEY
○○○○○	MAINTENANCE
○○○○○	FREEZE/STORE

CROPPING SEASON: LATE SPRING–MID-AUTUMN

The strawberry has got to be one of the easiest fruits to grow. These small plants can be fitted into any garden – even window boxes will happily take a few plants – and their fruits are bright, fragrant and sweetly flavoured.

They're perfect for larger fruit gardens too. If you manage to keep the weeds off, a row of strawberry plants will provide kilos of fruit throughout the summer.

The large red strawberries we know today have been bred from the Chilean strawberry and the North American strawberry. A relatively new fruit compared to most, it wasn't until the early 20th century that breeding really took off. Today, however, they're a favourite in both gardens and supermarkets, and there are a wide range of varieties and types to choose from.

Succulent strawberries
A couple of years after planting, your strawberry plants will be rewarding you with kilos of fruit through the summer months.

Strawberry plants don't last that long, however; traditionally they're grown for just three years. At that point you dig out the old plants and start again. But as they're simple to propagate, you shouldn't have to buy any more.

Minimum temperature range
-40°C (-40°F) to 5°C (40°F).

Where to grow
Strawberries are a bit fussy when it comes to soil. They don't like it too wet, or too alkaline or too sandy. If you don't have perfect loam, the best solution is to add plenty of well-rotted organic matter.

The berries have a tendency to rot off if left on the soil surface too. Traditionally, growers would spread straw underneath the developing fruits to protect them. Nowadays strawberries are often grown through plastic sheeting that both keeps the soil warm and weed-free and protects the fruit.

If you don't have a large area to devote to strawberries, they can be added to your vegetable garden as a one- or two-year crop, or even grown in the ornamental garden. The leaves, flowers and small fruit of the alpine strawberry are extremely pretty in themselves and will thrive in a dry, shady spot.

Strawberries can also do well in containers, as long as they're well looked after. Using a large container will cut down on the amount of watering that's required, and in the summer they'll need feeding with a tomato feed to encourage flowering and fruiting. In a window box or hanging basket, go for the alpine strawberry.

Types and varieties
Strawberries have been bred to fruit at different times. You'll often see varieties advertised as early, mid-season or late varieties. In reality, this can mean picking your fruit from

Delicate alpine strawberries
Smaller alpine strawberries are intensely flavoured, and are also good for dry, shady areas of the garden.

Container strawberries
Strawberries make excellent container plants. Keep them well fed and watered and they'll reward you with an excellent harvest, free from slug and snail damage.

late spring to midsummer. To extend your harvest, it's a good idea to choose a couple of varieties of different seasons. There are also varieties known as perpetual. These varieties typically fruit for longer – often into autumn.

The best time to buy strawberries is late summer to autumn. Planted at this time, the plants will be able to settle in and start cropping well the following year. Strawberries are often sold throughout the year, and many nurseries will sell right into early summer and promise a crop for that year.

Pests and diseases Strawberries can suffer from a range of pests and diseases. To keep these at bay, encourage good, strong growth by ensuring the soil is weed-free, fertile and water-retentive.

Aphids can be a problem and here you'll need to spray with an organic pesticide. Slugs can feed on the fruit. Use a sprinkling of organic slug pellets to keep these at bay. Vine

weevil can eat the roots of plants, particularly those kept in containers or under plastic sheeting. You can use a nematode biological control if they cause you a real problem. Grey mould can be a problem in wet areas. Thin out the leaves on plants to encourage some air movement and remove affected fruit. Remove runners as they develop and once cropping is finished it's a good idea to cut down all the old foliage and destroy. New, clean shoots will soon regrow.

Harvesting and storage
Strawberries can be picked ripe between spring and autumn. Growing a crop in the greenhouse can also extend the harvest. Plants should be picked over at least twice a week. Strawberries can be frozen, but are not anywhere as good as when fresh.

In the kitchen If you sicken of fresh strawberries, either on their own or with a

PROPAGATING STRAWBERRIES

1 After a couple of years, your strawberry crop will start to decline. In the summer, plants will produce runners – long stems from the main plant. Select a runner and cut off in order to create the new plant.

2 Along each runner will be small plants developing with their own leaves and the start of some roots. Cut a single plant off and plant into small pots filled with multi-purpose compost. Water well and leave in a sheltered spot.

3 By autumn the plants can be planted out in the garden. Plant strawberry plants every 45 cm (18 in). Although their crop will be small in the first year, it will increase dramatically by the second year.

'Eros'
A mid-season cropper with attractive berries, which have a conical shape and a well-balanced flavour.

VARIETY SELECTOR

New varieties are being bred all the time and released each year.

Early season

- 'Rosie', 'Honeoye', 'Elsanta'.

Mid-season

- 'Alice', 'Amelia', 'Eros'.

Late season

- 'Sophie', 'Rhapsody', 'Symphony'.

Perpetual

- 'Mailing Pearl', 'Flamenco', 'Evie 2'.

dollop of cream, and you're tired of fruit puddings and pavlovas, excess strawberries can be made into jam, which will give you the taste of summer in the depths of winter.

Pest protection
Keep the birds off your crop with fine mesh, which can either be supported with a series of hoops (see below) or draped right over the plants.

CALENDAR

EARLY SPRING

Pull back the mulch you applied in winter when growth begins.

SPRING

Strawberries are sold through most of the year and can be successfully planted in spring, autumn or even early summer. Prepare the soil by digging over well and removing any weeds. Add some well-rotted organic matter. You can lay a row of black plastic sheeting over the soil and bury the edges in the soil using a spade, ensuring the surface is kept tight to avoid puddles collecting. Cut slits in the plastic and plant every 45 cm (18 in).

SUMMER

In dry weather, water through the planting hole under the plastic. Avoid watering onto the foliage directly as this can encourage diseases to spread. Consider giving a liquid feed to the strawberries, such as a tomato feed, which will encourage more fruit to set.

If you haven't used plastic sheeting, you can apply a mulch around the plants. This can be anything from straw to cardboard, or even 'strawberry mats' that you can buy. This helps to keep the fruits dry and stops them rotting as they ripen. Cut off runners if you don't need them for propagation and pick fruits as they ripen. If birds are getting to the crop before you, consider draping over some netting.

AUTUMN

You may still get a few fruits, but most should have finished by now.

WINTER

By the end of winter your plants will be looking fairly tatty. Cut back the old growth and new stems should soon appear.

Raspberry

Ripe, sweet raspberries just dropping off the plant are one of the joys of growing food. This plant is one not to be missed.

ooooo VALUE FOR MONEY
ooooo MAINTENANCE
ooooo FREEZE/STORE
CROPPING SEASON: EARLY SUMMER–MID-AUTUMN

Long-fruiting raspberry season
With careful selection of a couple of different raspberry varieties, it's possible to have fruit from early summer right into mid-autumn.

Raspberries are expensive to buy in the supermarket. This is because the fruits are tricky to pick and don't transport well. Fortunately, growing your own couldn't be easier.

They crop heavily too – each plant will produce well over 1 kg (2 lb) of fruit, and as you need only a small amount of space and the plants require little care and attention, they are definitely worth a go.

Minimum temperature range
-40°C (-40°F) to -13°C (9°F).

Where to grow
Raspberries prefer a slightly acidic soil of between pH 6–6.5. If your soil is more alkaline than this, add sulphur. They don't do particularly well on sandy or clay soil either, but you can improve your soil structure easily with the addition of well-rotted organic matter, such as homemade compost or composted bark, which tends to be a bit on the acid side.

Raspberries prefer a sheltered spot and will crop most heavily in full sun, although they'll thrive in partial shade too.

While autumn-fruiting types don't need any support, summer-fruiting types will need a series of stakes and horizontal wires to help keep their canes upright. As raspberries will remain in the same spot for many years, consider creating a special area for your raspberries: they'll need a bed around 1 m (3 ft 2 in) wide, but often a double row 2 m (6 ft 5 in) apart is better for netting and picking. Unfortunately, raspberries don't do well in a pot, so they're worth growing only if you have some outdoor space.

Types and varieties
Raspberries grow on canes, which grow from the base of the plant each year. One job each year will be to

TIP

If you've bought your plants but either not got the time to plant or the weather is too bad, you can wait until early spring. Just plant the canes in a trench making sure the roots are covered, and they'll happily sit there all winter.

Ripe raspberries
Fruit is ripe when the whole berry slips off the plant, leaving the core on the plant.

cut the old canes back, but how and when you do this will depend on the type you grow.

So, before you go any further with raspberries, you'll need to decide which type to grow. There are two main types and many people tend to grow both – this way you can extend the picking season.

The first type are known as floricane or summer-fruiting. They fruit on canes produced the previous year. They're a bit tricky to manage as while you're picking fruit off old canes, new canes will be growing, which you need to tie in.

The second type are much easier to look after. They are the primocane or autumn-fruiting raspberries. They fruit later in the summer, but fruit on the canes produced earlier in the year. As they don't have as much time to grow, the canes don't get as big and don't need supporting with posts and wires unlike summer-fruiting types.

How to grow The best time to buy raspberry canes is in the late autumn. They'll be sold as bare-rooted plants, usually in bundles of six, 10 or 12. Look for stout canes with tightly closed but →

PRUNING SUMMER- AND AUTUMN-FRUITING RASPBERRY BUSHES

SUMMER-FRUITING VARIETIES

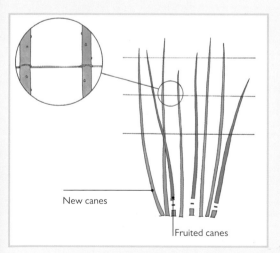

New canes

Fruited canes

Summer-fruiting raspberries carry their fruit on year-old stems. In the dormant season, cut out all those canes that have fruited, then tie in the new canes produced during the summer. If in time the clumps become congested, thin the canes to about 7.5 cm (3 in) apart.

AUTUMN-FRUITING VARIETIES

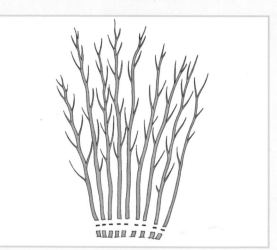

Autumn-fruiting varieties carry their fruit on the current season's growth, so pruning is extremely simple. Just cut all the canes down to ground level during the dormant season.

'All Gold'
This pale yellow variety of raspberry, 'All Gold', is good but not as productive as 'Autumn Bliss'.

healthy-looking buds. The roots should be dense and fibrous. Plants will need to be spaced at around 45 cm (18 in) between cane so your selected site will determine how man you buy.

Once you've chosen your site and bought your canes, you'll need to get them in the ground.

If you're growing summer-fruiting raspberries, you'll also need to create some support for the canes, and it's best to get this in place before planting (see below).

Dig over the soil and add plenty of organic matter. Raspberries don't like to be planted too deeply, and their roots spread just underground, so aim to plant just below the soil surface.

You won't get much of a crop in the first year, but if you prune appropriately and ever spring, add a couple of handfuls of a general-purpose fertiliser and a good mulch of garder compost, the plants should last for many year

SUPPORTING SUMMER-FRUITING RASPBERRIES

1 The easiest support consists of single posts and horizontal wires.

2 Using 2.4-m (7 ft 8 in) high posts, drive them into the ground by about 60 cm (3 ft), spaced 3 m (9 ft 8 in) apart.

3 Fix galvanised wire horizontally between the posts at 90 cm (3 ft) and 1.5 m (5 ft) high.

Pests, diseases and other problems

Although raspberries are among the easiest perennial fruit to prune, they do have a few enemies.

There are several fungal diseases that affect the canes of raspberries, such as cane spot and spur blight. The easiest way to manage raspberry diseases is to make sure that you cut out the old canes right down to the base each year and destroy them if they are diseased.

Birds may steal the fruit as it ripens. If birds are a problem, you'll have to consider building a structure around your canes so you can drape netting over during the fruiting season.

The other problem you may encounter is leaf mottling and poor growth. This is usually down to the growing conditions and availability of nutrients.

If the youngest leaves are yellowing, you'll need to feed with sequestered iron. If the older leaves are yellowing but the veins remain green, then Epson salts will provide the magnesium pick-me-up that they need.

Harvesting and storage

Raspberries can be harvested over a fairly long period, especially if you're growing both types. Fruit will be ready for picking when it's bright red and comes away easily from the plug. Picked berries will last longer if they're not squashed so choose a wide bowl or tray to keep them in – this also allows any bugs and small spiders to escape as you pick.

Once inside, raspberries can easily be frozen. Just bag them up in weighed amounts for jam making later, or lay them on a tray and freeze. If frozen on a tray, they keep their shape as you tip the frozen ones into a bag.

In the kitchen

Raspberries can be used fresh in summer desserts, sprinkled over ice cream or turned into purée. However, at some point during the season it's likely you'll have a glut. Fortunately raspberry jam is among the best-tasting of preserves.

CALENDAR

LATE AUTUMN
Buy your raspberry canes, improve the soil with organic matter, and plant shallowly.

SPRING/SUMMER
Mulch and add fertiliser each year in the spring. Water the plants in the first couple of years to get them established, especially during dry spells. They shouldn't need too much watering after that. You won't get much of a crop in your first year, but that will soon change. Follow advice for Year 1 for the type of raspberry you have, then subsequent years thereafter.

SUMMER-FRUITING RASPBERRIES
YEAR 1
As new canes grow out from the base, tie in new growth to horizontal wires.

YEAR 2
Canes grown last year and tied in will start to fruit. New canes will start to grow, which need to be roughly tied in. At the end of Year 2, cut down canes that have fruited to the ground. Spread out new canes along the horizontal wires and tie in.

YEAR 3 ONWARDS
Repeat Year 2.

AUTUMN-FRUITING RASPBERRIES
SUMMER YEAR 1
Cut down all last year's canes to the base at the beginning of the year. New canes will emerge. There's no need to tie in.

SUMMER YEAR 2
Cut down all last year's canes to the base at the beginning of the year. New canes will emerge. There's no need to tie in. They should start to fruit by late summer.

YEAR 3 ONWARDS
Repeat Year 2.

4 Plant in between the posts. As the canes grow, tie them onto the wires. If they grow above the wire, curve them over and tie them in along the top of the wire.

'Glen Ample'
'Glen Ample' is bred in Scotland, can survive tougher weather conditions and crops well through the summer.

Blackberry and hybrid berries

Juicy blackberries
Blackberries can be very productive, and if you don't have wild brambles growing nearby, it's worth having at least one plant in the garden.

You'll only need a single plant to produce enough dark, juicy clusters of fruit for the kitchen.

○○○○○	VALUE FOR MONEY
○○○○○	MAINTENANCE
○○○○○	FREEZE/STORE

CROPPING SEASON: MIDSUMMER–MID-AUTUMN

Blackberries and hybrid berries have the most delicious aroma and wild, juicy flavour, but their popularity in the garden is rather limited. It may be because the plants, on the whole, grow large, with some needing around 4 m (13 ft) of wall or fence space. It also may be because the spines of many are fierce, and pruning a blackberry becomes quite a tricky task. Or it may be because wild blackberries are often to be found growing nearby, giving the gardener free access to a large wild crop. If, however, you don't have a wild clump of brambles near your home, fortunately there are now smaller, better-behaved varieties of blackberries and hybrid berries that have been bred without spines, perfect for growing up a wall, or post.

Minimum temperature range
-29°C (-20°F) to -8°C (19°F).

Where to grow All blackberries and hybrid berries need some support for their

CARING FOR BLACKBERRIES AND HYBRID BERRIES

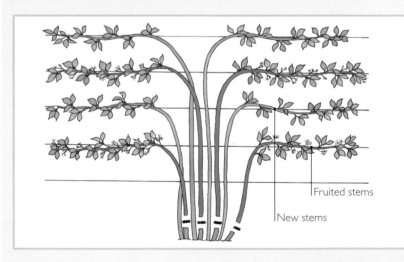

Fruited stems

New stems

1 As new stems emerge, tie them onto the horizontal wire frame using soft string.

2 Only last years stem's will fruit – pick the fruits as they become ready.

3 At the end of fruiting, cut back fruited stems to the ground (see above). Next year's fruit will come from this year's stems.

VARIETY SELECTOR

Best of the blackberries

- **'Chester'**: a cold-hardy, thornless blackberry.

- **'Black Butte'**: huge berries are produced by this variety, but you'll need to keep tying it to its supports.

- **'Triple Crown'**: a large-fruiting, thornless variety with excellent flavour.

VARIETY SELECTOR

Best of the hybrid berries

- **'Buckingham Tayberry'**: a spine-free version of the tayberry with large, red fruit from mid summer onward.s

- **'Boysenberry'**: the berries are much darker, producing large black berries. Needs plenty of space.

- **'Loganberry Thornless'**: another spine-free version of an old favourite, producing large, red fruit in the summer.

wild stems. A wall or fence is fine with horizontal wires attached. Alternatively, you can set up a series of posts and wires in open ground as with summer-fruiting raspberries. Another alternative is to allow plants to scramble over a pergola or arch. Whichever you go for, you'll have to be prepared for pruning throughout the year.

Blackberries do best in sun, but will also thrive with some shade too. They're not the most attractive of plants, so pick a spot that's out of the way and used for little else.

In the ground Wherever you decide to plant you'll need to get the soil prepared beforehand. On the whole, blackberries are fairly unfussy about the soil, however, plants do prefer it slightly acidic. They don't like waterlogged soils and prefer good, deep, rich soil. It's a good idea to add a few bucket loads of homemade compost before you plant.

They flower later than other fruits so are unlikely to be affected by frost. They're tough too, so are a good choice for cold gardens.

Types and varieties Wild blackberries have always grown along the edges of woodlands and on scrubby ground, particularly where the soil is good. Prior to 100 or so years ago very little breeding was carried out as these wild plants were bountiful enough on their own. More recently, however, breeding has attempted to increase the size of fruit, reduce the size of plants and remove the thorns. There are now a fairly large number of blackberry varieties available.

Hybrid berries are the result of the ability of the blackberry to cross with the raspberry. They grow in much the same way as blackberries and require the same amount of space and pruning regime, but their fruits are often larger and redder. The first hybrid berry to be discovered was the loganberry in 1883 in Santa Cruz, USA.

Since then, breeders have purposely crossed blackberries and raspberries to create plants that produce these blackberry-like fruits that are ready to harvest earlier in the season.

Pests and diseases Generally trouble-free, but birds can be a problem. Fine mesh will be your only solution to prevent birds from stealing your harvest.

Harvesting and storage Blackberries will start to ripen in midsummer, but may go on into autumn. The fruits will be ready for picking when they turn from red to a shiny black colour. It's harder to tell with hybrid berries, and depending on the variety they may still be bright red when ripe. Try picking a couple of berries to try before you start picking a whole plant. Some varieties can crop very heavily – you may get up to 10 kg (22 lb) of fruit from a single plant.

Lay the fruit out on a tray outside once picked. Any spiders or other bugs should escape before you take them into the kitchen.

Fresh fruit doesn't last long so should be eaten immediately. Alternatively, they can be laid on a tray and frozen. Once frozen, tip them into a freezer bag. This way their shape is kept intact.

In the kitchen The fantastic flavour and aroma of blackberries can be kept all year in a jar. Making jam with a large crop of blackberries is ideal. For smaller harvests, try adding to summer puddings, or for a later harvest, combine with apples to make crumbles and pies.

Loganberries
Hybrid berries are a cross between blackberries and raspberries. They generally produce larger fruit than blackberries but retain some of the aroma of wild brambles.

CALENDAR

SPRING

YEAR 1
Plant shallowly in the soil, spreading the roots to encourage the production of new shoots. Ensure you have wires in place to attach the new growth.

SUBSEQUENT YEARS
Add a good layer of mulch, such as homemade compost, and a handful of general-purpose fertiliser.

SUMMER

YEAR 1
As the new shoots emerge, tie them into the support system.

SUBSEQUENT YEARS
New shoots will need to be tied in, but keep these separate from last year's stems. Start to pick fruit from last year's stems.

AUTUMN

YEAR 1
There'll be no fruit in the first year, but don't prune back the plants.

SUBSEQUENT YEARS
Keep picking fruit.

WINTER

YEAR 1
Nothing to do.

SUBSEQUENT YEARS
Once fruiting has finished, cut out all fruiting canes at the base. Re-tie this year's growth, spreading it out along all the wires.

TENDER FRUIT

If you just can't help but try to grow something tricky, go for one of the tender fruits. You'll need hot, sunny conditions for long periods, but if you get good weather you may well be able to show off an exotic fruit salad to your dinner guests.

Kiwi

If you have a warm garden, a kiwi can add an exotic touch to your edible garden, but beware: they need plenty of space.

◖◖◗◗◗ VALUE FOR MONEY
◖◖◗◗◗ MAINTENANCE
◖◖◗◗◗ FREEZE/STORE
CROPPING SEASON: LATE AUTUMN

Kiwis are also often known as Chinese gooseberries – referring to where they grow in the wild. This large, rampant plant produces broad, downy leaves, fragrant white flowers and brown-skinned furry fruits with a sweet green pulp. Since they are exotic plants, they need a warm site and temperatures in between 5 and 25°C (41 and 77°F) to fruit. They will grow in colder areas, but the production of fruit may be limited. Kiwis grow into huge plants, so they need lots of space and pruning.

Minimum temperature range

-40°C (-40°F) to 5°C (40°F), depending on variety.

Where to grow

Kiwis twine and clamber as they grow and need appropriate supports to keep them from flopping. This is usually achieved by a series of posts and wires or even trellises attached away from the wall. The wall should be west- or south-facing, and away from any harsh winds, which kiwis hate. You could try growing them in a conservatory or greenhouse, but as they grow so large, they will soon take over. If you have plenty of room in a polytunnel, however, then it may be worth devoting some space.

Kiwis prefer a pH of 6–7 and good soil, rich in organic matter.

Tender vines
The kiwi needs warm temperatures to produce a good crop.

Types and varieties

In the past, you had to grow a male plant to pollinate a female plant. However, recent breeding means you can now buy self-fertile varieties which do away with the need for a male plant. Unfortunately, this has also resulted in the fruit on these varieties being somewhat smaller than those produced by the older types.

Pests and diseases

Kiwis are generally trouble-free.

Harvesting and storage

It will take three to eight years before vines start producing fruit. Kiwis should be ready for picking by the autumn, and a slight squeeze of the fruit will tell you whether they've softened and are ripe. They keep for weeks if picked slightly under-ripe.

In the kitchen

This fruit is best eaten fresh, added to fruit salads or cheesecakes or even turned into juice.

CALENDAR

WINTER
Plant kiwis at least 50 cm (20 in) away from a south- or west-facing wall, or against a series of horizontal wires fixed between sturdy posts. They'll need around 5 m (16 ft 4 in) of wall space.

SPRING
Mulch plants well with organic matter and sprinkle a handful of general-purpose fertiliser every year.

SUMMER
Train shoots onto the wires, tying in as you go. Kiwis fruit on shoots growing off one-year-old wood so it's best to create a framework of shoots that can be cut back each year.

AUTUMN
After a few years, your plant should be producing fruit that should ripen in early autumn.

WINTER
Cut back stems that have fruited back almost to your established framework along the wires. Make sure those stems produced this year (which should fruit next summer) have been tied in.

TIP

To boost your harvest, in early summer cut shoots which are bearing fruit to five leaves above where the fruit are developing. This encourages the fruits to swell and ripen.

VARIETY SELECTOR

- **'Jenny'**: a self-fertile variety that produces fairly small fruit.
- **'Solo'**: another self-fertile variety with vigorous growth and smallish fruit.

NUTS

There are not many nuts that are
worth growing in the garden, but
if you have the space, cobnuts and
filberts, almonds and walnuts are
worth trying. They need little care or
attention, but you may need to wait
a few years before you see any nuts.

PART 3: HOW TO GROW

Once you've selected the varieties you want to grow, you'll need to kit yourself and your garden out to make sure you're prepared for any eventuality. From the equipment you need to finding out more about your soil and how to improve it, it's worth learning more about the tools and techniques that make for a successful food garden.

BUY OR HIRE?

ROTOVATOR

Another piece of equipment that is very useful, especially on largers plots or allotments, is a rotovator. The petrol version is very expensive, and as you'll only be using it a couple of times a year when the beds are empty, this may not be cost-effective. You can rent rotovators from rental shops, but again, cost can be prohibitive. If you are part of a gardening club, allotment society, or just have gardening-friendly neighbours, consider chipping in together to get one to share. Aim for one that is easy to start and easy to maintain.

There's also another type of hoe, often used on the vegetable plot but more commonly used for drawing up soil and creating drills. Onion hoes or draw hoes can be useful for earthing up potatoes, say, or when you want to create long lengths of drills.

Trowel and hand fork Although a trowel is an essential piece of kit for planting, a hand fork is more useful for weeding on your hands and knees. They often come as a pair, and it's worth having them both in your armoury. Make sure the handles are comfortable. A wooden handle is usually the best, along with a stainless steel blade or tines. Trowels and hand forks are renowned for bending under pressure, so look at the shaft and make sure there are no weak joints.

Use a marker line
A marker line is useful when planting out to ensure you plant your seedlings in straight rows.

Tools for cutting

Cutting back soft fruit and pruning fruit trees requires a good pair of secateurs. Go for the bypass type. While anvils are more useful for cutting dead wood, bypass secateurs can cut both live and dead wood effectively. Select a pair that is comfortable to hold – they are sold in different sizes so try before you buy. And make sure the catch is easy to reach, whichever hand you use. Blades should be sharp and easily sharpened when necessary. The best secateurs will allow you to have blades replaced once worn out. Finally, go for a pair with bright handles as you'll often lose them in a pile of prunings.

Loppers, which are basically long-handled secateurs, are good for thicker stems and awkward-to-reach places. Again, a bypass pair is best. Pruning saws are a good choice too if you have a lot of fruit trees. They can give a cleaner cut than loppers and are sometimes easier to use in tricky-to-reach places. Blades often fold inside the handle for easy carrying.

Moving things around the garden

A plastic, flexible carry trug is one of the most useful recent introductions for the gardener. They are excellent for harvesting crops or collecting weeds or prunings. One of these is essential for a garden of any size, and as they come in such a wide range of colours, there'll be one to fit your style.

On top of this, a wheelbarrow is always a good investment – useful for carrying heavier or more awkward materials around the garden, such as compost and young plants. Go for one with a pneumatic tyre and a plastic pan. Make sure the handles are comfortable and that it has a good balance – you don't want it to tip over when it's full of your prize plants.

There is a range of other trolleys and pot movers available to the gardener, but most things can be carried in either a trug or barrow.

Measuring and planting equipment

A marker line, basically made of two pieces of wood with a string attached to each piece, is always useful when it comes to planting straight rows. Alternatively, use a wide plank, marked at spacing intervals. This can be kneeled on over the bed while you plant. Or use a narrower rod or ruler that can be used for spacing. Once you get your eye trained, you'll probably end up leaving this one in the shed, but it can be useful when you first start out.

Tools for harvesting

A sharp folding knife is really useful for the gardener. As well as using it to harvest crops such as courgettes, cucumbers and grapes, it's also useful for cutting string when you want to quickly tie something in. Choose a small one, with a comfy handle and a sharp blade that easily folds in and out. Other tools, such as a good pair of scissors or snippers, can also be useful for harvesting crops.

Hoe your plot

Spring and autumn are the key times for hoeing, but weeds can soon appear at any time following rain. It's best to keep your plot fairly weed free at all times to stop it getting out of hand.

MAINTAINING YOUR TOOLS

- Keep your tools somewhere dry. A shed or a garage is perfect.

- Try to keep them as clean as you can, which helps prevent them from rusting.

- For tools like secateurs, use an oily rag to keep them in good shape.

- Some tools will need to be sharpened – usually on an annual basis. There are a range of sharpeners available to the gardener – go for one that will allow you to sharpen all your tools.

SOWING SEED

Whatever container you're sowing seed in, you'll need to follow the germination advice provided here.

- First, select either a sowing or multi-purpose compost. Most vegetable seeds aren't too fussy, and you could use a good-quality peat-free version.

- When sowing seed on the surface of the compost, aim to sprinkle the seed evenly. When planting individual seeds, place in the middle of the pot, and for courgettes, cucumbers and other flat-seeded vegetables, it's best to place them on their side.

- In a module, you may want to plant two seeds, then if both come up, just pinch out the weaker one – this will ensure you don't have any gaps later.

- A fine sprinkling of compost can be used to cover the seed, helping to retain moisture, or alternatively you can use a dusting of vermiculite, which is useful for those seeds that require light to germinate, such as celery.

- Water with tap water and use a fine rose to ensure the seeds don't get washed down through the compost.

Prick out your seedlings
If you have sown your seeds in a seed tray, you will need to prick out young plants into individual pots.

Pots, trays and modules

Traditionally, seeds are sown in large seed trays, and once germinated, they can be pricked out into individual small pots. To save time, seed can either be sown directly into pots or into module trays. Module trays are trays that have been divided into separate growing units. They're usually square so you can fit plenty of plants into a single tray. For most people who want to raise a lot of plants but don't have lots of time and space, module trays are the best choice. These can also be fitted into propagators, or clingfilm can be placed over the surface of the tray until seedlings start to appear.

Pricking out

If you've sown individually in pots or modules, you won't need to prick out seedlings, but for those you sowed in open trays, once the seedlings have germinated they need to be transferred to individual pots. Fill small pots with multi-purpose compost and use a pencil to create a small hole in the centre. Then, using the pencil, plant label or similar, gently tease out the seedlings from the soil of the tray. Only pick up the seedling by the tip of the leaf, never the stem, which can be easily damaged. Then lower into the prepared hole and carefully firm up. These transplanted seedlings will need a bit of care and attention for the next few days until they settle into their new home.

Aftercare

Once plants have grown on in their pots and modules, they will be ready for planting out. Plants that you are keeping in a container can be planted out into larger containers as soon as they're ready. Other plants that are to be planted out in the soil, such as peas and broad beans, are fairly unfussy when they get planted out. Other tender vegetables, such as sweetcorn and runner beans, will need to be kept under cover until the conditions are right.

If you are keeping your plants in small containers for a long time, bear in mind that the fertiliser in the potting soil will only last for around five weeks. After this, it's a good idea to apply a liquid fertiliser or pot on into a larger container. It's also a good idea not to sow too early as they dislike being left in small pots for a long time, and sometimes struggle to recover once planted out.

Using covers

Covers can be used to cover the soil and raise the temperature to help seeds get a head start.

Fleece

The most economical cover, fleece can be used on the surface

Flourishing seedlings
In mid-spring your greenhouse should be packed with young plants and seedlings. Having a removable bench will allow you to squeeze more into the space you have available.

MAKING SOWING EASIER

Most seed comes in its natural state; however, some is treated to make sowing easier and more successful.

Seed mats These are mats that have been impregnated with seed. They're usually sold to fit into a small or large container for container growing, and are ideal for some herbs such as basil. It also means you don't need to handle small, tricky seeds.

Seed tapes For vegetables usually grown in rows, you can buy tape impregnated with seed every few centimetres. Typically, these are available for vegetables such as lettuce, carrot and parsnip, and again are ideal if you struggle to handle small seed. However, your choice of varieties may be limited.

Treated and pelleted seed Most seed available for amateur gardeners is not treated, but some may be treated with a fungicide. It will say on the packet if this is the case. Others may be pelleted (surrounded in a clay-like casing to make seeds bigger and therefore easier to handle).

of the soil after you've sown your crop. It will help lift the temperature underneath it by a few degrees and encourage germination. You'll need to anchor the edges with bricks or pieces of wood.

Plastic tunnels
Long tunnels or cloches are available that can be lifted over a row of newly sown seeds. Again, this warms the air within the tunnel and encourages germination, especially early in the season. They're easy to lift off and move to another part of the garden.

Individual cloches
Bell cloches or lantern cloches are more expensive but can be good for protecting individual larger plants, for example courgettes, cucumbers and melons.

Storing seed
If you've got seed left over or are storing your own, it's a good idea to store it properly so it can be used the following year.
- Use a plastic container with a sealed lid.
- Make sure your seed packets are labelled with the plant and variety name.
- Add a sachet of silica gel to help keep the moisture levels down.
- Keep in the fridge or somewhere cool and dark.

Growing in containers

Whatever size space you have, you'll be able to grow some fruit and vegetables, but pick what you grow wisely.

While many people have large plots at their disposal, there are even more with just a small patio, terrace, balcony or window box. Even if you do have a large garden, bringing it closer to your kitchen makes sense. Who wants to traipse down to the end of the garden to pick herbs, when a well-positioned container next to the back door can provide you with a decent supply? One of the problems of growing food on the patio is that, unlike flowering plants that can carry on flowering for months, for much of the time the pots and baskets containing edible crops don't look particularly good. However, choose your crops wisely and be a little creative, and your containers of fruit and vegetables will look attractive and appetising for much of the year.

How to grow

You can use multi-purpose compost for your containers, preferably peat-free. Growing bags often work out a little cheaper, and these are easy to carry. They're formulated for growing crops so do well for container vegetables. There shouldn't be any need for specialist compost for your crops, except perhaps with blueberries or cranberries. Here, it's best to go with an ericaceous compost. For any permanent, larger plants (such as trees), it's well worth using a soil-based compost as it will be heavier and prevent tall plants from toppling over.

If you want to save some money, homemade compost performs very well too (see pages 222–223). Make sure it's well

Fresh herbs
Growing herbs in containers on the patio can make attractive features as well as a useful supply for your kitchen.

Peppers on the patio
Peppers make attractive patio plants, despite not being
the most productive of crops.

WHERE TO GROW

Vegetables, salads, herbs and fruit can all be grown in
containers, but you'll need to select wisely.

Large planters Growing your own food is becoming
so popular that companies have started designing large
planters for patios. These are often raised off the ground
so no bending is required. They're a great idea if you
lack space in the ground but want to grow some larger
vegetables such as spinach, beetroot and shallots, as well
as rows of herbs and salads. If you do invest in a large
planter, think about where you'll site it, as once filled with
compost it will be difficult to move. A sunny spot is best.

Pots For most crops, opt for pots at least 30 cm
(12 in) in diameter. While quick crops such as salads will
do fine in shallow containers, plants that produce edible
roots, such as carrots, do better in a fairly deep container.
In general, the deeper the pot the better, as plants are less
likely to run out of water and you can water less often.
You can also use containers on the patio for fruit that you
can't grow in the ground, such as blueberries, or those
that need to be moved to a sheltered area in the winter,
such as citrus.

Baskets Baskets can be a good choice for vegetables
and salads. Although not many vegetables trail, cucumbers
and melons can prove successful in a basket, as can
tomatoes. Other crops can be successful too, but it's
best to go for short plants as anything too tall becomes
unwieldy. Try spherical carrots, dwarf beans and herbs
such as parsley and basil.

Window boxes Plants in window boxes are often the
most tricky-to-grow food. Their position usually means
they struggle for good light, and their width and depth
make them unsuitable for any but the smallest crops.
However, if you choose plants with pretty foliage, then
they can look good and be productive too. There are now
varieties of tomatoes to fit in window boxes; chillies can
look good; and a regular supply of radishes and salads
such as rocket and mizuna will soon help them fill out.

On the windowsill There's nothing wrong with
growing food on your windowsill. Small pots of herbs
can be kept for weeks on a windowsill; however, if you're
buying them from a supermarket it's best to pot up into
slightly larger containers and add some slow-release
fertiliser. The windowsill is a good place for sprouting
seeds too.

Watering in the garden

Some crops really do benefit from watering at certain times in their growth cycle, whereas others don't benefit from any additional watering. With containers, watering is essential, and sometimes necessary up to twice a day. There are techniques that make watering both quicker and easier, as well as more effective.

Rainwater or tap water?

For most people the water they get out of their taps is the easiest water to use in the garden. It's clean, cheap and easy to use with a hosepipe. However, if you water a lot and your supply is on a water meter, it could end up being more expensive than you think. Water from the water mains supply is often fairly alkaline too, so is not always ideal for certain crops such as blueberries.

To keep the cost (both environmental and economic) of watering down, consider investing in one or two water butts. These can be attached to the downpipes of your guttering using a rain diverter, and water from your roof is then diverted into the water butt. Place the water butt on bricks or a stand, so you can put a watering can underneath to fill up.

If you really value the water that falls on your house, you can even invest in larger, underground storage tanks. Electric pumps can also be fitted to remove the need to use a watering can and allow you to use a hose from your butt or tank.

Ways to water

Whichever source of water you use, you'll need to decide the way you'll water. There are pros and cons to each.

Watering can

This is the slowest way of watering, but also the most efficient as you water only where required. This is a good choice if you are using a water butt, but also good on an allotment or place where you don't have mains water available. A small can with a fine rose is useful for watering seedlings.

Hose

If you want to water quickly, a hose is the best bet. You'll still need to stand there to water so you can direct the hose to where the water is really needed, but it's much quicker than using a can. There are a range of nozzles available that allow

WAYS TO REDUCE WATERING

If you're finding yourself out every evening watering, here are a few tips to help keep watering to a minimum:

Mulches and membranes Use either thick layers of organic material or permeable or non-permeable weed-control fabrics. These help to keep the moisture in the soil and reduce evaporation.

Timing of crops If your crops need a lot of watering in midsummer, consider changing the timing of your growing. Start plants off earlier so they're ready for harvest before the very hot period.

Keep weeds down Weeds also use up water, so where necessary keep weeding regularly.

Soak in new plants
Watering shouldn't be a burden, but it's a good idea to give crops a good watering as they are first planted out.

HOW TO WATER

Whichever way you decide to water, there are a few other golden rules.

● Use only tap water for watering seedlings as this limits the spread of disease.

● When watering, try to do so either early in the morning or late in the evening.

● Try to direct the water to the roots of the plant. If the water is just running off, consider inserting an upside-down cut-off plastic drinks bottle next to the crop and water into that – this is particularly effective for large single plants such as courgettes or tomatoes.

● Try to avoid watering onto the plants themselves and water just at the base of the plant. This helps to discourage diseases from entering the plant.

These crops should be watered a few weeks before they're ready for harvesting or as the crop just starts to form to help swell the crop: calabrese, broad beans, French beans, peas, potatoes and sweetcorn.

The following crops do benefit from regular watering right through their growing season: aubergine, celery, courgette, cucumber, fennel, leek, lettuce, oriental salads, pepper, radishes, runner beans, spinach and tomatoes.

In general, fruit and nut trees shouldn't need to be watered. However, to aid good establishment they should certainly be watered for the first couple of years, especially in dry spells. After that, just applying a thick layer of mulch in early spring, as well as keeping any other plants and weeds away from the base of the tree, should be sufficient. Soft fruit, however, can benefit from additional watering, especially as the crop begins to form. Blackcurrants and raspberries, for example, will produce a larger crop if watered as they ripen. However, most plants, once established, should be able to fend for themselves, and again keeping weeds down and adding a layer of mulch or weed-control fabric should be sufficient in most areas to give you a decent crop.

you to change the spray pattern, which can be useful when you're watering containers and in the greenhouse to stop the plants from being blasted.

Sprinkler
A sprinkler is attached to your hose and left on for a few hours. It's fairly difficult to direct to exactly where you want it, and it can waste a lot of water. However, it does mean you can get on with other things in the meantime.

Irrigation systems and water timers
Irrigation systems are worth thinking about when designing your garden. Attached to the water mains pipe with a water timer, they can be programmed to switch on for a period each day or even twice a day. They are efficient in using water as they need to stay on only for a limited period and can save a lot of time and effort.

There are a couple of different types available. The first is a leaky hose system where the whole length of the hosepipe leaks water and this is good for along a bed. The second uses specific drippers, and is good for growing bags and containers. Whichever you use, it will mean having black pipes around your garden, so think about whether they'll end up being more trouble than they're worth.

What needs watering when?
These vegetable crops shouldn't need any additional watering, once established: artichoke, asparagus, beetroot, broccoli, Brussels sprouts, cabbage, carrots, cauliflower, garlic, kale, onions, parsnip, pumpkin, rhubarb, shallots and swede.

Hosepipe help
Young plants should be able to survive without too much additional watering, but in dry years, a good soak with a hose may be essential.

All about soil

The soil you have and the weather you experience in your garden can affect what you grow. While you can't do very much about the weather, there is much you can do to improve or alter the soil to make your crops healthier and your yields bigger.

Drainage

If you have a clay soil, you may need to improve drainage. Essentially, free-draining soil ensures the plants don't sit in waterlogged conditions and that there is plenty of air in the soil to allow the roots to breathe. To improve drainage, you can dig coarse sand into your soil, but probably the easiest option is to apply a 5-cm (2-in) layer of organic matter each year until it is suitably improved. Organic matter will be pulled underground by the soil micro-organisms and helps to create air spaces, improving the ability of water to move down the soil profile.

Fertility

All soils need to be fertile to support plant growth. There are a range of micronutrients that plants need, as well as a plentiful supply of nitrogen, phosphorus, potassium, calcium, magnesium and suphur. While most ornamental gardens have plenty of nutrients, in the vegetable and fruit garden where you are constantly taking out plants and harvesting crops, you will be removing nutrients from the soil. These need to be replenished. Organic matter again has plenty of these nutrients that are released slowly over time, ideal for growing plants. However, it may also be necessary to supplement with additional fertilisers.

Types of fertilisers
General-purpose fertilisers

These generally contain nitrogen, potassium and phosphorus. They should contain quantities of these fertilisers in the ratio of something like 7:7:7 (the ratio should be listed on the packs).

TYPES OF SOIL

It's worth thinking about the type of soil you have in your garden before you decide how you need to treat it.

Whether you have a stony, sandy, clay or even loamy soil, you'll need to constantly improve it. As plants grow they use nutrients, which need to be replaced. You'll also need to replace the organic matter in the soil that slowly disappears due to the actions of the soil micro-organisms.

Stony Soils that are stony are usually free-draining, so dry out quickly. They may also lack nutrients. You may find digging it over tricky too because of all the stones you hit. Root crops such as carrots and parsnips may find growing in stony soil a challenge as it will be difficult for their roots to grow straight.

Sandy Sandy soils are also free-draining and dry out quickly, but are much better for growing root crops as the roots can grow unimpeded. Sandy soils may also be easy to dig over. However, the fertility of sandy soils may be limited and will need improving.

Clay You know you have clay soil if you dig when the ground is wet and all the soil sticks to your spade. Essentially, clay soil is made up of very fine particles that easily stick together. It usually holds nutrients well, but can be difficult to drain. It can be slow to warm in the spring too.

Loamy Loamy soils are essentially the ideal soil for gardening. They contain some clay to hold nutrients, but some sand to help with drainage.

Know your soil type
The soil you have can affect what you grow, but adding plenty of well-rotted organic matter can help to improve even the worst of soils.

Chicken pellets, made from chicken manure, are a good example, though they tend to have slightly more nitrogen than potassium and phosphorus. However, they are good all-round fertilisers that can be used across your plot.

Straight fertilisers

These contain generally just one nutrient, such as nitrogen, in sulphate of ammonia. These can be useful if you know your garden is deficient in one nutrient. For instance, Epsom salts is a fertiliser that supplies magnesium and can be useful for crops such as tomatoes and raspberries if they show yellowing between the veins of leaves.

Seaweed extracts

These claim to provide plenty of micronutrients. They generally won't sustain the soil on their own, so should be supplemented with other fertilisers if used at all.

Soil pH

The pH of your soil describes how acid or alkaline it is. While some crops such as blueberries and raspberries prefer acid conditions, others are less fussy. You should be aiming for around pH 6.5–7. For brassicas, it's better if the soil is around pH 7.5.

To test the pH of your soil, you can buy a cheap pH testing kit from your garden centre. If your soil is too acid and you want to raise the pH, you can do something called liming. Adding ground limestone to your soil will help to raise the pH. You'll need to know the current pH of your soil first and what general type of soil you have (whether loamy, clay or sandy) to work out how much lime to add.

For soils with a high pH, reducing it is more difficult. Use sulphur chips to acidify the soil supplemented with some organic matter, such as composted bark, to slowly reduce the pH over time.

Supplementing soil with organic matter

Adding bulky organic matter to your soil will benefit your garden in many ways:
- It provides nutrients for your plants immediately as it will contain some nutrients in an available form.
- It helps with drainage and makes working your soil, such as digging it over, much easier.

Composted bark
Composted bark and other organic materials provide a long-term supply of slow-release nutrients as well as improving the soil structure for the roots of the plants.

● It also provides a slow-release fertiliser for your plants – micro-organisms slowly break down complex organic molecules and release nutrients for plants to take up.
● It helps to make the soil lighter and airy. This aids plant growth by providing plenty of air spaces in the soil around the roots.
● It encourages friendly micro-organisms to grow around the roots; they help to defend the plants from plant diseases.
● It holds on to water and so reduces how often you have to irrigate.

Bulky organic matter can be added as a mulch to your soil, often in the spring. But there are lots of different types out there, so how do you decide which to go for?

Homemade compost

Compost you make yourself is a good place to start, but you may not always have enough. It's free, hasn't travelled very far and is an extremely good soil improver. However, you may have weeds germinating from the compost.

Leaf mould
Compost should be well rotted before it's used in the garden.

Recycle your waste
Homemade compost (see pages 222–223) is a great way of recycling garden waste locally.

Leaf mould

Made just of leaves in your own garden, leaf mould shouldn't have any weed seeds in it. While it can be a good soil improver, it doesn't tend to hold much in the way of nutrients.

Horse or cow manure

Horse or cow manure is a rich organic matter with plenty of nutrients and ideal to really improve your soil if it is very deficient in nutrients. However, you must make sure that it has matured for a few months before you add it to your soil.

Spent mushroom compost

This material contains peat, straw, chicken manure and chalk. It's nutritionally very rich and is an excellent soil improver, but because it contains chalk, it should be used only where you don't mind if the pH of your soil goes up.

Composted bark

This is a waste product of the forest industry and tends to have a slightly lower pH, so is good for soils where the pH is too high.

Mulching or digging in
Compost can either be added as a layer on top of your soil (mulch) or dug into the ground.

Municipal green waste compost

More and more local authorities are collecting green waste from householders and composting this material. Some councils then sell it back. This material can make an excellent soil improver as it tends to be like homemade compost. Contact your local council to see whether they supply it in bulk.

PREPARING THE SOIL FOR PLANTING

No digging Some people think that gardening is all about digging, but many now believe that digging isn't necessary. If you have created narrow beds for your crops, it's unlikely you'll ever have to walk on the bed. This way you won't compact the soil.

Adding a mulch of organic matter in early spring of at least 5 cm (2 in) deep will help to reduce weed growth and provide a medium into which you can directly plant. Once the crops are established, you'll need to make sure the weeds are kept down by hoeing, so this way digging could be a thing of the past.

Single digging For those more traditionally minded, digging over your plot in early spring is part of the gardening calendar. Digging over can help to break up the large clods of soil, particularly when you have clay soil, as well as allowing you to remove stones. It's also a way of removing the weedy growth established through the less productive months.

Double digging This is a method of really getting to grips with your soil and improving it quickly. This is hard work, but if you're keen to improve the soil conditions rapidly, it can be worth it.

You need to dig out a single trench to a spade's depth, around 30 cm (12 in) wide and put the soil into a wheelbarrow. Then spread a layer of organic matter in the bottom of the trench. Dig another 30-cm (12-in) trench along the bed and put the soil from this trench on top of the organic matter. Repeat this along the bed, and in the last trench empty out your barrow of compost.

Making compost

A great way of recycling waste from your kitchen and garden – no garden should be without a compost heap.

Making your own compost is fun and rewarding, beneficial to the garden, as well as being extremely environmentally friendly. Garden compost has all sorts of uses – from improving the soil in your fruit and vegetable beds, to raising plants from seed and growing in containers. Recent studies have shown garden compost to be an excellent alternative to bought growing media – for growing vegetables like potatoes in pots. Not only does it save you a trip to the garden centre, but also it saves money in the process.

If you work hard you can have garden compost ready for use in as little as three months. For those wishing to take it at a more leisurely pace – and without much added work – compost made one season will be ready for use the next.

What type of bin?

There are a range of compost bins available, but they can be split into two main groups.

The first is the plastic cone or cylinder shape with a tight-fitting plastic lid – essential if you suffer from pests such as rats. These are a great choice if you have only a small garden and don't expect too much waste to be generated.

There are also large 'bay' type bins, often made from wood. These are a great idea if you intend to produce a lot of compost, and if you invest in more than one bay it means you can add, mix and remove the compost very easily. For a homemade bin, this style is perfect – try using old pallets or doors.

Where to site the bin

The best site for a compost bin is in a warm, sunny spot. This helps the compost to heat up and start to decompose. However, in most gardens you'll want to use the sunniest parts

Autumn leaves
It can take over a year to make good leaf mould. Use for acid-loving plants.

of your garden for either relaxing or growing plants. Composting will work on a shady site but will take more time. Also, make sure you site your bin on bare soil – not on a concrete surface.

What to add

You can compost almost all plant and vegetable matter – as long as it isn't cooked. Materials that you add to your compost are usually either rich in nitrogen – such as grass clippings and vegetable peelings; or rich in carbon – leaves, plant stems and even cardboard and newspaper. The best combination is a 50:50 mix of these two groups of ingredients. Other materials you can add include teabags and eggshells. You shouldn't add fish, meat, bones or any cooked food as this will attract vermin. Also avoid perennial weeds as the composting process may not kill them and you may accidentally introduce them to your garden.

To mix or not to mix

Ideally you should be adding a mix of materials whenever you fill up the bin. Add it bit by bit, or fill it up in one go. Composting will really speed up in summer; you should make sure the bin is kept moist and doesn't dry out.

Mixing is also recommended: use a garden fork to turn and aerate the compost. Mixing the heap will also help to bring uncomposted material at the edge of the heap into the middle, and the composting process will begin again. If you turn once a month in the summer, your compost will be ready in as little as three months. If you choose not to mix, you'll still get great compost – it will just take longer.

Uses

If the compost heap gets really hot, it can kill any seeds – flowers, vegetables or weeds. However it's unlikely it will kill all seed, so be prepared for some unwanted visitors. You can use compost to fill trenches for beans, where the compost is buried, or use it as a mulch in the vegetable garden – but be prepared to do some weeding, or cover the top with a weed-control fabric.

Compost can be used in pots and containers too. Sieving it will help remove large uncomposted pieces, and mixing it with good-quality garden soil in a 50:50 mix produces an excellent container-compost in which to grow all sorts of vegetables. Think about applying a mulch of coarse sand or bark to prevent weeds from germinating.

Bin it
Wooden bay-type bins needn't be an eyesore if they are painted to blend in with other outbuildings.

DO COMPOST

- Shredded paper (although not shiny magazine-type paper), cotton and woollen fabrics
- Uncooked vegetable trimmings, peelings and teabags
- Annual weeds
- Tops of perennial weeds
- Old bedding plants
- Soft hedge clippings
- Dead leaves
- Lawn mowings

DON'T COMPOST

- Woody material like prunings and Brussels sprout stems – these need to be put through a shredder first
- Synthetic fabrics
- Food scraps
- Meat or bones
- Diseased plant material
- Soil pests
- Any weeds with seed heads
- Perennial roots

OTHER TYPES OF COMPOSTING

There are a few other types of composting systems that can help you recycle all your kitchen and garden waste.

WORMERY

If you don't generate much garden waste, but plenty in the kitchen, including cooked food such as pasta and rice, a wormery may be for you. Add kitchen scraps to this type of compost heap filled with worms and you can produce extremely fertile compost. The easiest way to set up a worm bin is to buy a kit with worms included. Keep in a sheltered spot – and somewhere frost-free in winter – and the worms will reward you with rich compost all year round.

BOKASHI BIN

Kept in the kitchen, you can add all sorts of kitchen waste to a bokashi bin, including fish, meat and cooked food. Add a special type of bran and the compost can be transferred into the garden – either onto the compost heap or buried in your garden. Bokashi bins and the special bran are available by mail order and are a good way to recycle all manner of kitchen waste.

LEAF MOULD

A name given to compost produced entirely from leaves. Autumn leaves decompose more slowly than other materials and if you have a lot they can be composted on their own. Leaf mould is slightly acidic so can be used for acid-loving plants such as blueberries. It contains few nutrients so is also good for seed sowing. To make a leaf bin, use four wooden posts, with wire mesh. Alternatively you can fill black bin liners, tie up tight, and leave to one side.

PART 4: *PRESERVING YOUR CROP*

Whichever crops you have chosen to cultivate, it is likely that you will have seasonal gluts at various points in the year. Rather than risking the possibility of your lovingly tended crops going to waste simply because you can't eat them fast enough, it is a good idea to preserve them so they can be enjoyed at a later date. This section details popular ways of preserving: how to make jams, jellies, pickles and chutneys, and how to dry and freeze your crops.

Jams

When making jam, the amount of sugar that is added varies according to the sugar content of the fruit, but it normally accounts for 60 to 65 per cent of the weight of the finished jam.

Making jam

1 Put the jars in a low oven to keep warm. Put the sugar into a bowl and place it in the oven as well, and put a saucer in the fridge. Make sure the fruit is clean and free of blemishes, and prepare according to type. Put the fruit in the pan with the specified amount of water and heat.

2 Remove the pan from the heat and pour in the warm sugar. Then, heat gently, stirring with a wooden spoon, until the sugar has dissolved. A pat of butter can be added after the sugar to reduce the formation of scum.

3 Increase the heat and boil rapidly, without stirring, until the setting point is reached. This should take between 10 and 15 minutes. The correct temperature should be 104°C (220°F) on the sugar thermometer.

4 To test for a set without a thermometer, remove the pan from the heat and try either one of these methods. Drop a little of the jam onto the cold saucer and push it gently with a teaspoon or your fingertip. If the surface wrinkles, the setting point has been reached. Alternatively, lift some of the jam from the pan on a wooden spoon, let it cool slightly and then allow it to drip back into the pan. If the drops run together along the edge of the spoon and form one unified flake or sheet that breaks off sharply as it falls back into the pan, the jam is ready.

5 Skim any scum from the surface of the jam using a slotted spoon. Leave the jam to stand in the pan for about 10 minutes before filling the jars so the fruit is evenly distributed throughout and does not rise to the top of the jars. Prepare and fill the jars (see page 231), then heat-process in a boiling water canner (see page 231).

JAM-MAKING: WHAT YOU WILL NEED

EQUIPMENT

- Sterilised jars (see page 231)
- Heatproof bowl
- Small plate or saucer
- Sharp stainless steel knife (optional)
- Cutting board
- Large non-reactive pan
- Long-handled wooden spoon
- Sugar thermometer (optional)
- Teaspoon
- Baking sheet or wooden board
- Slotted spoon
- Heatproof ladle
- Flat, plastic spatula
- Clean dishcloth and hot soapy water
- Boiling water canner
- Labels

INGREDIENTS

- Sugar
- Slightly underripe, blemish-free fruit, unwashed for preference
- Lemon juice (optional)
- Pat of unsalted butter (optional)

PLUM JAM RECIPE

1.25 kg (2½ lb) plums, halved
300 ml (1¼ cups) water
1 kg (4½ cups) granulated sugar
  or preserving sugar
Pat of unsalted butter
Makes about 1.6 kg (3½ lb)

The colour of this jam varies depending on the type of plums used. Red-fleshed plums produce a richly red jam, while green-fleshed plums like gages or Italian plums make a greenish-yellow jam. If the plums are large, cut them into quarters rather than halves.

1 Put the plums in a non-reactive pan and add the water. Bring to the boil, then simmer for about 25 to 30 minutes, stirring occasionally, until the skins are soft and the fruit is really tender. The liquid should be well reduced.
2 Stir in the sugar until dissolved. Add the butter and bring the jam to the boil. Boil rapidly for 10 to 15 minutes, until the setting point is reached (see page 232).
3 Remove the pan from the heat, remove the pits and any scum from the surface with a slotted spoon, and leave to stand for about 5 minutes. Stir the jam gently.
4 Prepare and fill the jars (see page 231), and heat-process in a boiling water canner (see page 231). Leave to cool, label and store in a cool, dark, dry place for one month before eating. Keeps for up to two years.

3

5

Jellies

The basic method and principles of making jelly are much the same as for jam, but there are some extra points to watch for, and more time is needed. High-pectin fruits (see below) make the best jellies, although low-pectin fruits can be used if combined with other fruits that have a higher pectin content, or if jam sugar (sugar with pectin) is used.

Making jelly

1 Put the jars in a low oven to keep warm. Put the sugar into a bowl and place in the oven as well, and put the saucer in the refrigerator. Make sure the fruit is clean and that any blemishes have been completely cut out. Prepare the fruit according to type; there is no need to remove the peel, core or seeds. Put the fruit in the pan with the specified amount of water and simmer gently until the fruit is soft, stirring occasionally with a wooden spoon to prevent sticking.

2 Pour boiling water through the jelly bag or cheesecloth to scald it. Tie the bag to a stand and place a large bowl underneath. Pour the contents of the pan into the bag and leave it to drip in a cool place, undisturbed, for 8 to 12 hours until no more liquid comes through.

3 Measure the juice in the bowl and return it to a clean pan. Add 450 g (2 cups) warmed sugar for every 575 ml (2½ cups) juice. Heat gently, stirring with a wooden spoon, until the sugar has dissolved, then raise the heat and boil rapidly until the temperature reaches 104°C (220°F) on a sugar thermometer. Alternatively, use the setting point test (see page 232). Avoid stirring unless necessary, as it can cause air bubbles.

4 With the pan off the heat, skim any scum from the surface with a slotted spoon. If the jelly contains particles such as herbs, let it stand for 10 minutes before filling the jars so the particles are evenly distributed throughout the jelly.

5 Prepare and fill the jars (see page 231), then heat-process in a boiling water canner (see page 231).

PECTIN CONTENT OF FRUIT

High: Blackberries (mature but unripe), cooking apples, cranberries, gooseberries, citrus fruit, red currants.
Medium: Eating apples, apricots, blackberries (ripe), loganberries, mulberries, plums, raspberries.
Low: Bananas, blueberries, cherries, figs, grapes, melons, nectarines, peaches, rhubarb, strawberries.

JELLY-MAKING: WHAT YOU WILL NEED

EQUIPMENT

Sterilised jars (see page 231)
Heatproof bowl
Small plate or saucer
Sharp stainless steel knife (optional)
Cutting board
Large non-reactive pan
Long-handled wooden spoon
Jelly bag or triple thickness of cheesecloth and stand
Large non-reactive bowl
Sugar thermometer (optional)
Teaspoon
Slotted spoon
Baking sheet or wooden board
Heatproof ladle
Flat, plastic spatula
Clean dishcloth and hot soapy water
Boiling water canner
Labels

INGREDIENTS

Sugar
Slightly under-ripe fruit
Water

TARRAGON AND ORANGE JELLY

1.8 kg (4 lb) oranges, halved
  and sliced into semi-circles
450 g (1 lb) lemons, halved
  and sliced into semi-circles
2.8 L (12 cups) water
Granulated sugar or preserving
  sugar (see method)
2 tbsp tarragon leaves
Makes about 2.5 kg (5½ lb)

Golden, fragrant herb jellies like this one are ideal for serving with roast and grilled meats, poultry and game – either spooned on the plate or stirred into the cooking juices to make a light sauce. Herb jellies are also good with pâtés, and this one goes well with fish like salmon and trout. Other herbs, such as thyme or mint, can be used instead of tarragon.

1 Put the oranges and lemons in a non-reactive pan with the water. Bring to the boil, then simmer gently for about 1½ hours, until the fruit is soft.
2 Pour the contents of the pan into a jelly bag suspended over a non-reactive bowl and leave overnight in a cool place to drip.
3 Discard the pulp in the jelly bag. Measure the juice and pour into a clean pan. Add 450 g (2¼ cups) sugar for each 575 ml (2½ cups) juice. Add the tarragon. Heat gently, stirring, until the sugar has dissolved, then boil hard for about 15 minutes until the setting point is reached (see page 232).
4 Remove any scum with a slotted spoon and let the jelly stand for 15 minutes. Stir to distribute the tarragon. Prepare and fill the jars (see page 231), and heat-process in a boiling water canner (see page 231). Leave overnight. Label the cool jars and store in a cool, dark, dry place for up to one year.

3

Pickles

Pickles are made from fruits and vegetables that have been preserved in vinegar; sometimes the vinegar is spiced or sweetened. Vegetables may be pickled raw or cooked. Most raw vegetables must be brined or salted before being pickled to draw out their moisture, which allows the vinegar to better penetrate the food. When vegetables and fruits are cooked, the cooking boils off excess moisture, and salt is not necessary.

Making pickles

1 Prepare the vegetables or fruits as directed by the recipe. For raw vegetables, there are two options: either layer them, sprinkling salt between each layer, then cover with a plate and leave overnight; or completely cover and soak the vegetables in salted water. Put a weighted plate on the surface to ensure the vegetables are immersed in the brine. Leave overnight.

For cooked fruits and vegetables that are to be pickled, prepare them according to the recipe. Drain very well and leave to dry.

2 Prepare the pickling vinegar according to the recipe. Let the vinegar cool; the spices can be left in or removed, depending on the strength of flavour required. For raw vegetables that were layered with salt, rinse off in cold running water, dry thoroughly with a clean cloth and spread out on another clean, dry cloth and leave to air-dry completely. For raw vegetables that were soaked in brine, drain the brine, rinse the ingredients under cold running water, and dry thoroughly with a clean cloth to remove the rinsing water.

3 Put the sterilised jars on a baking sheet or wooden board. Pack the vegetables into the sterilised jars to within 2.5 cm (1 in) of the top. Be sure to pack them firmly so as not to leave too many air pockets, but not too tightly because the vinegar must be able to flow between them.

4 Depending on the type of pickle being made, whether a soft or crunchy result is desired or specified in the recipe, either use the pickling vinegar cold, or bring it to the boil. Pour or ladle into prepared jars (see page 231) to come to within 1.5 cm (½ in) of the top. Swirl the jars to expel any trapped air bubbles. If the pickles have a tendency to float to the tops of the jars, put a piece of crumpled baking paper in the top of the jar. Remove it after a couple of weeks. Cover the jars with acid-proof lids (see page 231). Store the pickles in a cool, dark, dry place for about two to three months before eating. The exception is red cabbage, which needs to be eaten within three to four months after it is made, as it softens upon storage.

PICKLE-MAKING: WHAT YOU WILL NEED

EQUIPMENT

Sharp stainless steel knife
Cutting board
Weighted plate (optional)
Non-reactive bowl (optional)
Large, non-reactive pan
Piece of cheesecloth or gauze (optional)
Long piece of string (optional)
Long-handled wooden spoon
Paper towels or dishcloths
Sterilised jars (see page 231)
Baking sheet or wooden board
Heatproof ladle or measuring cup
Non-reactive funnel
Clean dishcloth and hot, soapy water
Clean wide-necked jars, warmed
Baking paper
Acid-proof lids (see page 231)

INGREDIENTS

Fruit or vegetables
Salt (optional)
Spices
Vinegar
Granulated or brown sugar (optional)

RED CABBAGE WITH ORANGE

1 red cabbage weighing about 1 kg (2 lb), quartered, cored and shredded
1 large onion, peeled and thinly sliced
Salt
3 large oranges, zested and juiced

For the spiced vinegar
350 ml (1½ cups) red wine vinegar
175 ml (¾ cup) raspberry vinegar
1½ tsp whole allspice berries, lightly crushed
1½ tsp black peppercorns
1½ tsp whole cloves
2 bay leaves, torn in half
5-cm (2-in) long cinnamon stick
1 tbsp brown sugar
75 g (½ cup) raisins
Makes about 1 kg (2 lb)

This preserve is best eaten within three to four months after it is made, as the cabbage softens upon storage. It goes well with bread and cheese, smoked meats and casseroles.

1 Layer the cabbage and onion in a colander, sprinkling salt between each layer. Stand the colander on a plate and leave in a cool place overnight to drain. The next day, rinse the vegetables well, and dry thoroughly with a clean cloth. Spread out on another dry, clean cloth and leave to air-dry completely.
2 Meanwhile, make the spiced vinegar: put all the ingredients and the orange rind and juice in a non-reactive pan and heat gently, stirring with a wooden spoon, until the sugar has dissolved, then boil for 2 minutes. Remove from the heat and leave to cool.
3 Return the vinegar to the boil, then remove from the heat. Mix the raisins with the cabbage and onion and pack firmly into sterilised jars. Add the vinegar as you go, distributing the raisins and flavourings evenly, and pressing down firmly on the cabbage. Swirl the jars to expel any air bubbles, then seal them and leave to cool. Label the jars and store in a cool, dark, dry place for at least one month before eating. It will keep for up to one year but is best eaten within three to four months.

Drying

Traditionally, the drying effect of the sun or wind was used to extend the storage of fruit and vegetables. When home-drying, the choice is limited to specific fruits, vegetables and herbs, as well as some aromatics, such as orange peel.

Oven-drying

1 Select good-quality, firm ingredients that are free of blemishes. Fruit should be just ripe and peeled if necessary with cores or pits removed. Root and tuber vegetables usually dry better than leaves or stalks.

2 Thinly slice and blanch vegetables, except tomatoes, peppers, okra, mushrooms, beetroot and onions. Remove or trim mushrooms stalks. Halve tomatoes, and halve and pit peaches and plums.

3 Dip foods that discolour, such as apples and pears, in a solution of 6 tablespoons lemon juice to 1 L (4⅓ cups) water.

4 Put a wire rack on a foil-lined baking sheet. Arrange the food on the rack, leaving space between the pieces. Halved fruit should be set cut-side down. Set the oven to its lowest setting (it should not exceed 60°C/ 140°F); the warming oven of a cast-iron stove is ideal. Put the rack of food in the oven and prop the door slightly open (not applicable for a cast-iron stove).

5 Halfway through drying, turn the food over. If using more than one shelf at a time, swap the trays from one shelf to the other. Leave the food until it is dry and leathery.

6 Leave to cool before packing in layers between sheets of baking paper in airtight containers. Store in a cool place, but not the fridge.

Air-drying

1 Prepare the fruit or vegetables, and treat for discolouration, if necessary (see left).

2 Spread on racks on baking sheets. Thread onto lengths of thin sticks, and keep the food slightly separated to allow air to circulate around the pieces. Place across a roasting or baking pan.

3 Leave in a warm, dry place (not a steamy kitchen), for example, in a warm cupboard. The food is ready when it is dried and shrivelled.

DRYING: WHAT YOU WILL NEED

EQUIPMENT

Sharp stainless steel knife
Cutting board
Wire rack
Aluminium foil
Baking paper

INGREDIENTS

Foods to be dried

At home, the choice is limited to specific fruits, vegetables and herbs as well as some aromatics, such as orange peel. Sun and outdoor drying give the best flavour to foods, but most of us do not live in suitable climates with steadily warm, dry temperatures and plenty of ventilation and clean air.

Air-drying herbs

Herbs with firm leaves, such as thyme and rosemary, can be dried more successfully than soft, fleshy herbs like basil.

1 Choose herbs shortly before they come into flower. Pick them in the morning as soon as the dew has lifted but before the sun has become too hot. If drying the herbs in bunches, pick stems as long as possible.

2 To dry in bunches, tie the herbs loosely in small bundles with thick thread and suspend in a warm, dry place out of direct sunlight. They should be ready in three days.

3 Alternatively, spread the herbs on a wire rack covered with cheesecloth (which allows the air to circulate) and leave in a warm place, preferably enclosed, for three to five days.

4 Herbs can also be dried tied in paper bags with small holes cut in the bags, and left in a warm, dry place for three days.

5 Herbs are ready when the stems and leaves are brittle but retain their green colour, and crumble easily when rubbed between the fingers. Either keep the stems and leaves intact, or strip the leaves off and store in an airtight container in a cool, dark, dry place.

OVEN-DRYING TIMES

Apple rings	6 to 8 hours
Apricots, halved and stoned	36 to 48 hours
Bananas, peeled and halved lengthways	10 to 16 hours
Berries, left whole	12 to 18 hours
Cherries, stoned	18 to 24 hours
Herbs, tied and bound	12 to 16 hours
Peaches, peeled, halved, stoned	36 to 48 hours
and sliced	12 to 16 hours
Pears, peeled, halved and cored	36 to 48 hours
Pineapple, cored and cut into	36 to 48 hours
5-mm (¼-in) rings	
Plums, halved	18 to 24 hours
Vegetables, cut into 5-mm (¼-in) slices	2 hours
Vegetables, cut into 1.5-cm (¾-in) slices	7 to 8 hours

Freezing

Freezing at a temperature below -18°C (0°F) preserves food by immobilising the bacteria that can spoil food, and slows down the enzyme activity that can cause quality deterioration. Food should be frozen quickly to prevent the formation of large ice crystals that damage cell walls, so that the thawed food doesn't lose its liquid and 'collapse'. Conversely, thawing should be done slowly.

1 If freezing more than 1 kg (2 lb) of food, turn the freezer thermostat to 'fast-freeze'. Choose heavyweight, vapour- and moisture-proof containers and wrappings to protect the food from freezer burn – for example, thick polythene bags, clingfilm, foil and plastic boxes.

2 Prepare the food as necessary and make sure that it is completely cold.

3 Vegetables should be blanched to preserve their colour, flavour, texture and nutritional content, and to destroy the enzymes that would otherwise cause deterioration during frozen storage. Put the prepared vegetables, in batches if necessary so that the pan is not crowded, in a wire basket. Plunge into a large saucepan of boiling water, cover and return quickly to the boil. Boil for the specified time. Remove the basket and immediately plunge it into a large bowl of water with some ice cubes in it. When cold, drain the vegetables very well.

4 Blackberries, black- and red currants, blueberries, gooseberries and raspberries can be 'open-frozen' by spreading them on trays lined with baking paper and freezing before packing as normal.

4

5 Pack the food into suitable containers. If solid food is in a rigid container that it does not fill, fill the gap with crumpled tissue paper. Leave 2.5-cm (1-in) headspace in rigid containers of liquids to allow for expansion, then fill the space if necessary.

6 Sauces, soups, purées, casseroles, etc. can be poured into polythene bags set in freezer-proof rectangular or square containers, with 2.5-cm (1-in) headspace to allow for expansion. Freeze until solid, then remove the bag from the container, seal and label.

7 When the food is frozen, return the thermostat to the normal setting.

6

8 To freeze herbs, open-freeze the herb sprigs, then pack into freezer-proof polythene bags without crushing the herbs, and tie the bags fairly loosely. Chopped herbs can be frozen individually or combined into blends, such as Provençal – with basil, oregano, thyme, parsley and rosemary – and then either packed into small freezer bags or small containers and put inside a labelled freezer box. Or put the herbs (preferably in useful quantities, such as 2 tablespoonfuls) into ice cube trays, cover with water and freeze. The frozen cubes can be put into freezer bags or boxes. Use frozen herbs straight from the freezer without thawing.

FREEZING: WHAT YOU WILL NEED

EQUIPMENT

Freezer-proof containers
Polythene bags
Clingfilm
Aluminium foil
Plastic boxes

STORAGE TIMES

VEGETABLES	
Most vegetables	8–12 months
Onions	3–6 months
Herbs	6 months
Not recommended: Lettuce and other salad leaves, salad onions, radishes and sweetcorn without husks.	
FRUIT	
Most fruit	8–12 months
Citrus fruit	4–6 months

FREEZER RASPBERRY JAM

700 g (1½ lb) raspberries
1 kg (4½ cups) caster sugar
125 ml (½ cup) liquid pectin
Makes 1.6 kg (7 cups)

Freezer jams are not boiled, so they have a fresher, more natural taste and a brighter, clearer colour than cooked jams. For a change, instead of using ordinary caster sugar, try using vanilla sugar, which can be bought or homemade. Simply insert a vanilla bean in a jar of sugar and leave for two weeks before using; the vanilla bean can be left in the jar, or used in another recipe.

1 Place the raspberries in a bowl and gently stir in the sugar using a fork, lightly mashing the berries. Leave for 20 minutes, stirring occasionally.
2 Pour in the liquid pectin and stir continuously for three minutes.
3 Ladle the jam into clean, freezer-proof containers, filling them to 1 cm (½ in) from the top. Seal, label and leave to cool for about five hours.
4 Put the containers in the fridge and leave for 24 to 48 hours until the jam 'gels'.
5 Put the containers in the freezer and store for up to six months.
6 To serve, leave at room temperature for about one hour, depending on the size of the container.

Sowing summary

A quick-reference guide to vegetable sowing information to help you plan your food garden calendar.

VEGETABLE	DEPTH OF SOWING	DISTANCE APART	DISTANCE BETWEEN ROWS	SOWING SEASON	CROPPING SEASON
Asparagus crowns	10 cm (4 in)	45 cm (17¾ in)	90 cm (36 in)	Mid-spring	Mid-spring–Late spring
Aubergine	0.5 cm (¼ in)	46 cm (18 in)	50–75 cm (20–30 in)	Early spring–Mid-spring	Late summer–Mid-autumn
Beetroot	1.5 cm (⅝ in)	2.5 cm (1 in)	20–30 cm (8–12 in)	Mid-spring–Early summer	Early summer–Mid-autumn
Broad beans	5 cm (2 in)	20 cm (8 in)	20–30 cm (8–12 in)	Late autumn or Mid-spring	Early summer–Late summer
Broccoli	1 cm (½ in)	40–60 cm (16–24 in)	40–60 cm (16–24 in)	Early spring–Late spring	Midsummer–Mid-spring
Brussels sprouts	1 cm (½ in)	90 cm (3 ft)	80–90 cm (32–36 in)	Late spring	Mid-autumn–Late-winter
Cabbage	1 cm (½ in)	15–50 cm (6–20 in)	80–90 cm (32–36 in)	Early spring	All year round
Carrot	1 cm (½ in)	2.5 cm (1 in)	50 cm (20 in)	Early spring–Early summer	Late spring–Late autumn
Cauliflower	1 cm (½ in)	40 cm (16 in)	85 cm (34 in)	Spring	All year round
Celeriac	Surface	30 cm (12 in)	30 cm (12 in)	Early spring	Early autumn–Late winter
Celery	Surface	20 cm (8 in)	70 cm (28 in)	Spring	Early summer–Late autumn
Chicory and Endive	1 cm (½ in)	30 cm (12 in)	20–40 cm (8–16 in)	Mid-spring–Early summer	Midsummer–Early winter
Chilli	1 cm (½ in)	30 cm (12 in)	30 cm (12 in)	Early spring	Midsummer–Mid-autumn
Chinese cabbage	1 cm (½ in)	30 cm (12 in)	30 cm (12 in)	Early summer–Midsummer	Late summer–Early winter
Climbing beans	5 cm (2 in)	40 cm (16 in)	50 cm (20 in)	Mid-spring	Early summer–Mid-autumn
Courgette	1 cm (½ in)	50 cm (20 in)	1 m (40 in)	Late spring	Early summer–Mid-autumn
Cucumber	2.5 cm (1 in)	15 cm (6 in)	10–12 cm (4–6 in)	Late spring	Midsummer–Mid-autumn
Dwarf beans	2 cm (¾ in)	5 cm (2 in)	30 cm (12 in)	Mid spring–Midsummer	Early summer–Mid-autumn
Edible flowers	Check specific instructions on your seed packet				All year round
Fennel	1 cm (½ in)	30 cm (12 in)	30 cm (12 in)	Mid-spring–Late spring	Late spring–Early autumn
Garlic	3 cm (1¼ in)	7.5 cm (3 in)	40 cm (16 in)	Autumn or Early winter	Late spring–Early autumn
Globe artichoke and Cardoon	1 cm (½ in)	75 cm (30 in)	75 cm (30 in)	Late winter	Late spring–Early summer
Jerusalem artichoke tubers	10–15 cm (4–6 in)	30 cm (12 in)	30 cm (12 in)	Late winter–Mid-spring	Late autumn–Winter
Kale	1 cm (½ in)	45 cm (17¾ in)	45 cm (17¾ in)	Mid-spring	Early autumn–Late winter
Kohlrabi	1 cm (½ in)	10 cm (4 in)	40 cm (16 in)	Spring–Early summer	Late spring–Early winter
Leek	0.5 cm (¼ in)	15 cm (6 in)	60 cm (24 in)	Spring	Late summer–Early spring

VEGETABLE	DEPTH OF SOWING	DISTANCE APART	DISTANCE BETWEEN ROWS	SOWING SEASON	CROPPING SEASON
Lettuce	0.5 cm (¼ in)	1.5 cm (⅝ in)	30 cm (12 in)	Early spring–Autumn	Early summer–Late autumn
Mangetout and Sugar-snap peas	5 cm (2 in)	10 cm (4 in)	7.5–15 cm (3–6 in)	Early spring–Midsummer	Late spring–Mid-autumn
Marrow	1 cm (½ in)	50 cm (20 in)	1 m (3 ft 2 in)	Late spring	Midsummer–Mid-autumn
Microgreens	0.5 cm (¼ in)	2 mm (¹⁄₁₆ in)	N/A	All year round	All year round
Mizuna and Mibuna	1 cm (½ in)	2.5 cm (1 in)	40 cm (16 in)	Early spring–Early autumn	Midsummer–Mid-winter
Onion	1 cm (½ in)	10 cm (4 in)	20 cm (8 in)	Spring and Autumn	Early summer–Early autumn
Pak choi	1 cm (½ in)	20 cm (8 in)	30 cm (12 in)	Mid-spring–Late summer	Late summer–Early winter
Parsnip	1 cm (½ in)	15 cm (6 in)	20–30 cm (8–12 in)	Early spring	Early autumn–Late winter
Peas	2.5 cm (1 in)	5–10 cm (2–4 in)	7.5–15 cm (3–6 in)	Early spring–Midsummer	Late spring–Mid-autumn
Pepper	1 cm (½ in)	30 cm (12 in)	30 cm (12 in)	Early spring	Midsummer–Mid-autumn
Perpetual spinach and Swiss chard	1.5 cm (⅝ in)	30–50 cm (12–20 in)	30–50 cm (12–20 in)	Mid-spring	Early spring–Late autumn
Potato (earlies)	10 cm (4 in)	40 cm (16 in)	50 cm (20 in)	Early spring–Mid-spring	Early summer–Late summer
Potato (second earlies)	10 cm (4 in)	40 cm (16 in)	24 cm (60 in)	Early spring–Mid-spring	Midsummer–Early autumn
Potato (maincrop)	10 cm (4 in)	40 cm (16 in)	75 cm (30 in)	Early spring–Mid-spring	Late summer–Late autumn
Radish	1 cm (½ in)	2.5 cm (1 in)	15 cm (6 in)	Early spring onward	Late spring–Late autumn
Rocket	1 cm (½ in)	1 cm (½ in)	20–30 cm (8–12 in)	Mid-spring–Early autumn	Late spring–Mid-autumn
Salad onion	1 cm (½ in)	2–5 cm (¾–2 in)	30 cm (12 in)	Early spring–Midsummer	Late spring–Late autumn
Shallot	1 cm (½ in)	15 cm (6 in)	30 cm (12 in)	Early spring	Late summer–Mid-autumn
Spinach	1 cm (½ in)	20 cm (8 in)	30 cm (12 in)	Early spring	Early summer–Mid-autumn
Sprouting seeds	N/A	N/A	N/A	All year round	All year round
Squash and Pumpkin	2.5 cm (1 in)	15 cm (6 in)	1 m (40 in)	Spring	Midsummer–Mid-autumn
Swede	1 cm (½ in)	30 cm (12 in)	65 cm (26 in)	Mid-spring–Late spring	Mid-autumn–Early winter
Sweetcorn	2.5 cm (1 in)	blocks of 3 x 3 or 5 x 5	35 cm (14 in)	Mid spring	Late summer–Early autumn
Sweet potato	Grow as plants	45 cm (17¾ in)	45 cm (17¾ in)	N/A	Mid-autumn–Late autumn
Tomato	0.5 cm (¼ in)	45–60 cm (17¾–23 in)	1 m (40 in)	Late spring	Midsummer–Mid-autumn
Turnip	2 cm (¾ in)	20 cm (8 in)	15 cm (6 in)	Early spring onward	Early summer–Mid-autumn

Crop selection summary

A quick-reference guide to the characteristics of each crop to help you decide what to grow.

VEGETABLE	VALUE FOR MONEY	MAINTENANCE	FREEZE/STORE
Asparagus	✿✿✿✿✿	✿✿✿✿	✿✿
Aubergine	✿✿✿✿	✿✿	✿✿
Beetroot	✿✿✿✿✿	✿✿✿✿	✿✿✿
Broad beans	✿✿✿✿✿	✿✿✿✿	✿✿✿✿
Broccoli	✿✿✿✿	✿✿✿	✿✿
Brussels sprouts	✿✿✿✿	✿✿✿	✿✿
Cabbage	✿✿✿✿	✿✿✿	✿✿✿
Cardoon	✿✿✿	✿✿✿✿	✿✿
Carrot	✿✿✿✿✿	✿✿✿✿	✿✿✿✿✿
Cauliflower	✿✿✿	✿✿✿	✿✿
Celeriac	✿✿✿✿	✿✿✿	✿✿✿
Celery	✿✿✿	✿✿✿✿	✿✿
Chicory	✿✿✿✿✿	✿✿✿	✿✿
Chilli	✿✿✿✿	✿✿	✿✿✿✿
Chinese cabbage	✿✿✿✿	✿✿	✿✿
Climbing beans	✿✿✿✿✿	✿✿✿✿	✿✿✿✿
Courgette	✿✿✿✿✿	✿✿✿✿	✿✿
Cucumber	✿✿✿✿✿	✿✿✿	✿✿
Dwarf beans	✿✿✿✿✿	✿✿✿✿	✿✿✿✿
Endive	✿✿✿✿✿	✿✿✿	✿✿
Fennel	✿✿✿	✿✿✿	✿✿
Garlic	✿✿✿✿✿	✿✿✿✿	✿✿✿✿✿
Globe artichoke	✿✿✿	✿✿✿✿	✿✿
Jerusalem artichoke	✿✿✿✿✿	✿✿✿✿	✿✿✿✿
Kale	✿✿✿✿✿	✿✿✿✿	✿✿
Kohlrabi	✿✿✿✿	✿✿✿	✿✿✿
Leek	✿✿✿✿✿	✿✿✿✿	✿✿✿

VEGETABLE	VALUE FOR MONEY	MAINTENANCE	FREEZE/STORE
Lettuce	✿✿✿✿✿	✿✿✿✿	✿✿
Mangetout	✿✿✿✿	✿✿✿	✿✿✿✿
Marrow	✿✿✿✿✿	✿✿✿	✿✿✿
Microgreens	✿✿✿	✿✿	✿✿
Mizuna and Mibuna	✿✿✿✿✿	✿✿✿✿	✿✿
Onion	✿✿✿✿✿	✿✿✿✿	✿✿✿✿✿
Pak choi	✿✿✿✿	✿✿	✿✿
Parsnip	✿✿✿✿✿	✿✿✿✿	✿✿✿✿✿
Peas	✿✿✿✿✿	✿✿✿✿	✿✿✿✿
Pepper	✿✿✿	✿✿	✿✿
Perpetual spinach	✿✿✿✿✿	✿✿✿✿	✿✿
Potato	✿✿✿✿✿	✿✿✿✿	✿✿✿✿✿
Pumpkin	✿✿✿✿✿	✿✿✿✿	✿✿✿✿
Radish	✿✿✿✿✿	✿✿✿✿	✿✿
Rocket	✿✿✿✿✿	✿✿✿✿	✿✿
Salad onion	✿✿✿✿✿	✿✿✿✿	✿✿
Shallot	✿✿✿✿✿	✿✿✿✿	✿✿✿✿✿
Spinach	✿✿✿✿✿	✿✿✿✿	✿✿
Sprouting seeds	✿✿✿✿	✿✿	✿✿
Squash	✿✿✿✿✿	✿✿✿✿	✿✿✿✿
Sugar-snap peas	✿✿✿✿	✿✿✿	✿✿✿✿
Swede	✿✿✿✿	✿✿✿	✿✿✿✿
Sweetcorn	✿✿✿✿	✿✿✿✿	✿✿
Sweet potato	✿✿✿	✿✿✿	✿✿
Swiss chard	✿✿✿✿✿	✿✿✿✿	✿✿
Tomato	✿✿✿✿✿	✿✿	✿✿✿
Turnip	✿✿✿✿✿	✿✿✿	✿✿✿

HERB	VALUE FOR MONEY	MAINTENANCE	FREEZE/STORE
Basil	●●●●●	●●	●●●
Bay	●●●●●	●●●●●	●●●
Chervil	●●●●	●●●●	●●●
Chives	●●●●●	●●●●	●●●
Coriander	●●●●●	●●●	●●●
Dill	●●●●	●●●	●●●
Fennel	●●●●	●●●	●●●
Lovage	●●●●	●●●●	●●●
Mint	●●●●●	●●●●	●●●
Oregano	●●●●●	●●●●	●●●
Parsley	●●●●●	●●●●	●●●
Rosemary	●●●●●	●●●●●	●●●
Sage	●●●●●	●●●●	●●●
Tarragon	●●●●●	●●●●	●●●
Thyme	●●●●●	●●●●	●●●

FRUIT AND NUTS	VALUE FOR MONEY	MAINTENANCE	FREEZE/STORE
Acid cherry	●●●●●	●●●	●●●
Almond	●●●●	●●●	●●●●
Apple	●●●●●	●●●	●●●●●
Apricot	●●●	●●●	●●
Black currant	●●●●	●●●●	●●●
Blackberry and hybrid berries	●●●	●●●	●●●
Blueberry	●●●	●●●●	●●●
Citrus	●●●	●●	●●●
Cobnut	●●●	●●●●	●●●
Cranberry	●●●●	●●	●●●
Damson	●●●●●	●●●	●●●
Fig	●●●●	●●●●	●●●
Filbert	●●●	●●●●	●●●
Gage	●●●●●	●●●	●●●
Gooseberry	●●●●	●●●	●●●
Grapes	●●●●	●●●	●●●
Kiwi	●●●	●●●	●●
Melon	●●●●	●●●●	●●
Nectarine	●●●	●●●	●●
Passion fruit	●●●	●●●	●●
Peach	●●●	●●●	●●
Pear	●●●●●	●●●	●●●●
Physalis	●●●	●●●	●●
Plum	●●●●●	●●●	●●●
Raspberry	●●●●●	●●●●	●●●
Red currant	●●●●	●●●●	●●●
Rhubarb	●●●●●	●●●●	●●
Strawberry	●●●●●	●●●●	●●●
Sweet cherry	●●●●●	●●●	●●●
Walnut	●●●●	●●●●	●●●
White currant	●●●●	●●●●	●●●

Hardiness zones

Remember that hardiness is not just a question of minimum temperatures. A plant's ability to survive certain temperatures is affected by many factors, such as the amount of shelter given and its position in your garden.

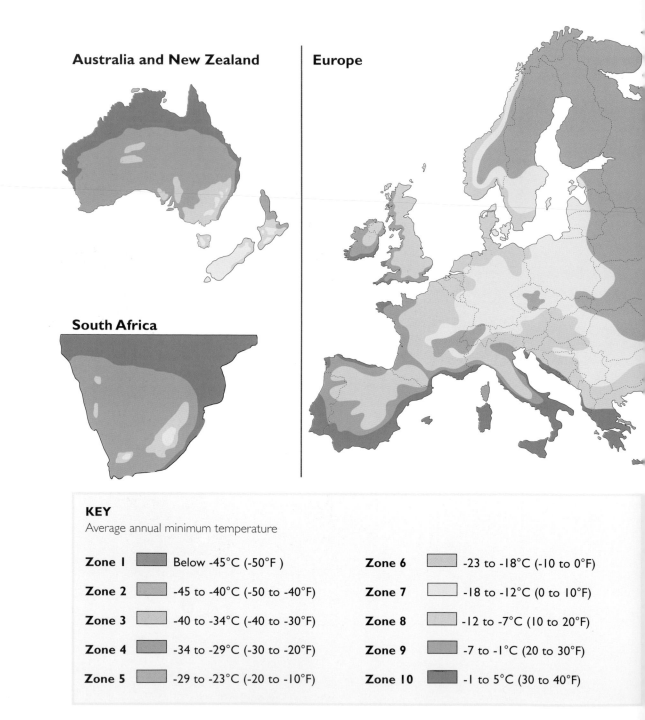

Australia and New Zealand

Europe

South Africa

KEY

Average annual minimum temperature

Zone 1		Below -45°C (-50°F)	**Zone 6**		-23 to -18°C (-10 to 0°F)
Zone 2		-45 to -40°C (-50 to -40°F)	**Zone 7**		-18 to -12°C (0 to 10°F)
Zone 3		-40 to -34°C (-40 to -30°F)	**Zone 8**		-12 to -7°C (10 to 20°F)
Zone 4		-34 to -29°C (-30 to -20°F)	**Zone 9**		-7 to -1°C (20 to 30°F)
Zone 5		-29 to -23°C (-20 to -10°F)	**Zone 10**		-1 to 5°C (30 to 40°F)

United States of America

Index

A

acid cherries 150–151
alfalfa 114
almonds 189, 192
apples 138, 139–143
  planting tree 140
  rejuvenating tree 142
  rootstocks 139–141
  tree forms 141
apricots 152–153
asparagus 98, 110–111
aubergines 88–89

B

balconies 14, 23
basil 117, 118, 120–121
baskets 211
bay 118, 119
beans 10, 22, 68
  broad beans 72–73
  climbing beans 69–70
  dwarf beans 71
beetroot 40
berries 137, 205
  hybrid berries 164–165
blackberries 164–165
blackcurrants 166–167
blueberries 170–171
  planting pit 171
bokashi bins 223
borage 117
brassicas 22
broccoli 98, 99–100
  microgreens 115
Brussels sprouts 56
buying plants 204–205

C

cabbages 52, 53–55
  red cabbage with orange 237
calendar
  apples 143
  apricots 153
  asparagus 111
  aubergine 89
  basil 121
  bay 119
  beetroot 40

blackberries 165
blackcurrants 167
blueberries 171
broccoli 100
Brussels sprouts 56
cabbage 55
carrots 37
cauliflower 101
celeriac 51
celery 109
chervil 122
chicory 66
chillies 93
Chinese cabbage 61
chives 123
citrus fruit 187
climbing beans 70
coriander 124
corn 87
courgette 79
cranberries 172
cucumber 85
dill 125
dwarf beans 71
endive 66
fennel 103, 125
figs 155
garlic 49
globe artichokes 113
gooseberries 177
grapes 175
Jerusalem artichokes 50
kale 57
kiwi 181
kohlrabi 102
leeks 105
lettuce 65
lovage 126
mangetout and sugar-snap peas 77
marrows 82
melons 185
mint 129
mizuna and mibuna 59
nectarines 153
nuts 191, 192, 193
onions 47
oregano 127
pak choi 61
parsley 131

parsnips 39
passion fruit 182
peaches 153
pears 145
peas 75
peppers 91
perpetual spinach 63
physalis 182
potatoes 34
pumpkins 81
radishes 43
raspberries 163
red and white currants 169
rhubarb 179
rocket 67
rosemary 132
sage 133
salad onions 107
shallots 48
spinach 62
squashes 81
strawberries 159
swede 44
sweet cherries 149
sweet potatoes 35
Swiss chard 63
tarragon 114
tomatoes 97
turnips 41
cardoons 112–113
carrots 36–37
cauliflower 101
celeriac 51
celery 108–109
chervil 122
  microgreens 115
chicory 66
chillies 92–93, 212
Chinese cabbage 60–61
chives 117, 123
chutneys 228, 238–239
citrus fruit 186–187
clay soil 218
clothing 196
clubroot 55
cobnuts 189, 190–191
cold frames 25
companion planting 226

compost 220, 221
 compost bins 222, 223
 composting materials 222, 223
 making compost 222–223
 mixing 223
composted bark 220, 221
conservatories 24
containers 9, 11, 210–212
 appearance 213
 apricots 153
 beetroot 40
 carrots 36–37
 chervil 122
 coriander 124
 crops that do well 212
 lettuces 64–65
 melons 185
 nectarines 153
 pak choi 60
 peaches 153
 potatoes 32–33
 salad onions 106–107
 successful growing 213
cordons 141
coriander 118, 124
corn salad 'Cavallo' 58
courgette 78–79
 edible flowers 117
 courgette chutney 239
cranberries 172
crop families 22
crop rotation 23, 226
crop selection 10, 11, 28, 246–247
cucumber 68, 83–85
cucurbits 68
currants 156

D

daisies 117
daylilies 117
design 20–21
digging 221
 tools 197
 weed control 224
dill 125
diseases 9
 apples 141–143
 apricots 153
 blackcurrants 166
 blight 33
 brassicas 55
 celery 109

courgette 79
cucumber 84–85
downy mildew 46, 55
fungal diseases 227
gooseberries 176
grapes 174
greenhouse hygiene 25
lettuce 64–65
melons 184
mint 129
nectarines 153
nuts 192
onions 46
organic gardening 217
peaches 153
pears 144
perpetual spinach 63
plums 147
potatoes 32–33
radishes 42
raspberries 163
red and white
 currants 168–169
rhubarb 179
salad onions 107
scab 33
spinach 62
strawberries 158
swede 44
sweet cherries 149
Swiss chard 63
tarragon 114
tomatoes 96–97
viruses 227
white rot 46
draw hoes 197
drying 228
 air-drying 127, 240–241
 oven-drying 240, 241

E

edible flowers 116–117
endive 52, 66
equipment 194, 196–199
espaliers 141

F

fans 148, 151
feeding plants 216–217
fennel 98, 103
fenugreek 114
fertilisers 8, 218–219

figs 154–155
 planting pit 154
filberts 189, 190–191
fleeces and fine meshes 159
 making 53
footwear 196
forks 197
freezing 228, 242–243
 red and white currants 186
fruit 8, 9, 137
 soft fruit 156
 tender fruit 180
 tree fruit 137, 138, 205

G

gardens 12, 14–15
 choosing site 18–19
 designing 20–21
 growing undercover 24–25
 kitchen gardens 16, 22–23
 patio gardens 17, 23
garlic 49
globe artichokes 98, 112–113
gloves 196, 197
gooseberries 176–177
grapes 173–175
green manures 225
greenhouses 9, 24, 25
growing bags 83, 94–95
guttering 201

H

hand forks 197, 198
hand trowels 197, 198
hardiness zones 248–249
harvesting 11, 226
 acid cherries 151
 apples 143
 apricots 153
 asparagus 111
 aubergines 89
 basil 120
 bay 119
 beetroot 40
 blackberries 165
 blackcurrants 167
 blueberries 171
 broad beans 72
 broccoli 99–100
 Brussels sprouts 56
 cabbage 54
 carrots 37

cauliflower 101
celeriac 51
celery 109
chervil 122
chicory 66
chillies 92–93
Chinese cabbage 61
chives 123
citrus fruit 187
climbing beans 70
coriander 124
courgettes 79
cranberries 172
cucumber 85
dill 125
dwarf beans 71
edible flowers 116
endive 66
fennel 103, 125
figs 155
garlic 49
globe artichokes 113
gooseberries 176–177
grapes 175
Jerusalem artichokes 50
kale 57
kiwi 181
kohlrabi 102
leeks 105
lettuce 65
lovage 126
mangetout and sugar-snap peas 77
marrows 82
melons 185
microgreens 115
mint 129
mizuna and mibuna 59
nectarines 153
nuts 191, 192, 193
onions 46
oregano 127
pak choi 61
parsley 131
parsnips 39
peaches 153
pears 145
peas 74
peppers 91
perpetual spinach 63
physalis 182
plums 147
potatoes 34

pumpkins 81
radishes 42
raspberries 163
red and white currants 168, 169
rhubarb 179
rocket 67
rosemary 132
sage 133
salad onions 107
shallots 48
spinach 62
squashes 81
strawberries 158
swede 44
sweet cherries 149
sweet potatoes 35
sweetcorn 87
Swiss chard 63
tarragon 114
thyme 115
tomatoes 97
tools 199
turnips 41
herbs 118, 205
    air-drying 127, 241
hoeing 199, 225
hoes 197–198
hosepipes 214–215
hygiene 25, 226

I
interplanting 87, 226
irrigation systems and water timers 215

J
jams 228, 232–233, 243
jellies 228, 234–235
Jerusalem artichokes 50

K
kale 52, 57
kitchen gardens 16, 22–23
kitchen uses
    acid cherries 151
    apples 143
    apricots 153
    asparagus 111
    aubergines 89
    basil 120
    bay 119
    beetroot 40
    blackberries 165

blackcurrants 167
blueberries 171
broad beans 72
broccoli 99–100
Brussels sprouts 56
cabbage 54
carrots 37
cauliflower 101
celeriac 51
celery 109
chervil 122
chicory 66
chillies 92–93
Chinese cabbage 61
chives 123
citrus fruit 187
climbing beans 70
coriander 124
courgettes 79
cranberries 172
cucumber 85
dill 125
dwarf beans 71
edible flowers 116
endive 66
fennel 103, 125
figs 155
garlic 49
globe artichokes 113
gooseberries 176–177
grapes 175
Jerusalem artichokes 50
kale 57
kiwi fruit 181
kohlrabi 102
leeks 105
lettuce 65
lovage 126
mangetout and sugar-snap peas 77
marrows 82
melons 185
microgreens 115
mint 129
mizuna and mibuna 59
nectarines 153
nuts 191, 192, 193
onions 46
oregano 127
pak choi 61
parsley 131
parsnips 39
peaches 153

pears 145
peas 74
peppers 91
perpetual spinach 63
physalis 182
plums 147
potatoes 34
pumpkins 81
radishes 42
raspberries 163
red and white currants 168, 169
rhubarb 179
rocket 67
rosemary 132
sage 133
salad onions 107
shallots 48
spinach 62
squashes 81
strawberries 158
swede 44
sweet cherries 149
sweet potatoes 35
sweetcorn 87
Swiss chard 63
tarragon 114
thyme 115
tomatoes 97
turnips 41
kiwi fruit 181
kohlrabi 102

L
lavender 117
leaf mould 220, 221, 222, 223
leeks 104–105
lettuce 52, 64–65
loamy soil 218
loganberries 165
loppers 197
lovage 126

M
mangetout and sugar-snap peas 76–77
manure 221
marker lines 198, 199
marrows 82
measuring equipment 199
melons 184–185
membranes 214
microgreens 115
mint 128–129

mizuna and mibuna 52, 58–59
modules 201, 202
mulches 214, 221
    weed control 224
mung beans 114
municipal green waste compost 221
mushroom compost 221
mustard 'Red Frills' 58

N
nasturtiums 117
nectarines 152–153
nuts 189, 190–191, 192, 193

O
onions 22, 45–47
oregano 127
organic gardening 216–217

P
parsley 118, 130–131
parsnips 38–39
passion fruit 182
patios 14, 17, 23
peaches 152–153
pears 138, 144–145
    rejuvenating old tree 145
    rootstocks 144
peas 22, 68, 74–75
    germinating 74–75
    mangetout and sugar-snap peas 76–77
    pea sticks 77
    pea tendrils 76
pectin 234
penknives 197
peppers 90–91, 211
perpetual spinach 63
pests 9, 226–227
    aphids 55, 73, 227
    apples 141–143
    apricots 153
    asparagus 111
    aubergines 89
    bay 119
    birds and mammals 227
    blackberries 165
    blackcurrants 166
    blueberries 171
    brassicas 55
    broad beans 72
    cabbage root fly 55
    cabbage white butterflies 55

carrot root fly 37, 38
carrots 37
cauliflower 101
celery 109
Chinese cabbage 61
citrus fruit 187
climbing beans 70
coriander 124
courgettes 79
cucumber 84–85
dwarf beans 71
fennel 103
figs 155
flea beetles 55
flying insects 227
gooseberries 176
grapes 174
greenhouse hygiene 25, 226
lettuce 64–65
lovage 126
melons 184
nectarines 153
nuts 191
organic gardening 217
pak choi 61
parsnips 38
passion fruit 182
peaches 153
pears 144
peppers 91
plums 147
rabbits 55
radishes 42
raspberries 163
red and white
    currants 168–169
rocket 67
slugs and snails 227
spinach 62
strawberries 158
swede 44
sweet cherries 149
sweetcorn 87
turnips 41
physalis 183
pickles 228, 236–237
pinks 117
planters 211
planting 11
    apple tree 140
    asparagus 110
    blackcurrants 166

blueberries 171
fig tree 154
peas 75, 77
plum tree 146
sweet potatoes 35
tools 197, 199
plots 9, 10, 14, 15, 22
plums 138, 146–147
plum jam 233
rootstocks 146
pollination 152, 192
polytunnels 24–25
pot marigolds 117
potagers 16, 22–23
potatoes 22, 30–34
pots 201, 202, 211
powdery mildew 55
preserves 228
preserving equipment 230–231
pruning 11
apricots 153
acid cherries 150–151
bay 119
figs 155
gooseberries 177
grapes 174
nectarines 153
peaches 153
pears 144
plums 146
secateurs 197
sweet cherries 148, 149
pumpkins 80–81

R

radicchio see chicory
radishes 27, 42–43
sprouting seeds 114
raised beds 225
raising plants 216
rakes 197
raspberries 156, 160–163
freezer raspberry jam 243
red and white
currants 168–169
red mustard 115
rhubarb 178–179
rocket 67
root trainers 201
rosemary 118, 132
roses 117
rotovators 198

S

sage 133
salad leaves 27, 212
salad onions 106–107
sandy soil 218
seaweed extracts 219
seed 9, 204
aftercare 202
cabbages 54
celery 108
onions 45
preparing the soil 200
pricking out 202
propagators 201
seed mats 203
seed tapes 203
seed trays 201, 202
sowing 11, 201, 202, 244–245
sowing in pots 201
sowing in the ground 200
sprouting seeds 114
storage 203
thinning 200
thyme 115
timing 200
tomatoes 96, 97
treated and pelleted
seed 203
using covers 202–203
ways to sow 201
seedlings 203
shade 18
shallots 48
sloping sites 19
soaking in new plants 214
soil 9, 18, 194
drainage 218
fertility 218–219, 226
organic matter 219–221
soil pH 219
soil types 218, 219
spades 197
spinach 52, 62
sprouting seeds 114
squashes 68, 80–81
step-overs 141
stony soil 218
storage 11, 226
acid cherries 151
apples 143
apricots 153

basil 120
bay 119
blackberries 165
blackcurrants 167
blueberries 171
broccoli 99–100
Brussels sprouts 56
cabbage 54
carrots 37
cauliflower 101
celeriac 51
chervil 122
chicory 66
Chinese cabbage 61
citrus fruit 187
climbing beans 70
coriander 124
cranberries 172
cucumber 85
dwarf beans 71
endive 66
garlic 49
gooseberries 176–177
Jerusalem artichokes 50
kiwi 181
lettuce 65
lovage 126
marrows 82
mint 129
nectarines 153
nuts 191, 192, 193
onions 46
oregano 127
pak choi 61
parsley 131
parsnips 39
peaches 153
pears 145
peppers 91
potatoes 34
pumpkins 81
radishes 42
raspberries 163
red and white
currants 168, 169
rhubarb 179
shallots 48
squashes 81
strawberries 158
swede 44
sweet cherries 149
sweet potatoes 35

sweetcorn 87
tarragon 114
turnips 41
strawberries 156, 157–159
sun 18
sunflower seeds 114
swede 44
sweet cherries 148–149
sweet potatoes 35
sweet rocket 117
sweet violets 117
sweetcorn 86–87
Swiss chard 63

T

tarragon 134
    tarragon and orange
        jelly 235
temperature 19
thyme 115
timing of crops 214
tomatoes 10, 94–97
tools 194, 196, 225
    cutting 198
    essential tools 197–198
    harvesting 199
    maintenance 199
    moving things 198
turnips 41

V

varieties 11, 226–227
    acid cherries 150
    apples 141
    apricots 153
    asparagus 111
    aubergines 89
    basil 121
    beetroot 40
    blackberries 164, 165
    blackcurrants 167
    blueberries 170–171
    broad beans 72, 73
    broccoli 99, 100
    Brussels sprouts 56
    cabbage 53
    carrots 36, 37
    cauliflower 101
    celeriac 51
    celery 109
    chicory 66
    chillies 92, 93

Chinese cabbage 60
chives 123
citrus fruit 187
climbing beans 69–70
coriander 124
courgettes 78–79
cucumber 84, 85
dill 125
dwarf beans 71
edible flowers 117
endive 66
fennel 103, 125
figs 155
garlic 49
globe artichokes 112, 113
gooseberries 176
grapes 174, 175
hybrid berries 165
Jerusalem artichokes 50
kale 57
kiwi 181
kohlrabi 102
leeks 105
lettuce 64, 65
mangetout and sugar-snap peas 76
marrows 82
melons 184, 185
mint 128–129
mizuna and mibuna 58, 59
nectarines 153
nuts 190–191, 192, 193
onions 45–46
oregano 127
pak choi 61
parsley 130–131
parsnips 39
passion fruit 182
peaches 153
pears 144
peas 74, 75
peppers 90, 91
perpetual spinach 63
plums 146–147
potatoes 31–32
pumpkins 80–81
radishes 43
raspberries 160–161, 162
red and white currants 169
rhubarb 178–179
rocket 67
rosemary 132
sage 133

spring onions 107
squashes 80–81
strawberries 159
swede 44
sweet cherries 149
sweet potatoes 35
sweetcorn 86, 87
Swiss chard 63
tarragon 114
thyme 115
tomatoes 94, 97
turnips 41
vegetables 8
    leafy crops 52
    perennial vegetables 205
    root crops 22, 30
    stem and flower crops 98
    young plants 204–205

W

walnuts 189, 193
watering 9, 18
    hoses 214–215
    how to water 215
    irrigation systems
        and timers 215
    rainwater or tap? 214
    reducing watering 214
    sprinklers 215
    timing 215
    watering cans 214
weeding 9, 214
    covering 224
    digging 224
    hand weeding 225
    hoeing 225
    mulches 224
    spraying 224
    tools 197, 225
    types of weeds 224
wigwam supports 77
    making 70
wildlife gardening 217, 227
wind 18
window boxes and
    sills 211
winter salads 58
wormeries 223

Acknowledgements

Quarto would like to thank the following photographers and agencies for supplying images for inclusion in this book:

Jenny & Colin Guest
p.32b–33b, 34, 36, 37, 38bl/br, 39t/bl, 40, 40b, 42b, 43b, 44b, 46b, 47bl, 48t, 49b, 54, 56br, 58, 59cr, 62cr, 64b–65b, 65t, 70, 71b, 72b, 73, 74b–75b, 78b, 79b, 82t, 84b, 87, 88b, 90bl, 100, 101br, 104bc, 105br, 106b–107b, 120b, 122b, 123b, 124bl/bc, 127b, 132b, 133b, 134b, 135t, 161t, 168b, 169b, 183, 214, 215, 227

Mark Winwood
p.31, 35, 45t, 47br, 48b, 52, 53b, 60b, 63bl, 66, 69, 77, 82b, 83, 86, 88t, 89br, 93br, 96bc/br, 97t, 98, 104, 108b, 110b, 112, 113b, 119b, 124br, 135b, 140, 146b, 152bl, 154b, 155, 158t/bl, 171b, 177b, 178b, 179b, 185, 199t, 204

John Grain
p.2, 3c/b, 11, 80b, 154t, 162b, 163bl

Jenny Steel www.wildlife-gardening.co.uk
p.216

Key Sexton http://blog.gardening-tools-direct.co.uk
p.226

Photolibrary
p.12–13, 16, 17, 19t, 50b, 61, 81, 92, 94br, 95b, 111t, 128, 129tl/tr, 129bl, 130, 131bl, 150, 162, 163br, 165, 198b, 213, 223t/bl/br

Getty Images
p.33tl/tr, 43t, 103b, 106t

Quintet Publishing
Images: p.230tl/br, 231tl, 232, 233, 234, 235, 236, 237, 238, 239, 240, 241, 242, 243
Text: p.230–243